President Lincoln in the War Department telegraph office, writing the first draft
of the Emancipation Proclamation

LINCOLN
IN THE TELEGRAPH OFFICE

RECOLLECTIONS OF THE UNITED
STATES MILITARY TELEGRAPH
CORPS DURING THE CIVIL WAR

BY
DAVID HOMER BATES

MANAGER OF THE WAR DEPARTMENT TELEGRAPH
OFFICE, AND CIPHER-OPERATOR, 1861–1866

Introduction to the Bison Books Edition
by James A. Rawley

University of Nebraska Press
Lincoln and London

Introduction to the Bison Books Edition © 1995 by the
University of Nebraska Press
Manufactured in the United States of America

☉ The paper in this book meets the minimum require-
ments of American National Standard for Information
Sciences—Permanence of Paper for Printed Library
Materials, ANSI Z39.48-1984.

First Bison Books printing: 1995
Most recent printing indicated by the last digit below:
10   9   8   7   6   5   4   3   2

Library of Congress Cataloging-in-Publication Data
Bates, David Homer, b. 1843.
Lincoln in the telegraph office: recollections of the United
States Military Telegraph Corps during the Civil War / by
David Homer Bates.
p.   cm.
Originally published: New York: Century Co., 1907.
Includes index.
ISBN 0-8032-6125-X (alk. paper)
1. United States. Military Telegraph Corps.   2. Lincoln,
Abraham, 1809–1865.   3. United States—History—Civil
War, 1861–1865—Communications.   4. Military tele-
graph—United States—History—19th century.   I. Title.
E608.B28   1995
973.7—dc20
95-10908   CIP

Reprinted from the original 1907 edition by The Century
Co., New York.

CONTENTS

CONTENTS

LIST OF ILLUSTRATIONS

LIST OF ILLUSTRATIONS

INTRODUCTION TO THE BISON BOOKS EDITION

James A. Rawley

Day after day "his tall, homely form could be seen cross-ing the well-shaded lawn between the White House and the War Department." So wrote David Homer Bates, manager of the telegraph office of the War De-partment during the Civil War.

Abraham Lincoln, the "tall, homely form," was the first president and commander in chief to be able to be in almost instant touch with armies in distant fields of war. Countless observers—politicians, reporters, dia-rists, visitors—black and white, male and female, for-eign and domestic—recorded impressions of Lincoln. In his *Lincoln in the Telegraph Office* Bates provides a firsthand portrait of Lincoln the commander in chief, away from the official surroundings of the White House, agonizing over military reverses, generals' ineptitude, holding high-level emergency meetings, writing the Emancipation Proclamation, and endlessly telling sto-ries.

The telegraph, marvel of nineteenth-century electric communication, had been invented only in 1844, but by 1861 much of the United States had been wired into a network that transformed the lives of citizens and sol-diers. Newspapers speedily received dispatches from throughout the country, simultaneously knitting together the nation and contributing to a dissolution of the Union by publishing ordinances of secession one after another to slave states in the dark winter of 1860–61.

Congress in 1843—the year Bates was born in Steubenville, Ohio—had appropriated $30,000 to construct an experimental telegraph line. A dramatic step in the technological revolution in communications, the electromagnetic telegraph system was used the next year to transmit news of the national political party conventions from Baltimore to Washington. "What hath God wrought?" queried Samuel F. B. Morse, the telegraph's inventor from the Supreme Court room in Washington to his partner in Baltimore. Alfred Vail returned the same words to Washington.

Despite the political and public importance of the telegraph, Congress declined to appropriate additional funds and private enterprise developed a national network. In 1861 the first transcontinental line was completed; the continent had been wired by the codified sound of dots and dashes. Attempts to connect North America and Europe did not succeed until 1866.

The military telegraph was both novel and necessary to the Union aim to conquer the Confederacy. Military operations extended from Maryland to Texas. Couriers and visual communication were inadequate. The U.S. Signal Corps' system—flags by day and torches by night—stood inadequate to the vast terrain and the huge, dispersed forces engaged in the struggle.

The electric telegraph maintained speedy, almost instantaneous communication between Washington and armies in distant fields. Wires clicked news, orders, strategy, coordinated movements, and dispatched reinforcements, ordnance, and commissary supplies. Waging an offensive war in enemy territory, the Union needed the telegraph more than the Confederacy did. By the war's end the Union had strung over fifteen hundred miles of military telegraph line, the Confederacy about one thousand.

BISON INTRODUCTION

In February 1862, Lincoln established control of the nation's telegraph lines. The following year the United States Military Telegraph was created, separated from the United States Signal Corps, with which it had suffered some friction. The prewar commercial network had connected cities, but armies often fought and moved outside cities. Portable, front-line electric communication for field operations was required. General U. S. Grant praised the work of the telegraph service in the field. "The signal service was used on the march," he said, and the moment the troops went into the camp the telegraph service, never needing orders, would set to work to put up its wires. "In a few minutes longer time than it took a mule to walk the length of its coil [of wire], telegraphic communication would be effected between all the headquarters of the army." An estimated 6,500,000 Union messages passed over the wires during the war at a cost of about forty cents a message.

Ciphers of two kinds were commonly employed for military telegrams. The service arbitrarily assigned significance to certain words or letters, or arranged words in a false position, throwing in meaningless words to confuse readers. Ingenuity and inventiveness characterized the ciphers. Lincoln is thought to have devised the following cipher telegram.

"HEADQUARTERS ARMIES OF THE U.S., CITY POINT (VA)
8:30 A.M., April 3, 1865

To CHARLES A. TINKER, War Dept., Washington, D. C.:—

A. Lincoln its in fume a in hymn to start I army treating there possible if of cut too forward pushing is he so all Richmond aunt confide is Andy evacuated Petersburg reports Grant morning this Washington Sec'y War.

(Signed) S. H. Beckwith."

xi

Read backwards, stressing phonetics instead of spelling, the meaning becomes clear.

With the outbreak of fighting in 1861, Secretary of War Simon Cameron turned to a civilian, Thomas A. Scott, general manager of the Pennsylvania Railroad, and gave him charge of railroads and telegraph lines needed for the war. Scott in turn brought to Washington young Andrew Carnegie, then superintendent of the Pittsburgh Division of his railroad. These knowledgeable businessmen coordinated the many separately owned telegraph lines and began development of a military telegraph system that spread each year of the war. Congress was not in session and in the absence of an appropriation the president of the American Telegraph Company, which did much of the construction, operation, and maintenance of the system, advanced funds.

General George B. McClellan, who had studied military telegraphs used on a limited scale in the Crimean War, contributed to the developing system. Commanding the Department of the Ohio, he gave charge of all lines in his department to Anson Stager, the general superintendent of Western Union. A man of great business capacity, Stager coordinated the private lines in the department. In addition, he organized a field telegraph system that moved with McClellan's advance into western Virginia—"the first field telegraph that ever advanced with an army in America."

Scott became assistant secretary of war, Carnegie returned to the private sector and making a personal fortune, and McClellan, victorious in western Virginia, was summoned to Washington to command the Union army repulsed and demoralized at First Bull Run. McClellan, a skilled engineer and organizer, established a centralized military telegraph bureau in Washington. He called Stager to his side, made him superintendent of military telegraphs, and he in turn placed management of operations in the hands of Thomas T. Eckert, who later became president of Western Union. These two highly capable men did yeoman work in organizing and developing the military telegraph during the Civil War. They made it fundamental to military operations and a vital factor in Federal victory.

Within five months Stager reported that his service had strung 1,137 miles of wire for military use; "in many instances the wires followed the march of the army at the rate of 8 to 12 miles per day." Growth was rapid— by the end of the fiscal year 1862, 3700 miles were in operation; 1800 miles were added the following year, 3700 in 1863, another 3300 in 1864, and 2000 more in the final fiscal year. Altogether, the military telegraph lines were enough to stretch more than half-way away around the earth—a prodigious achievement of American technology and organizational skill.

Bates, only seventeen years of age when the war broke out, employed in the telegraph department of the Pennsylvania Railroad, was ordered by his superintendent to take up duties in the War Department telegraph office in April 1861. Less than a year later the youth became manager and cipher-operator of the office. He remained in that capacity until August 1866.

His wartime diary formed the heart of a series of articles he published in *The Century Magazine* in 1907 and shortly after in book form. *Lincoln in the Telegraph Office* is a staple of Lincoln biographers and Civil War historians.

The military telegraph was housed in the War Department, a short walk from the White House. Bates saw Lincoln daily, sometimes several times a day, as the commander in chief came for the latest news from the field. On occasion during a crisis he would stay all night. At times the cabinet met at the War Department. In cool weather Lincoln characteristically appeared with a gray plaid shawl carelessly draped over his shoulders. He would hang the shawl over a door top and then eagerly pore over the most recent dispatches filed in a small drawer in the cipher desk. During critical battles he would hover over the shoulder of a cipher operator, reading the translation of the Morse code.

Telegrams from the field were essential to Lincoln's expansive conception of his role as commander in chief. He was an active commander in chief, enabled by the new electromagnetic telegraph to follow and supervise military actions.

When spring operations opened in 1862, Bates recounts that on 24 May Lincoln sent ten or twelve dispatches to various generals, as many again the next day, and from one to a dozen nearly every following day for months. Frustrated by the long duration of the war and the inability of general after general to end it, he often communicated directly with his generals, sometimes bypassing both the secretary of war and the general in chief. His secretaries John George Nicolay and John Hay observed, "His thought by day and anxiety by night fed upon the intelligence which the telegraph brought."

For the only major battle of 1861, First Bull Run, the military telegraph set the scene in Washington. An improvised telegraph line had been extended to Fairfax Courthouse; from there mounted couriers carried news between General Irvin McDowell's headquarters and the telegraph office. Attended by his military advisers, with "deep anxiety" Lincoln awaited this first important test of Union arms. When the telegraph announced, "Our army is retreating," the group dispersed; but Lincoln kept returning past midnight.

The extended, often strained, relationship between Lincoln and General George B. McClellan was conducted by wire, after the president had prodded "Tardy George" into moving his forces out of Washington. The telegraph office once played a significant part in softening the general's dispatches, which, Lincoln said, "do not offend me, [but] do pain me very much." Ever calling for more troops, failing to score a decisive victory, McClellan bitterly ended a wire to Secretary of War Stanton: "If I save this army now, I tell you plainly that I owe no thanks to you or to any other persons in Washington." Major Edward Sanford, supervisor of telegrams, astounded by these words, took the liberty of suppressing them before delivering a copy to Stanton.

At last Lincoln's patience with McClellan snapped; he relieved the general of command of the Army of the Potomac and entrusted it to General John Pope. In late summer of 1862, Pope's army clashed with the Confederates in the second battle of Bull Run. Lincoln stayed all night in the telegraph office on 26 August. During the next anxiety-filled days he dispatched inquiries time and again, typically asking, "What news?" or "Did you hear any firing this morning?" An officer in the field to whom he addressed a number of his queries later recalled, "Inquiries came from him at all hours of the night asking for the latest news from the front."

One of the most notable sections of Bates's book is his description of the writing of the Emancipation Proclamation. Issued 17 September 1862, it began a laborious, pensive existence as a draft in June. Day after day the author of one of the most momentous documents in United States history seated himself at a desk in the cipher room of the War Department, free from the demands made on him at the White House. Using sheets of foolscap, with many pauses for reflection, the Great Emancipator penned a line or two at a time.

Each day he left his draft sheets in the office, asking Major Thomas Eckert, chief of the telegraph staff, to lock them up. All the while there rose an increasing clamor for the president to act. He concealed his purpose from most persons, disclosed it to his cabinet, and on the sagacious Seward's advice withheld it until a Union victory gave the proclamation to free rebels' slaves some plausibility. When the formal proclamation was announced on 1 January 1863, telegraph wires diffused the word to the troops and the country. But for the president to proclaim that slaves not under Federal control were free was one thing; to attain and preserve black freedom was another. That night Lincoln, though he had experienced a tiring day, including the customary New Year's Day reception at the White House, returned to the telegraph office to peruse the dispatches. General U. S. Grant seemed baffled about how to capture Vicksburg, the Confederate Gibraltar; and General William B. Rosecrans, assailed by Confederate General Braxton Bragg, anticipated renewal of the indecisive fighting at Murfreesboro. All the while the North was smarting from General Ambrose Burnside's drubbing by General R. E. Lee at Fredericksburg.

The Union outlook at last brightened in the first days of July. Lee having defeated another Union general, Joseph Hooker, at Chancellorsville, ventured a daring invasion of the North. Lincoln promptly replaced Hooker with George G. Meade, and hovered in the telegraph office through the tense days until on the Fourth of July he joyously announced "a great success to the cause of the Union." Three days later the wires brought news that Grant had captured Vicksburg, dissipating the skepticism Lincoln had held about Grant's campaign strategy.

But clouds darkened the skies almost immediately. "I left the telegraph office a good deal dissatisfied," Lincoln on 6 July confided to Henry W. Halleck, his general in chief. He was apprehensive that Meade, like McClellan, would not pursue the retreating enemy. As apprehension deepened he paced the floor of the telegraph office, wringing his hands, in unaccustomed sarcasm exclaiming of Meade and his officers, "They will be ready to fight a magnificent battle when there is no enemy there to fight."

In late September 1863 Rosecrans engaged in battle against Bragg's forces south of Chattanooga at Chickamauga. Clearing Confederates from Tennessee, which held many loyalists, was dear to Lincoln's heart. Through anxious days Lincoln abided in the telegraph office. On 20 September Rosecrans wired him, "We have no certainty of holding our position." Lincoln reassured him, "Be of good cheer. . . . We shall do our utmost to assist you."

But where was assistance to come from? General Burnside in northeast Tennessee did not heed Lincoln's, "Go to Rosecrans . . . without a moment's delay." When Burnside dallied and replied from distant Jonesboro, Lincoln in the only profanity Bates heard from his lips in the telegraph office, swore, "Damn Jonesboro!" The wires conveyed further gloomy dispatches from Rosecrans and the assistant secretary of war who had been sent to observe and report. In a single day Charles Dana sent eleven telegrams to Stanton.

In this crisis the military telegraph saved the situation. Secretary of War Stanton in great alarm sent copies of the distressing telegrams to Lincoln, who was spending the still warm September nights at the Soldiers Home, two miles or so from the White House. Stanton appealed an immediate meeting. Under a moonlit sky the president rode back to Washington for a crisis conference in the War Department.

Stanton proposed to meet the crisis by sending 30,000 men from Meade's Army of the Potomac in Virginia, saying they could join Rosecrans within five days. Halleck rejoined that it would take three months; Lincoln worried over weakening Meade's forces. Meanwhile, Bates and other telegraphers were poring over maps and railroad schedules. They concluded the movement could be consummated in much less time than Halleck's estimate. The conferees agreed to send reinforcements, and the long wires from Washington to distant places hummed orders to organize trains and men for the most dramatic troop movement of the Civil War. Lincoln and cabinet members spent 24 September arranging details. Cars had to be found and assigned, gauges changed, supplies provided, traffic cleared, and generals ordered to cooperate. With extraordinary efficiency, wire and rail sped 20,000 men to a railway station only twenty-six miles from Chattanooga where Rosecrans had retreated and lay under siege. Other troops followed and, thanks to the telegraph, catastrophe was averted. Stanton's biographers describe the event as "the greatest transportation feat in the history of warfare up to that time."

Chattanooga was claimed by the Union forces, thanks in part to the reinforcements and in part to Grant, who soon took charge of freeing eastern Tennessee of rebel forces. Now the way opened for Grant to assume supreme command of Union armies as general-in-chief, develop an overall strategy while supervising Meade's Army of the Potomac facing Lee in Virginia, and encourage General W. T. Sherman to ravage Georgia.

On the success of Union arms hinged Lincoln's re-election. During the 1864 military operations Confederate General Jubal A. Early drove his forces to the outskirts of the District of Columbia. The intrepid, perhaps foolhardy president visited the scene of fighting and became a target for Confederate skirmishers. A Union soldier within a few feet of the president fell dead, and Lincoln yielded to a shout from young Oliver Wendell Holmes, later associate justice of the U.S. Supreme Court, "Get down, you damn fool." It was, Bates notes, perhaps the only time a president "has been exposed to the fire of the enemy's guns in battle." After returning safely to the War Department telegraph office, Lincoln, drawing a diagram, gave a picturesque account of the situation.

The military telegraph figured in the election of 1864. It was in the telegraph office Lincoln received word he had been renominated. He laconically remarked to a telegrapher after reading the message: "Send it right over to the Madam. She will be more interested than I am." The sluggish progress of Union arms and the nomination by the Democrats of the warrior General George B. McClellan made a second term problematical. By telegraph the Lincoln administration exerted itself strenuously to enable soldiers in the field to vote.

Pivotal elections took place in such states as Pennsylvania, Ohio, and Indiana three weeks earlier than the November elections in most states. The president, looking "unusually weary and depressed," arrived at the telegraph office election night, 11 October, and sank into "his accustomed seat at Major Eckert's desk." He remained in the office until after midnight, reading dispatches, sending inquiries to political leaders in crucial states. Their projections trickled in, failing to assure the president; after two days of disconcerting reports he took a blank telegraph form and set down his prediction of the final electoral count. Under the headings "Supposed Copperhead Vote" and "Union Vote for President" he listed the states, his retentive memory recalling the number of each state's electoral vote, and noted those states he expected to vote for McClellan and for him.

He assigned himself a close margin of three votes, not counting Nevada, which three weeks later he proclaimed admitted to the Union, anticipating its three electoral votes would be added to the Union Vote for President. His estimate, product of a murky moment, proved far off from reality as Sherman captured Atlanta, thereby changing voters' outlook on the war's progress. In November Lincoln won 212 of 233 electoral votes. With little show of elation on election night he perused the telegrams bearing details of his reelection.

The military telegraph figured interestingly in effecting the great Union victory at Nashville, crushing rebel resistance west of the Appalachian mountains. Failing to hold Atlanta, Confederate General John B. Hood had set out to retake Nashville. General William T. Sherman responded by detaching forces under George H. Thomas to pursue him. Reaching Nashville, Thomas failed to attack, pleading bad weather.

No friend of Thomas or advocate of his delay, Grant wrote out two telegrams to remove the general from command. Lincoln and his conferees suspended the first telegram to afford Thomas a last chance to move. Grant, in Washington on 15 December, supervised personally the second telegram ordering removal. Major Eckert, awaiting word from Nashville—where on 14 December the lines had been temporarily cut—refrained on his own responsibility from dispatching the order. In a timing worthy of an ancient Greek drama, on 15 December Thomas telegraphed news of his smashing victory over Hood. A relieved Eckert and an exultant Stanton hastened to the White House and routed Lincoln from bed. The commander in chief, wearing his nightdress, holding a candle at the second floor landing, rejoiced in the good news.

Bates's final chapters describe the Hampton Roads peace conference, contrast Lincoln's benign manner with Stanton's brusqueness, and provide a facsimile of one of the last, ominous telegrams Lincoln sent. Responding to Stanton's concern for his safety, Lincoln said, "I will take care of myself."

The book illuminates the fact that the military telegraph was vital to the waging of the Civil War. It also was vital to the distinctive and forceful manner of Lincoln's wielding his authority as commander in chief. His youthful and admiring secretary, John Hay, wrote in his diary in September 1863: "some well-meaning newspapers advise the President to keep his fingers out of the military pie: and all that sort of thing. The truth is, if he did, the pie would be a sorry mess. The old man sits here and wields like a backwoods Jupiter the bolts of war and the machinery of government with a hand equally steady & equally firm." The wires stretching out from the War Department telegraph office to the generals in the field were vehicles to transmit Lincoln's bolts of war.

LINCOLN
IN THE TELEGRAPH OFFICE

LINCOLN IN THE
TELEGRAPH OFFICE

I

INTRODUCTION

ABRAHAM LINCOLN has been studied from almost every point of view, but it is a notable fact that none of his biographers has ever seriously considered that branch of the Government service with which Lincoln was in daily personal touch for four years—the military telegraph; for during the Civil War the President spent more of his waking hours in the War Department telegraph office than in any other place, except the White House.[1] While in the telegraph office he was comparatively free from official cares, and therefore more apt to dis-

---

[1] During the Civil War the Executive Mansion was not as now connected by telegraph, and all the President's telegrams were handled at the War Department.

close his natural traits and disposition than elsewhere under other conditions.

It is hard to realize that an entire generation
has been born into the world, and that a second
generation is nearing maturity, since the death
of Lincoln—

> "The kindly, earnest, brave, foreseeing man,
> Sagacious, patient, dreading praise, not. blame,
> New birth of our new soil, the first American."[1]

The earliest date which the writer has been able
to find relating to Lincoln's presence in a telegraph office is supplied by Charles A. Tinker,
one of the cipher-operators in the War Department during the Civil War, in his "Personal Reminiscences of Abraham Lincoln." He says that in
the month of March, 1857, he was employed as
telegraph-operator in the Tazewell House, Pekin,
Illinois, which was the headquarters during successive terms of the judge of the circuit, and of
the lawyers in attendance on court. On one occasion, after watching young Tinker's expert
manipulation of the Morse key, and seeing him
write down an incoming message, which he received by sound, an unusual accomplishment in
those early days, Lincoln asked him to explain

[1] Lowell's Harvard Commemoration Ode, July, 1865.

4

the operation of the new and mysterious force. Tinker gladly complied with the request, going into details, beginning at the battery, the source of the electric current, which, in its passage through the coils of the magnet, serves to attract an iron armature connected with a retractile spring, which pulls back the armature from the magnet whenever the electric current is broken. By this means, as Tinker explained to Lincoln, the now more familiar dots and dashes of the Morse telegraph signals are sent and received.

Tinker says that Lincoln seemed to be greatly interested in his explanation, and asked pertinent questions showing an observing mind already well furnished with knowledge of collateral facts and natural phenomena; and that he comprehended quite readily the operation of the telegraph, which at that time was a comparatively new feature in business and social intercourse; for it should be remembered that before that time wires had been extended west of the Alleghany Mountains only five or six years.

From this early period until the day of his death, eight years afterward, Lincoln's connection with the telegraph was very close and intimate.

Napoleon's meteoric career extended from the Reign of Terror to Waterloo, twenty-one years; Grant's from Donelson to McGregor, twenty-three years; Washington's public life covered twenty-four years, Jackson's thirty, Jefferson's fifty, while Gladstone's extended over sixty years. Frederick Trevor Hill, in "Lincoln the Lawyer" [p. 262], says his national reputation dates from his Cooper Union speech (February 27, 1860). I should be inclined to go farther back, to June 16, 1858, when in his celebrated Springfield speech at the Illinois Republican State Convention (by which he had been named as a candidate for United States Senator) he announced his creed: " . . . I believe this Government cannot endure permanently half slave and half free. I do not expect the Union to be dissolved . . . but I do expect it will cease to be divided."

Thank God that long since, from the Lakes to the Gulf and from the Atlantic to the Pacific, that creed has been accepted by his countrymen, and the Union has proven itself to be "one and inseparable."

But even thus, Lincoln's national career comprised less than seven years, four of which were

spent in the presidential chair. Already Roose-
.velt, who was born in 1858, the year of Lincoln's
prophetic speech above mentioned, has seen much
longer public service.

During the last four years of Lincoln's national
career, even until the day before its tragic ending, the writer was fortunate in being able to see
him and talk with him daily, and usually several
times a day; for he visited the War Department
telegraph office morning, afternoon, and evening,
to receive the latest news from the armies at the
front. His tall, homely form could be seen crossing the well-shaded lawn between the White
House and the War Department day after day
with unvaried regularity.

In cool weather he invariably wore a gray plaid
shawl thrown over his shoulders in careless fash-
ion, and, upon entering the telegraph office, he
would always hang this shawl over the top of the
high, screen door opening into Secretary Stanton's room, adjoining. This door was nearly always open. He seldom failed to come over late
in the evening before retiring, and sometimes he
would stay all night in the War Department.
When returning to the White House after dark,
he was frequently accompanied by Major Eckert,

and nearly always by a small guard of soldiers. He sometimes protested against this latter precaution as unnecessary, but Secretary Stanton's orders to the guard were imperative.

It was in the War Department telegraph office that Lincoln received from the writer's hands, on May 24, 1861, the message announcing the shooting of his young friend, Colonel Ellsworth, at the Jackson House, Alexandria; and it was Lincoln's own despatch in cipher, from City Point on April 3, 1865, that gave us in Washington our earliest news of Grant's capture of Petersburg and Richmond.

Therefore it seemed fitting that after his assassination, when the entire country was searching for the murderer, the first authentic news of Booth's whereabouts should come from Grant's cipher-operator, Samuel H. Beckwith, who telegraphed from Port Tobacco, Maryland, April 24, 1865, to General Eckert, Chief of the War Department telegraph staff, that Booth had been traced to a swamp near by. Thirty-six hours after Beckwith's despatch reached Washington the assassin was hunted down and shot.[1]

[1] On April 20, 1865, the Secretary of War offered a large reward for Booth's arrest, and there were so many claimants for the

INTRODUCTION

Lincoln's daily visits to the telegraph office were therefore greatly relished by him and of course were highly prized by the cipher-operators. He would there relax from the strain and care ever present at the White House, and while waiting for fresh despatches, or while they were being deciphered, would make running comments, or tell his inimitable stories. Outside the members of his cabinet and his private secretaries, none were brought into closer or more confidential relations with Lincoln than the cipher-operators. Of his official family not one now survives; and of the leading generals who met Lincoln in person, there remain only Howard, Sickles, and Dodge; but there are still living (1907), at least five witnesses of those stirring scenes, namely: Thomas T. Eckert, Charles A. Tinker, Albert B. Chandler, and the writer—who served as cipher-operators in the War Department telegraph office—and Albert E. H. Johnson, custodian of military telegrams. Eckert was our chief and Johnson facetiously called the others the "Sacred Three." Each of this little company has heretofore written some more

fund that its distribution was referred to the Committee on Claims in Congress, who awarded five hundred dollars to Beckwith for his part in the service leading to Booth's apprehension.

or less desultory recollections of the Civil War period, and has been from time to time importuned to place on record, while it is possible, a fuller and more orderly account of our unique experiences in the War Department, which it is my present effort to do. A few of the incidents mentioned in this volume have heretofore appeared in print, but their repetition now is clearly justified, since they properly belong to any detailed account of "Lincoln in the Telegraph Office." In fact such an account would be incomplete without them. And also because of their collateral interest, and for the purpose of throwing light upon the general subject, certain data relating more particularly to the United States military telegraph are included.

WE read with unfailing interest of the wars of Alexander, of Frederick the Great, and of Napoleon, but in their day there was no electric telegraph or other means of quick communication. The events of history succeeding their mighty conflicts were slow in movement, and the knowledge of those events slower still in reaching distant points. Even in our own country's short history, it is recalled that Jackson fought and won the battle of New Orleans, January 8, 1815, two weeks after the Treaty of Ghent had been signed. On the other hand, the Treaty of Portsmouth, August, 1905, was flashed to the uttermost parts of the civilized world in less than forty minutes, the space of time in which Puck said he could "put a girdle round about the earth."

In our Civil War the Morse telegraph was for the first time employed to direct widely separated armies and move them in unison, and news of victories or defeats was flashed almost instantly all over our broad land. In fact the history of our Civil War was largely recorded by the telegraph, and that branch of the service Stanton, the great War Secretary, called his "right arm." In his annual report, December 5, 1863, he used this language:

> The military telegraph, under the general direction of Colonel Stager and Major Eckert, has been of inestimable value to the service and no corps has surpassed—few have equaled—the telegraph-operators in diligence and devotion to their duties.

The operations of the United States Military Telegraph Corps, as described by Grant in his memoirs, Volume II, page 205 *et seq.,* were no doubt closely studied by the quick-witted Japanese in preparing plans for their recent campaign against Russia, which were so favorably commented upon by Emperor William in his Strasburg speech (March 12, 1905). In that address he specially commended Marshal Oyama for "remaining away from the scene of actual conflict at the battle of Mukden, and directing the widely extending struggle, receiving telegraphic reports and sending telegraphic orders while sitting quiet, like a chess-player who can at once follow move by move."

As throwing additional light upon the work of our corps during the Civil War, the following brief references, taken at random from voluminous data bearing upon the subject, are quoted:

QUARTERMASTER-GENERAL MEIGS, in his report to the Secretary of War, November 3, 1864, says:

> The operators have shown great zeal, intrepidity, fidelity, and skill. Their duties are arduous and the trust reposed in them great. I have seen a telegraph-operator in a tent in a malarious locality shivering with ague, lying upon his camp cot with his ear near the instrument, listening for messages which might direct or arrest movements of military armies. Night and day they are at their posts. . . .

Senator Scott of West Virginia in a speech to the Senate, February 8, 1906, on House bill 8988, said:

12

INTRODUCTION

. . . The military telegraphers came under the immediate direction of President Lincoln as Commander in Chief through the Secretary of War. The movements of the armies, the secrets of the nation, were intrusted to them, and yet not one was ever known to betray that knowledge and confidence in the most remote degree. History records no other war where the armies were so widely scattered and where prior to ours they were so well informed of each other's movements.

II

ORGANIZATION OF THE MILITARY TELEGRAPH CORPS

FORT SUMTER'S fateful signals had not ceased reverberating over the hills and valleys of the North before the electric telegraph flashed a message from Washington calling for telegraph operators for service in defense of the Union. This message and its answer are reproduced from memory, as follows:

Washington, D. C., April 22, 1861.

DAVID MCCARGO,
   Supt. Telegraphs, Penna. Railroad Co., Altoona, Pa.

   Send four of your best operators to Washington at once, prepared to enter Government telegraph service for the war.

   (Signed)   ANDREW CARNEGIE.
19 Words paid, Govt.

Altoona, Pa., April 23, 1861.

ANDREW CARNEGIE,
   War Department, Washington, D. C.

   Message received.   Strouse from Mifflin, Brown from

14

Pittsburgh, O'Brien from Greensburg, and Bates from Altoona, will start for Washington immediately.

    (Signed)   DAVID McCARGO, *Supt. Telegraph.*

20 Words collect, Govt.

These are the earliest official despatches in our service which can be definitely recalled.

At the outbreak of the Civil War, the writer was employed in the telegraph department of the Pennsylvania Railroad at Altoona, Pennsylvania. On April 14, 1861, the first Sunday after Sumter's fall, the Rev. Samuel Creighton, my pastor, —who is still living at Markleton, Pennsylvania, —preached a patriotic sermon in the little Methodist church, and during the following week recruiting for the army under the terms of the President's call for 75,000 militia, dated April 15, was actively carried on, the inspiring sounds of fife and drum being heard all day long. My ardor rose almost to the enlisting point, when I received orders from my superintendent to start at once for Washington to report for duty in accordance with the telegraphic correspondence quoted above.

Andrew Carnegie was then superintendent of the Pittsburg Division of the Pennsylvania Railroad, but at that time was in Washington, acting as assistant to Colonel Thomas A. Scott, who had just been appointed general manager of military railroads and telegraph-lines by Secretary of War Cameron. My companions were David Strouse, Samuel M. Brown, and Richard O'Brien. We left on April 25, 1861, traveling via Philadelphia, stopping over at Harrisburg long enough to have our pictures taken by the now old-fashioned ambrotype process; and the writer still cherishes, with other war-time relics, his copy of that old picture.

Reaching Perryville, Maryland, we found that a force of Southern sympathizers from Baltimore, under Marshal Kane and a man named Isaac R. Trimble,[1] a former superintendent of the Philadelphia, Wilmington & Baltimore Railroad, recently appointed chief of the police force of Baltimore, had destroyed the railroad bridges over the Bush and Gunpowder rivers, so that we were compelled to go by water to Annapolis, sailing on the steamer *Maryland,* at that time used for transporting railroad cars across the Susquehanna River. (This boat, since rebuilt, may still be seen in similar daily service

[1] See Wm. Bender Wilson's "History of the Pennsylvania Railroad," Vol. I, p. 319.

From an ambrotype

Samuel M. Brown
David Strouse   Richard O'Brien
David Homer Bates

First four operators in the United States Military
Telegraph Corps, April, 1861

in New York harbor.) She had just returned from her first trip to Annapolis with the Eighth Massachusetts. On the voyage we met Ormsby M. Mitchel, noted astronomer and soldier, and our sleeping accommodations, like his, were odorous coffee-bags. At Annapolis, after reporting to General Benjamin F. Butler, in command, the quartet of operators loitered about the old railroad station until we could find room on one of the crowded trains to Washington, all troops from the North having been ordered to proceed by that route instead of through Baltimore, because of the opposition of citizens of that city to the passage of Federal troops, and also because of the destruction of railroad bridges north of Baltimore.

Although a native of Steubenville, Ohio, the writer during his boyhood had never crossed the Ohio River into Virginia, then a slave state, and had never seen a slave. It was therefore a new experience for him, a boy in years, as he walked the streets of Maryland's capital, to be curtsied to by colored women, and to observe colored men, old and young, lift their hats or caps and bow obsequiously as they passed by. We had learned at Annapolis that Carnegie, with his corps of workmen, had repaired the single-track railroad to Annapolis Junction and was then on the line somewhere near Washington.

The following account of Mr. Carnegie's work in connection with the United States military telegraph was prepared after a recent interview with him, and has received his indorsement:

In the month of April, 1861, just after Sumter's fall, Simon Cameron, then Secretary of War, requested President Thomson of the Pennsylvania Railroad to spare Vice-President Thomas A. Scott for a time, to get the railroad and telegraph service under proper control. Colonel Scott asked that Andrew Carnegie, then superintendent of the Pittsburg Division, should accompany and assist him. President Thomson acquiesced. This was just before the Sixth Massachusetts, on April 19, 1861, was assaulted while passing through the streets of Baltimore en route to the capital.

Mr. Carnegie went to Washington via Philadelphia and Perryville, thence to Annapolis by the ferry-boat *Maryland,* which also carried the Eighth Massachusetts.[1] He had drafted from

[1] Captain J. P. Reynolds, who served with the Eighth Massachusetts in the Civil War, furnishes the following notes of its journey to Washington:

his railroad division, and brought with him, the nucleus of a strong railroad force, so that the Government would be able at once to take possession of and operate the railroads about Washington. This force consisted of conductors, trainmen, trackmen, road-supervisors, bridge-builders, etc.

Arriving at Annapolis, Samuel F. Barr of Pittsburg, who was made commissary, took possession of a fine mansion which the owners had deserted, and the entire force made that ancient town its headquarters for the time being. Their first work was to repair the railroad and telegraph-line which had been wrecked by a band of raiders from Baltimore. This occupied them several days. Skilled men detailed from the Eighth Massachusetts rendered valuable service. Meanwhile General Benjamin F. Butler with his staff was the first to pass over the repaired line. Carnegie was on the locomotive, and, when approaching Washington, he saw that the enemy had torn down the telegraph-line, and

"Left Boston April 18, 1861, Jersey City, April 19. Stopped over night at Girard House, Philadelphia. Left Philadelphia April 20. Took Steamer *Maryland* at Perryville for Annapolis. Arrived Annapolis April 21. Arrived Washington, D. C., April 26. Reviewed by President Lincoln, marched to the Capitol, and quartered in the Rotunda."

21

at one place had pinned the wires to the ground between two poles. Stopping the train, he jumped off, and, pulling the stake toward him, the released wires struck him in the face, knocking him over. He came into Washington bleeding profusely. We have always claimed that, so far as is known, the Military Telegraph Corps thus furnished the third man who bled for his country in the Civil War, the two Massachusetts men assaulted by the mob in Baltimore being the first and second. Mr. Carnegie has not yet applied for a pension.

When Carnegie reached Washington his first task was to establish a ferry to Alexandria and to extend the Baltimore & Ohio Railroad track from the old depot in Washington, along Maryland Avenue, to and across the Potomac, so that locomotives and cars might be crossed for use in Virginia. Long Bridge, over the Potomac, had to be rebuilt, and I recall the fact that under the direction of Carnegie and R. F. Morley,[1] the railroad between Washington and Alexandria was completed in the remarkably short period of seven days. All hands, from

[1] Morley, the first military railroad superintendent, and Strouse, the first military telegraph superintendent, literally worked themselves to death. They both died before the year was out.

From a photograph by J. E. McClees, Philadelphia.   Half-tone plate engraved by H. Davidson

Andrew Carnegie in 1861

Carnegie down, worked day and night to accomplish the task set before them.

At the same time the telegraph-lines were extended, and communication by wire was opened with outlying points. Telegraphers were in great demand, and were called for from all the leading systems, but chiefly from the Pennsylvania Railroad, which was drained of many of its best men. Telegraph offices were opened at Alexandria, Burke's Station, Fairfax, and other points.

Carnegie remained at the capital until November, continuing his work of organizing and perfecting the military railroad and telegraph service, which by that time had been placed on such a firm basis that he could be spared to return to his former duties at Pittsburg, which post had become of prime importance because of the increasing demands of the Government in the matter of transporting troops and supplies for McClellan's army.

The four boy operators, heretofore mentioned, reached Washington on Thursday, April 27, 1861, and after securing rooms at the old National Hotel on Pennsylvania Avenue at Sixth Street where the New York Seventh, recently arrived, were quartered, proceeded to the War

Department and reported to Thomas A. Scott, who had just been commissioned colonel of volunteers, and who, on August 1, 1861, was appointed Assistant Secretary of War.

The telegraph instruments were in Chief Clerk Sanderson's room, adjoining that of the Secretary of War. Upon entering, we could see through the open door two very tall, slim men, President Lincoln and Secretary Cameron, and General Winfield Scott, the old Mexican hero, who was massive as well as tall. To tell the truth, Lincoln's homely appearance did not at first impress us favorably. We had heard of him as "Old Abe the rail-splitter," and he seemed to us uncouth and awkward, and he did not conform to our ideas of what a president should be; while old General Scott, with his gold epaulets, sash, and sword, made a magnificent presence. But as afterward I saw Lincoln almost daily, often for hours at a time, I soon forgot his awkward appearance, and came to think of him as a very attractive and, indeed, lovable person.

This, then, was the beginning, and the four young operators I have named, formed the nucleus of the United States Military Telegraph Corps, which later, at its maximum strength, contained over fifteen hundred members. In 1907, when these pages were written, the survivors numbered less than two hundred.[1]

The United States Military Telegraph Corps was a special organization, and its members were not considered an integral part of the army (excepting only ten or twelve holding commissions, to enable them officially to receive and disburse funds and property), nor were we under military control proper, our orders coming direct from the Secretary of War.

Our first superintendent was David Strouse.[2] His health was poor when he reached Washington, and he overworked himself during the succeeding months, dying in November of that year. Samuel M. Brown, another of the original group, died in 1877. James R. Gilmore succeeded Strouse, and he in turn was succeeded by Thomas T. Eckert, Gilmore having resigned. Gilmore helped to organize the 126th Pennsylvania Volunteers, and was with that regiment until after Antietam and Fredericksburg. He then re-

[1] One of the recent deaths was that of Edward Rosewater, proprietor of the Omaha "Bee," who died in 1906 soon after his return from Rome, where he represented the United States as one of two delegates in the International Postal Congress.
[2] His official appointment bears date May 15, 1861.

joined the Military Telegraph Corps, with which he was connected until a year after the war, serving chiefly as superintendent in the Department of the South, under General Quincy A. Gillmore. He is still living at his old home, in Chambersburg, Pennsylvania.

My first assignment to duty was at the Navy Yard under Captain, afterward Rear-Admiral, Dahlgren, who directed the sergeant of the guard to keep a sentry in front of the door leading to the telegraph room, and to allow no one to enter or leave. These orders were obeyed literally, and for four days I was virtually a prisoner, my frugal meals being sent to me. The confinement became so irksome that on one occasion I locked the door and climbed out of the window; but on my return by the same route, the sentry overheard the noise I made, and when I opened the door he warned me that the manœuver could be repeated only at the risk of a shot from his gun.

Early in May I was transferred to Annapolis Junction, where on the night of the tenth I was roused from bed by General Butler, who ordered me to open the telegraph office and keep the railroad track clear to Annapolis for the train carrying Ross Winans, whom he had that day arrested in Baltimore for treason. I continued to call the Annapolis office for several hours, but finally concluded that General Butler's train had either safely reached its destination or had encountered obstacles which I could not hope to remove. A fortnight later I returned to the War Department, and remained there on continuous duty until a year after the close of the war, excepting for two weeks in June, 1864, when I served as cipher-operator for General Grant at City Point.

My second meeting with Abraham Lincoln was on May 24, 1861, my first service at that time being to record and deliver to him in person a telegram from an advance office in Virginia, beyond Long Bridge, announcing the shooting of Colonel Ellsworth of the Fire Zouaves (Eleventh New York) at the Marshall House, Alexandria. Ellsworth had been a student in Lincoln's office before the war, and was held in high esteem by Lincoln, who, upon hearing the sad news of his death, wrote a touching letter of condolence to his parents from which the following extract is quoted:

Washington, D. C., May 25, 1861.
To the Father and Mother of Colonel Elmer E. Ellsworth.
My DEAR SIR AND MADAM: In the untimely loss of your

noble son, our affliction here is scarcely less than your own. . . . In the hope that it may be no intrusion upon the sacredness of your sorrow, I have ventured to address you this tribute to the memory of my young friend and your brave and early fallen child.

May God give you that consolation which is beyond all earthly power.

Sincerely your friend in a common affliction,

A. LINCOLN.

The entire letter shows the great man's sympathy with human sorrow and his close reliance upon God, which traits appear like golden threads running all through his published utterances and were exhibited in his every-day walk and conversation. My fellow telegrapher, Charles A. Tinker, thinks that Ellsworth, while studying law in Lincoln's office at Springfield about 1859, drew up the Illinois militia law. I am unable to confirm this. Ellsworth accompanied Lincoln on his journey from Springfield to Washington in February, 1861.

Amasa Stone of Cleveland, Ohio, whose daughter afterward became the wife of John Hay, was a director and large holder of stock in the Western Union Telegraph Company, of which Anson Stager was general superintendent. Stone recommended Stager to Secretary of War Cameron as a suitable person to take general charge of military telegraph matters. Meantime Stager had voluntarily coöperated with General McClellan in Ohio and Western Virginia, in the operation of telegraph-lines required for military purposes. In accordance with Stone's suggestion Cameron telegraphed Stager to come to Washington, which he did at once. Upon his arrival, he submitted a brief but comprehensive plan for a military telegraph service which was referred by Thomas A. Scott, Assistant Secretary of War, to the President, who returned it on the same day with this indorsement:

Washington, D. C., Oct. 28, 1861.

I have not sufficient time to study and mature an opinion on this plan. If the Secretary of War has confidence in it and is satisfied to adopt it, I have no objections.

A. LINCOLN.[1]

The Secretary of War formally approved the plan, and on November 11 Stager was appointed captain and assistant-quartermaster, and on November 25 was assigned in Special Orders 313 to duty as general manager of military telegraph-lines. Stager was commissioned colonel in the army on February 26, 1862, and brevet brigadier-general

[1] Plum's "Military Telegraph," Vol. I, p. 129.

on March 13, 1865, for meritorious service. Special Orders 313 must have been lost in the hurry and excitement of war preparations, for on February 25, 1862, Stager was appointed "Military superintendent of all telegraph-lines and offices in the United States," and on April 8, 1862, we find that General Order 38 appoints him assistant quartermaster and military superintendent of telegraph-lines throughout the United States. Each of these orders placed all lines and employees under the control of the Secretary of War, and required commanding officers to "furnish rations and give all necessary aid to Colonel Stager and his assistants in the construction, repair, and protection of military telegraph-lines."

Stager from time to time appointed assistants, who were also given commissions in the Quartermaster's Department, to enable them to handle government property and cash. Major Eckert was Colonel Stager's principal assistant, in immediate charge of telegraph operations at Washington and in the Department of the Potomac. Colonel Stager visited Washington occasionally, but resided in Cleveland, and after October, 1863, he made that place his per-

From a photograph by C. M. Bell, Washington, D. C.

Major Albert E. H. Johnson

Custodian of military telegrams, War Department, 1862-9

From a war-time photograph

Brigadier-General Edwards S. Sanford

Military supervisor of telegrams during the Civil War

manent headquarters and from that point directed the operations of the corps generally, giving particular attention to matters in the West and Southwest, his principal assistant in that section being Colonel Robert C. Clowry, who was stationed first at Little Rock and afterward at St. Louis. On March 13, 1865, Clowry was appointed brevet lieutenant-colonel for "meritorious service and devoted application to duty," a characterization that all who know him consider well bestowed. For many years Colonel Clowry was vice-president, and he is now president, of the Western Union Telegraph Company.

There was no government telegraph organization before the Civil War. In the month of April, 1861, the American Telegraph Company, whose lines reached Washington from the North, extended its wires to the War Department, Navy Yard, Arsenal, Chain-Bridge, and other outlying points. There was no appropriation to meet the expenses of a government telegraph service, and for six months or more Edwards S. Sanford, President of the American Telegraph Company, paid all the bills, aggregating thousands of dollars, for poles. wires, instruments, salaries of operators, etc. This was a generous and patriotic act on the part of Sanford, which was gratefully acknowledged by the President and Secretary Cameron and by the latter's successor, Stanton. The American Telegraph Company was, of course, reimbursed later through an appropriation by Congress.

Efforts have been made from time to time to have Congress pass an act giving us officially what we always claimed was our real status in the United States army, but not until thirty-two years after the war closed was even partial justice done. On January 26, 1897, President Cleveland approved an act authorizing and directing the Secretary of War to issue certificates of honorable service to all members of the United States Military Telegraph Corps, or to the representatives of deceased members. The act was carefully drawn, however, to exclude us from receiving pensions. The certificates issued to Richard O'Brien and the writer bear the date of entry into government service as of April 27, 1861, which is the earliest shown on the War Department records. We have not yet received the honor of membership in the Grand Army of the Republic, although we are in fact honorably discharged members of the United States army, by virtue of the special act above specified which mention our corps by name.[1]

---

[1] Additional information relating to the Military Telegraph Corps may be found in the Appendix. See also William R. Plum's two volumes, "The Military Telegraph in the Civil War," and Senate Document 251, 58th Cong., 2d Session.

III

THE telegraph office in the War Department was first located in Chief Clerk Sanderson's room adjoining that of the Secretary of War, on the second floor of the building in the southeast corner. In May, 1861, it was transferred to the entresol at the head of the first stairway, where it remained until August, when it was moved to a room on the first floor, north front, to the east of the main entrance from Pennsylvania Avenue.

In October, 1861, the telegraph office was moved to the first floor room west of the rear entrance, opposite the Navy Department. The final change was made soon after the *Monitor-Merrimac* fight in March, 1862, when Secretary of War Stanton directed the office to be located in the old library room, on the second floor front, adjoining his own quarters, which consisted of three rooms, each having two win-

38

dows. The library room had five windows, and about one half of the floor space was taken up with alcoves containing many rare volumes of great value including among others a perfect elephant folio edition—of Audubon's[1] "Birds of America." The alcove doors were securely locked, but the telegraph operators managed to obtain access to the books, from which we made selections for reading and study. It was in this old library—which Librarian Cheney tells me was founded in 1800—that I first came across a copy of Roget's "Thesaurus," to which we thereafter made frequent reference, especially during the time when Charles A. Dana, Assistant Secretary of War, was at Grant's and Rosecrans's headquarters, from each of which he sent long cipher-despatches containing words with meanings new and obscure to the telegraph boys.

Not long after the instruments had been moved to the library room, Secretary Stanton gave up the adjoining room for the use of the cipher-operators. We remained in these quarters until after the close of the war.

From January, 1862, when Stanton entered the cabinet, until the war ended, the telegraphic

[1] Four volumes, size 25 x 39 inches, London imprint, 1827-1830.

reins of the Government were held by a firm and skilful hand. Nicolay and Hay, in their "Abraham Lincoln,"[1] say that Stanton "centered the telegraph in the War Department, where the publication of military news, which might prematurely reach the enemy, could be supervised, and, if necessary, delayed," and that it was Lincoln's practice to go informally to Stanton's office in times of great suspense during impending or actual battles, and "spend hour after hour with his War Secretary, where he could read the telegrams as fast as they were received and handed in from the adjoining room." He did not always wait for them to be handed in, but made the cipher-room his rendezvous, keeping in close touch with the cipher-operators, often looking over our shoulders when he knew some specially important message was in course of translation.

When in the telegraph office, Lincoln was most easy of access. He often talked with the cipher-operators, asking questions regarding the despatches which we were translating from or into

---

[1] Vol. V, pp. 141–142. See also Vol. VI, p. 114: "His thoughts by day and anxiety by night fed upon the intelligence which the telegraph brought. . . . It is safe to say that no general in the army studied his maps and scanned his telegrams with half the industry—and it may be added with half the intelligence—which Mr. Lincoln gave to his."

cipher, or which were filed in the order of receipt in the little drawer in our cipher-desk.

Lincoln's habit was to go immediately to the drawer each time he came into our room, and read over the telegrams, beginning at the top, until he came to the one he had seen at his last previous visit. When this point was reached he almost always said, "Well, boys, I am down to raisins." After we had heard this curious remark a number of times, one of us ventured to ask him what it meant. He thereupon told us the story of the little girl who celebrated her birthday by eating very freely of many good things, topping off with raisins for dessert. During the night she was taken violently ill, and when the doctor arrived she was busy casting up her accounts. The genial doctor, scrutinizing the contents of the vessel, noticed some small black objects that had just appeared, and remarked to the anxious parent that all danger was past, as the child was "down to raisins." "So," Lincoln said, "when I reach the message in this pile which I saw on my last visit, I know that I need go no further."

In the White House, Lincoln had little or no leisure, but was constantly under a severe strain from which, as he often told us, he obtained welcome relief by his frequent visits to the telegraph office, which place was in fact his haven of rest, his Bethany. There only was he comparatively free from interruption and he would frequently remain for hours, and sometimes all night, awaiting news that might mean so much to the country, and in the intervals of waiting he would write messages of inquiry, counsel and encouragement to the generals in the field, to the governors of the loyal states and sometimes despatches announcing pardon or reprieve to soldiers under sentence of death for desertion or sleeping on post. He almost lived in the telegraph office when a battle was in progress, and on other occasions would drop in, as he sometimes jocosely remarked, to get rid of the pestering crowd of office-seekers.

The War Department telegraph office was the scene of many vitally important conferences between Lincoln and members of his cabinet, leading generals, congressmen and others, who soon learned that when the President was not at the White House he could most likely be found in the telegraph office.

The staff of the War Department telegraph office consisted at first of a few operators only,

Colonel William B. Wilson

Manager of the War Department telegraph office,
May 1861 to March 1862

Colonel James R. Gilmore

Superintendent of the United States Military Telegraph
Corps in August, 1861

our manager from May, 1861, to March, 1862, being William B. Wilson who in the service of the Commonwealth of Pennsylvania had opened on April 17, 1861, in Governor Curtin's office at Harrisburg the first military telegraph office on the continent. Later, in the Antietam and Gettysburg campaigns, and during Early's raid, Wilson rendered important scouting service, carrying with him a telegraph instrument which he utilized in sending reports over the wires by cutting in when opportunity offered.

On March 29, 1903, the State of Pennsylvania awarded to Wilson a gold medal bearing this inscription: "In recognition of his Important and Delicate Service as Military Telegraph Operator and Scout during the Raids and Invasions into the State, 1862–3 and 4." The same Act gave him a commission as colonel of Pennsylvania volunteers. Colonel Wilson is the only member of the Civil War Military Telegraph Corps who to-day holds a commission, all other officers in that corps having been mustered out after the close of the war.

I succeeded manager Wilson in March, 1862, soon after Major Thomas T. Eckert was appointed chief of the War Department telegraph staff, which office he held until August, 1866. I continued to hold the position of manager until the latter date, serving also as cipher-operator with Charles A. Tinker, Albert B. Chandler, George W. Baldwin, and Frank Stewart. Baldwin and Stewart died years ago. As the telegraphic work increased the staff was enlarged, until at one time there were ten or twelve day and, as needs required, two or three night operators. It was not always an easy matter to procure enough skilled telegraphers for the service, and whenever we learned of enlisted soldiers or drafted men who could telegraph we took immediate steps to secure an order from the Secretary of War detailing such men for our service.

One instance, described in the following letter, will suffice to show at once our great need of operators and the method of speedy transfer to our corps:

Pittsburgh, Pa., May 1, 1907.

One day early in June, 1864, I was ordered to Wilmington, Delaware, on special duty for my Battery. While there I happened to meet Martin Buell, who had charge of the military telegraph-line down the Eastern shore leading to Fort Monroe. In a brief conversation he learned that I was a telegraph-operator and he remarked, "We need you in our service." How quickly this apparently casual remark bore fruit is shown by the following correspondence:

WAR DEPARTMENT TELEGRAPH OFFICE

"Fort Delaware, June 7, 1864.

"Mr. M. V. B. Buell, Wilmington.

"SIR: If you design endeavoring to have J. W. Boyd of this command transferred elsewhere I would respectfully state that it will be impossible for me to spare him from here, he being a clerk in my office.

"Very respectfully, A. SCHOEF, Brig. Gen. Comdg."

"War Department, A. G. O.,
"Washington, D. C., June 8, 1864.

"Special Orders 201.

" . . . Private Joseph W. Boyd, Battery G, Independent Pennsylvania Artillery, now at Fort Delaware, Del., is hereby granted a furlough without pay or emoluments to enable him to enter the U. S. Military Telegraph Corps. He will be borne on his Company Rolls as on furlough and will report in person without delay for duty to Mr. M. V. B. Buell at Dover, Del.

"The quartermaster will furnish the necessary transportation.

"By order of the Secretary of War.

"E. D. TOWNSEND, Asst. Adjt. Genl."

I served on this detail as military telegraph operator until September, 1865, but was mustered out with my Battery on June 15, 1865.

JOSEPH W. BOYD.

All military telegraph despatches from or to Washington of necessity passed through the War Department office. The operators were fully occupied in the work of transmitting and receiving these messages over the wires, and the cipher-operators in translating the more important ones into and out of cipher. There was no time to spare for the task of filing them away in an orderly, careful manner, but the Government was fortunate in having the right man for such an important duty, and historians of the Civil War for all time will have cause to be grateful to Major Albert E. H. Johnson for his preliminary work toward the great array of volumes of the "Official Records" published by authority of Congress, which contain thousands of military telegrams all carefully filed by him.

Johnson before the war was a clerk in Stanton's law office and came with him to the War Department as his private secretary in January, 1862. He remained in that capacity, and as custodian of military telegrams, until Stanton left the cabinet in 1868. Over eighty years of age, he is still living in Washington, and to him the writer is indebted for authentic data concerning many of the incidents recorded herein.

IV

ANSON STAGER was the author of the first Federal ciphers, which he devised for General McClellan's use in West Virginia, in the summer of 1861, before McClellan came to Washington. They were very simple, consisting merely of cards, about three inches by five, on which was printed a series of key-words and arbitraries, the former indicating the number of lines and columns and the route or order in which the messages might be written, the arbitrary words being used to represent names of places and persons. When an important despatch was intrusted to a cipher-operator for transmission, he first rewrote it carefully in five, six, or seven columns, as the case might be, adding extra or blind words on the last line, if it was not full. A key-word was then selected to indicate the number of columns and lines and the order in which the words of the message were to be copied for transmission by wire.

For instance, a certain key-word would represent the combination of seven columns and eleven lines, and the route would be up the sixth column, down the third, up the fifth, down the seventh, up the first, down the fourth, down the second. At the end of each column a blind word would be inserted, provided the code so directed, and at the end of the despatch one or more blind words might be added at the discretion of the cipher-operator, for the purpose of increasing the difficulty of translation by unauthorized persons. The key-word and the blind words would be discarded by the cipher-operator when translating the despatch into English. The total number of words in a cipher-message in the above-mentioned combination would be $7 \times 12 + 1 = 85$, provided no extra words were added at the end, as above indicated.

This somewhat crude but really effective method was improved upon from time to time by the War Department staff of cipher-operators.

Mr. William R. Plum, in his history, "The Military Telegraph," Vol. I, p. 60, says:

The Cipher System, originated by Anson Stager, and developed mainly by him, but in no small degree by others, more particularly T. T. Eckert, A. B. Chandler, D.

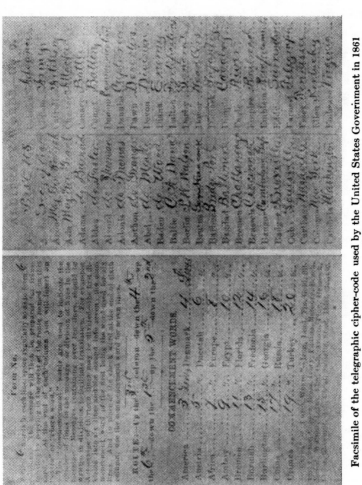

Facsimile of the telegraphic cipher-code used by the United States Government in 1861

The original of this card-form was devised by General Anson Stager, and the arrangement as above was made by Cipher-operator Charles A. Tinker (Copyright, 1907, by Charles A. Tinker)

Homer Bates and Charles A. Tinker, was eminently successful. Copies of cipher messages quite often reached the enemy, and, some were published in their newspapers, with a general request for translation, but all to no purpose. To the statement that in no case did an enemy ever succeed in deciphering such messages, let us add that neither did any Federal cipher-operator ever prove recreant to his sacred trust, and we have, in a sentence, two facts that reflect infinite credit upon the corps.

It is not within the scope of this history to describe in detail the various cipher-codes used in the military telegraph service during the Civil War, as Plum's history contains a full and accurate account, to which little can be added except in the way of incident. It will suffice here to say that from time to time the War Department staff issued successive printed editions of this cipher-code, numbering twelve in all, in the form of a book of a size suitable for the pocket, containing at first sixteen printed pages, and in the last edition, forty-eight pages. The front part was taken up with key-words, in different order and various combinations. The remainder of the book contained a series of printed arbitrary words opposite which, in each case, respectively, we wrote the name of a person, place, or short phrase most likely to be used in military despatches.

To the President, cabinet officers, and leading generals two, three, and in some cases half a dozen arbitrary words were assigned, so that in any despatch prepared for transmission it would not be necessary to use a given word more than once. This precaution was also followed in the key-word section, several different words being set apart to represent each separate combination. Arbitrary words were also used to indicate the month, day, and hour of each cipher-message when ready for transmission.

On page 55 is given one example from Plum's history which will suffice to show the general plan followed in all our cipher work.

The combination selected was indicated by the key-word "Blonde" in No. 12 cipher, effective at that time between the War Department and the Army of the Potomac, ex-Secretary Cameron being then on a visit to Genèral Meade's headquarters, south of Gettysburg.

This key-word "Blonde" indicated the combination of columns, lines, and word route specified above. Following these directions, the despatch, when prepared for transmission by wire, was in this form:

EXAMPLE FROM PLUM'S HISTORY

SHOWING GENERAL PLAN FOLLOWED IN MILITARY TELEGRAPH CIPHER WORK

Washington, D. C,	July	15th	18	60	3	for
Sigh	man	Cammer	on	period	1	would
give	much	to be	relieved	of the	impression	that
Meade	comma	Conch	comma	Smith	and	all
comma	since	the	battle	of	get	ties
burg	Comma	have	striven	only	to	get
the enemy	over	the river	without	another	fight	period
please	tell	me	if	you	know	who
was	the	one	corps	commander	who	was
for	fighting	comma	in the	council	of	war
on	Sunday	night	signature	A. Lincoln	Bless	him

55

LINCOLN IN THE TELEGRAPH OFFICE

Washington, D. C., July 15, 1863.

A. H. CALDWELL, *Cipher-operator,*
    Gen. Meade's Headquarters:

Blonde bless of who no optic to get an impression I madison square Brown cammer Toby ax the have turnip me Harry bitch rustle silk adrian counsel locust you another only of children serenade flea Knox county for wood that awl ties get hound who was war him suicide on for was please village large bat Bunyan give sigh incubus heavy Norris on trammeled cat knit striven without if Madrid quail upright martyr Stewart man much bear since ass skeleton tell the oppressing Tyler monkey.

BATES.

Total, eighty-five words.

By comparing the two copies one may discover the several arbitrary words used to represent names of persons, places, dates, words and phrases. The blind words may also be readily found.

Captain Samuel H. Beckwith, General Grant's cipher-operator during his four campaigns, was an expert with the pen, as will be seen from the specimen of his work shown by the facsimile of two pages of his cipher-book, which is truly a work of art. It was his habit all through the war to recopy with a pen the contents of each new edition of our cipher-book as fast as supplied to him, and his written copy would be so embellished

56

with extraneous matter as to make it not only attractive from a chirographical point of view,

Facsimile of two pages of the last cipher-book in the War Department series, printed for the first time in "Century Magazine" for June, 1907

The original is in the handwriting of Captain Samuel H. Beckwith, General Grant's cipher-operator, and was used in transmitting Lincoln's telegrams to and from City Point and Richmond, March 25 to April 8, 1865

but also wholly unintelligible to any one but a shrewd cipher-operator. By the use of ink of various colors he combined two or three different codes in one book.

The one from which these two pages were taken was the last in the War Department series, having been sent to Beckwith on March 23, 1865, and it was this cipher that he used for Lincoln's despatches during his two weeks' stay at City Point and Richmond, March 25 to April 8, 1865, after which time none of the President's telegrams was put in cipher. For this reason Beckwith's cipher-book is of historic interest.

During Burnside's Fredericksburg campaign at the end of 1862, the War Department operators discovered indications of an interloper on the wire leading to his headquarters at Aquia Creek. These indications consisted of an occasional irregular opening and closing of the circuit and once in a while strange signals, evidently not made by our own operators. It is proper to note that the characteristics of each Morse operator's sending are just as pronounced and as easily recognized as those of ordinary handwriting, so that when a message is transmitted over a wire, the identity of the sender may readily be known to any other operator within hearing who has ever worked with him. A somewhat similar means of personal identification occurs every day in the use of the telephone.

At the time referred to, therefore, we were certain that our wire had been tapped. In some way or other the Confederate operator learned that we were aware of his presence, and he then informed us that he was from Lee's army and had been on our wire for several days, and that, having learned all that he wanted to know, he was then about to cut out and run. We gossiped with him for a while and then ceased to hear his signals and believed that he had gone.

We had taken measures, however, to discover his whereabouts by sending out linemen to patrol the line; but his tracks were well concealed, and it was only after the intruder had left that we found the place where our wire had been tapped. He had made the secret connection by means of fine silk-covered magnet wire, in such a manner as to conceal the joint almost entirely. Meantime, Burnside's cipher-operator was temporarily absent from his post, and we had recourse to a crude plan for concealing the text of telegrams to the Army of the Potomac, which we had followed on other somewhat similar occasions when we believed the addressee or operator at the distant point (not provided with the cipher-key) was particularly keen and alert. This plan consisted primarily of sending the message backward, the individual words being misspelled and otherwise garbled. We had practised on one or two despatches to Burnside before the Confederate operator was discovered to be on the wire, and were pleased to get his prompt answers, couched also in similar outlandish language, which was, however, intelligible to us after a short study of the text in each case. Burnside and ourselves soon became quite expert in this home-made cipher game, as we all strove hard to clothe the despatches in strange, uncouth garb.

In order to deceive the Confederate operator, however, we sent to Burnside a number of cipher messages, easy of translation, and which contained all sorts of bogus information for the purpose of misleading the enemy. Burnside or his operator at once surmised our purpose, and the general thereupon sent us in reply a lot of balderdash also calculated to deceive the uninitiated.

It was about this time that the following specially important despatch from Lincoln was filed for transmission:

CIPHER–CODES AND MESSAGES

Executive Mansion, Washington,
November 25, 1862. 11:30 A.M.

MAJOR-GENERAL BURNSIDE, Falmouth, Virginia: If I should be in boat off Aquia Creek at dark to-morrow (Wednesday) evening, could you, without inconvenience, meet me and pass an hour or two with me? A. LINCOLN.

Although the Confederate operator had said good-by several days before, we were not sure he had actually left. We therefore put Lincoln's telegram in our home-made cipher, so that if the foreign operator were still on our wire, the message might not be readily made out by the enemy. At the same time extra precautions were taken by the Washington authorities to guard against any accident to the President while on his visit to Burnside. No record is now found of the actual text of this cipher-despatch, as finally prepared for transmission, but going back over it word for word, I believe the following is so nearly like it as to be called a true copy:

Washington, D. C., November 25, 1862.

BURNSIDE, Falmouth, Virginia: Can Inn Ale me withe 2 oar our Ann pas Ann me flesh ends N. V. Corn Inn out with U cud Inn heaven day nest Wed roe Moore Tom darkey hat Greek Why Hawk of Abbott Inn B chewed I if. BATES.

By reading the above backward, observing the phonetics, and bearing in mind that flesh is the equivalent of meat, the real meaning is easily found. It cannot be said that this specimen exhibits specially clever work on the part of the War Department staff, nor is it likely that the Confederate operator, if he overheard its transmission, had much trouble in unraveling its meaning. As to this we can only conjecture.

Burnside readily translated this cryptogram, if it may be dignified with so high-sounding a name, and replied in similar gibberish that he would meet Lincoln at the place and time specified. At that meeting on the steamer *Baltimore* was discussed the plan of a movement against Lee's intrenchments which was made three weeks later, and which resulted in our army being repulsed with the loss of many thousands of lives.

Another instance may be referred to in which a telegram from Lincoln was put into crude cipher form of the sort described above. On his last visit to the army he wrote a despatch to the Secretary of War, which Grant's cipher-operator did not put in our regular cipher, but, instead, transmitted in the following form:

CIPHER–CODES AND MESSAGES

City Point, Va., 8:30 A.M., April 3, 1865.

TINKER, War Department: A Lincoln its in fume a in hymn to start I army treating there possible if of cut too forward pushing is He is so all Richmond aunt confide is Andy evacuated Petersburg reports Grant morning this Washington Secretary War.   BECKWITH.

The probable reason for adopting this crude form was to insure its reaching its destination without attracting the special attention of watchful operators on the route of the City Point-Washington wire, because at that crisis every one was on the *qui vive* for news from Grant's advancing army, and if the message had been sent in plain language, the important information it conveyed might have been overheard in its transmission and perhaps would have reached the general public in advance of its receipt by the War Department.

It is not necessary to give the translation of this cipher-message. To use a homely term, "Any one can read it with his eyes shut." In fact, the easiest way would be for one to-shut the eyes and let some one else read it backward, not too slowly. The real wording then becomes plain.

An earlier cipher-despatch with which Lincoln had to do during his visit to City Point, was from Sheridan to Grant, about March 26, 1865. Sheridan, with his entire cavalry command, was finishing up his great raid from the Shenandoah Valley to join Grant's army on the James, his special object being to cut the railroad and canal to the west of Richmond and then strike to the north for the Pamunkey at White House. By the time he reached that point his horses would be in great need of forage and new shoes. Accordingly, Sheridan wrote a long despatch to Grant, telling him just when to expect him at White House, and asking him to direct General Ingalls, quartermaster, to meet him with plenty of forage for men and horses, as well as horse-shoers with their kits. Sheridan then selected three of his best scouts, each taking a different route, one south of Richmond, one directly through that city, and the third to the north of Lee's army. Each man had a copy of the despatch to Grant, which Sheridan's expert cipher-operator, McCaine, had written in small but legible characters on tissue-paper. The copy was then rolled up, incased in tin-foil, and secreted on the scout's person, in one instance resting in front of his upper teeth.

Lincoln, with Mrs. Lincoln and Tad, had just reached City Point from Washington. The party had been supplied with tents close to the telegraph office. Beckwith—Grant's cipher-operator —told the writer in November, 1906, that a few days after the President's arrival at Grant's head-quarters, the flap of the telegraph tent was slowly turned back and there appeared at the opening a tall, slim, long-haired, typical Virginian, who quietly entered, and closed the flap, asking the only other occupant of the tent if his name was Beckwith. Upon receiving an affirmative an-swer, the stranger, who was dressed in butternut clothing, soiled and worn and incredibly dusty, without further word took a small, round, tin-foil-covered roll from his person and handed it to Beckwith with the single word, "McCaine."

Beckwith grasped the meaning at once, and thinking to give the messenger a little pleasure in return for his faithful service, said: "You have risked your life in the cause. Would you not like to deliver this document direct to President Lin-coln, who is now in the next tent?" The scout's eyes lighted up and he nodded assent. Beckwith then went into Lincoln's tent and told him there was a man in the telegraph office who had brought a cipher-despatch from Sheridan, and he thought it would be pleasant to have him deliver it direct to the President. Lincoln took in the situation, and returning with Beckwith to the other tent, greeted the scout pleasantly. The latter then handed the cipher-roll to the President, who slowly and carefully unwound it and pressing out the tissue-sheet, glanced at it long enough to see that the despatch was in cipher. He then passed it over to Beckwith, remarking to the scout that he guessed this young man would have to do some work on it before it would be of any use.

The President then asked about Sheridan's whereabouts, and the route taken by the scout. The latter told where he had last seen Sheridan when he received the little packet, and added that he was a native Virginian, and had been able to come through the city of Richmond without detection. After some further conversation and an expression of thanks from the President, the scout backed out of the tent and disappeared forever, so far as Beckwith knew. The other two scouts were never heard from, and were probably captured by the enemy. Sheridan's despatch was most welcome to Lincoln and Grant, and 20,000 horseshoes and other much-needed supplies were soon on their way to the Pamunkey.

A few days later, Sheridan, with his chief of staff, Captain Forsyth, rode over from White

House to City Point. Robert Lincoln informed his father, who was on the *River Queen,* that "Little Phil" had arrived. The President hastened ashore and went to Colonel Bowers's tent to express his personal congratulations to Sheridan, which he did in the most sincere and graceful manner, winding up with this remark: "General Sheridan, when this peculiar war began I thought a cavalryman should be at least six feet four high; but"—still holding Sheridan's hand in his earnest grasp and looking down upon the little general—"I have changed my mind—five feet four will do on a pinch." Sheridan measured five feet four and a half, and at this time weighed only one hundred and forty-one pounds on the ground; but in the saddle "he weighed a ton," as his soldiers were wont to say. At the meeting with Lincoln he appeared without sword, sash, belt, or epaulets, and with his old brown slouch-hat in his hand.

V

CONFEDERATE CIPHER-CODES AND INTERCEPTED DESPATCHES

LINCOLN took a personal interest in our translation of the enemy's cipher-despatches, intercepted and brought to the War Department for translation, and whenever he saw the three of us with our heads together he knew that we had something on hand of special interest. At such times his anxiety would lead him to ask whether there was anything of importance coming through the mill. One of these occasions was in 1863, during the siege of Vicksburg. General Grant's scouts had captured several cipher-despatches from General Joe Johnston, addressed to General Pemberton. The letter inclosing one of them is as follows:

Headquarters Department of the Tennessee,
Near Vicksburg, May 25, 1863.

Col. J. C. Kelton, Assistant Adjutant-General ,
Washington, D. C.

COLONEL: Eight men, with 200,000 percussion caps, were arrested whilst attempting to get through our lines into

Vicksburg. The inclosed cipher was found upon them. Having no one with me who has the ingenuity to translate it, I send it to Washington, hoping that some one there may be able to make it out. Should the meaning of this cipher be made out, I request a copy be sent to me.

Very respectfully,

U. S. Grant, Major-General.

INCLOSURE

Jackson, May 25, 1863.

Lieutenant General Pemberton: My X A F V. U S L X was V V U F L S J P by the B R C Y A (I) J 200 000 V E G T. S U A J. N E R P. Z I F M. It will be G ꜰ O E C S Z O (Q) D as they N T Y M N X. Bragg M J T P H I N Z G a Q R (K) C M K B S E. When it D Z G J X. I will Y O I G. AS. Q H Y. N I T W M do you Y T I A M the I I K M. V F V E Y. How and where is the J S Q M L G U G S F T V E. H B F Y is your R O E E L. J. E. Johnston.

When Grant's communication reached Washington, nearly a week after its date, it was turned over to the cipher-operators, who soon translated it almost verbatim, as follows:

Jackson, May 25, 1863.

Lieutenant-General Pemberton, Vicksburg: My——— was captured by the picket. 200,000 caps have been sent. It will be increased as they arrive. Bragg is sending a division. When it joins I will come to you. What do you think the best route? How and where is the enemy operating? What is your force? J. E. Johnston.

At various other times our troops intercepted despatches, sent from one Confederate general to another, containing important information in cipher. As a rule, we were able to translate these ciphers after more or less labor. They were generally ordinary letter ciphers, the letters of the alphabet being transposed in various ways. For instance, the foregoing despatch from General Johnston of May 25, was put into a cipher the key-words of which were "Manchester Bluff." In arranging the message, Johnston wrote it out with the letters well spaced, and then on a line above he wrote in order the letters forming the key-words "Manchester Bluff," repeating them as often as necessary to the end of his real message. Then, by means of an alphabet square, he found one by one the cipher letter for each real letter, thus: beginning with the first letter of the key-word, "M," on the top line of the alphabet square, he ran down the "M" column until he came to the first letter of his real message, then turning to the left or right, as prearranged, he found the end letter (in the A or Z column of that line), and took that end letter as the first for his cipher-despatch; and so on until all the letters had thus been couched in cipher. The reverse method would, of course, be followed by the addressee.

In translating Johnston's despatch we did not have the key-word to guide us, but guessed at the meaning, trying first one word and then another until by analogy we had worked out the entire message. In 1884 the War Records Office published our translation, together with a true copy of the despatch in connection with the key-words as above.[1] The official copy is the same as our translation, with two or three slight differences.

In other cases the Confederates did not use the alphabet square, with a key-word, but adopted the "Slater" code method of going ahead or back in the regular alphabet a certain number of letters, as prearranged. This latter plan was followed by Johnston in another despatch to Pemberton, dated June 30, 1863, only four days before the surrender of Vicksburg, which was captured by Grant's scouts on the day of its date, and deciphered by Michael Mason of Waterhouse's Chicago Battery. My records do not show the particular code used in preparing this despatch.

On December 21, 1863, the War Department cipher-operators were called upon to unravel a

[1] See "Official Records," Vol. XXIV. Part 1, pp. 39–40.

Confederate cipher-letter written in New York City by a man named J. H. Cammack, and inclosed in an envelop addressed to Alex. Keith, Jr., Halifax, Nova Scotia. It had been dropped in the post-office at New York, and intercepted and forwarded to the War Department by the postmaster, Abram Wakeman, who had been instructed by the authorities to keep a sharp lookout for communications addressed to Keith. The despatch itself, when we had translated it, was found to be intended for Judah P. Benjamin, Confederate Secretary of State, Richmond, Virginia. This cipher (see facsimile on page 73) was wholly unlike any we had ever been called upon to translate, and the "Sacred Three" puzzled their brains for hours before they succeeded in making full sense out of the jargon, while the President hovered about us, anxious to know the sequel of our united cogitations. A few days later a second cipher despatch, also inclosed in an envelop bearing Keith's address as above, was intercepted and forwarded to Washington. This one was dated New York, December 22, 1863, and bore on the inside in cipher characters the address of Benjamin H. Hill, Secretary of War, Richmond. It was also quickly deciphered, and

CONFEDERATE CIPHER-CODES

Facsimile of a Confederate cipher-letter

This letter was dropped in the post-office at New York, December 18, 1863, addressed to Alex. Keith, Jr., Halifax, N. S. It was sent by the New York postmaster, Abram Wakeman, to the War Department where it was quickly translated by the cipher-operators—Tinker, Bates and Chandler—without the aid of the cipher-key, a copy of which will be found on page 77

proved to be even more important than the first one. The translations of the two despatches, according to the record in my war diary, were as follows:

LINCOLN IN THE TELEGRAPH OFFICE

N. Y., Dec. 18, 1863.

Hon. J. P. Benjamin, *Secretary of State,* Richmond, Va.:

Willis is here. The two steamers will leave here about Christmas. Lamar and Bowers left here via Bermuda two weeks ago. 12000 rifled muskets came duly to hand and were shipped to Halifax as instructed.

We will be able to seize the other two steamers as per programme. Trowbridge has followed the President's orders. We will have Briggs under arrest before this reaches you. Cost $2000. We want more money. How shall we draw. Bills all forwarded to Slidell and rects recd. Write as before.

J. H. C.

The second cipher was prepared in the same way as the first, and its translation is as follows:

New York, Dec. 22, 1863.

Hon. Benj. H. Hill, Richmond, Va.

Dear Sir: Say to Memminger that Hilton will have the machines all finished and dies all cut ready for shipping by the first of January. The engraving of the plates is superb.

They will be shipped via Halifax and all according to instructions.

The main part of the work has been under the immediate supervision of Hilton, who will act in good faith in consequence of the large amount he has and will receive. The work is beautifully done and the paper is superb. A part has been shipped and balance will be forwarded in a few days.

Send some one to Nassau to receive and take the machines and paper through Florida. Write me at Halifax. I leave

74

first week in January. Should Goodman arrive at Nassau please send word by your agent that he is to await further instructions.

Yours truly,

J. H. C.[1]

The man Cammack, who signed the two cipher-letters, made use of six different sets or alphabets of cryptograms, but made the error—fatal to his purpose—of confining himself, as to any given word, to one particular code or alphabet, instead of using the six sets of hieroglyphics inter-changeably.

Our fortunate and prompt translation of the first of these two important despatches resulted in an immediate visit of Assistant Secretary Dana to New York for conference with General Dix, with the result that in less than a week six or eight of the conspirators were arrested, and a quantity of arms and ammunition seized, which had been packed in hogsheads ostensibly containing pro-visions, and which the cipher-despatches indicated were meant to be shipped on Atlantic liners, a number of the conspirators taking passage at the same time, their intention being to suddenly over-power the crew after sailing, and then use the

[1] A more detailed account of these two cipher-despatches appeared in "Harper's Magazine" for June, 1898.

vessel as a privateer or run the blockade with the cargo into a Southern port.

WHEN Richmond fell into our hands in April, 1865, Assistant Secretary of War Charles A. Dana found among the Confederate archives, in addition to the alphabet square code used by Booth, referred to in the latter part of this chapter, a more complicated cipher-code identical with the key in the hands of Cammack, the Confederate agent in New York, and which was used by him in his two letters of December 18 and 22, 1863, above referred to. A facsimile of the code is shown on page 77. This code was also used between Canada and Richmond for important despatches from and to Jacob Thompson and his associates, notably the despatch hereinafter referred to, dated October 13, 1864, from Thompson to Davis, and the latter's reply of October 19. The War Department operators, however, managed to decipher all these despatches without the aid of an official key.

My colleague, Mr. Tinker, has recently shown me a letter which he wrote to his mother on December 27, 1863, giving an account of the translation of the two Confederate cipher-de-

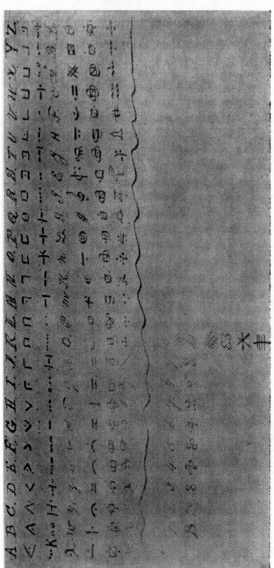

Facsimile of the Confederate cipher-code found on April 6, 1865, by Charles A. Dana, among the archives of the Confederate State Department in Richmond, printed for the first time in "Century Magazine" for June, 1907

This cipher was used in the correspondence between the highest Confederate officials and the Confederate agents in Canada and New York City. The letters signed "J. H. C." on pages 74 and 75, were written in a commingling of these six sets of hieroglyphics. From a consideration of such intricacy the reader may judge how remarkable was the feat of the cipher-operators in translating these despatches without any other clues than those derived from ingenuity and patience spatches of December 18 and 22, 1863, from which the following extract is taken:

On December 21, after we had worked out the first rebel cipher-letter, it was found to be of such importance that a special cabinet meeting was called, and Asst.-Secretary of War, Chas. A. Dana, was sent by night train to New York to find and arrest the conspirators, which was soon accomplished. On December 24, the second rebel cipher was translated by us and proved to be almost as important as the first one. Secretary Stanton told Major Eckert he would n't give his cipher-operators for the whole clerical force of the Government. Asst.-Secretary of War Watson came into the cipher-room and congratulated us in person upon our mysterious success. He said he would like to make us a Christmas gift, but could not do so because there was no appropriation for such a purpose. He said, however, that the three of us who translated the Cammack-Keith ciphers would receive an increase in our pay from December 1.

In order to keep itself informed upon political and military matters in the North, the Confederate government employed agents, with headquarters in Canada, who maintained secret communication with Richmond, chiefly by means of spies, who went through our lines to and fro in the performance of their very dangerous task. One of these messengers was also in the service of our Government. and as he passed through

Washington on his way north or south, he found it necessary on each occasion to rest and recuperate for a few hours, during which interval he would communicate with Major Eckert, and allow him to inspect his budget, which was always in cipher, and which, on his northward trip, was usually addressed to Jacob Thompson, one of the Confederate agents at Clifton, Ontario. Two extracts from my war diary will suffice to show the situation:

Sunday, October 16, 1864.

A rebel cipher, dated Clifton, Canada, October 13, was brought to the War Department to-day from Jake Thompson in Canada, addressed to Jeff Davis, Richmond.

Thompson says that Washington is sufficiently garrisoned to resist any attack until reinforced; that the re-election of Lincoln is almost certain and he urges upon Davis the necessity for the South gaining advantages over the Northern armies.

Sunday, October 23, 1864.

The rebel cipher intercepted on October 16th has been to Richmond and a reply from Jeff Davis, dated October 19, returned, the carrier very kindly traveling via Washington and allowing us to make a copy of his precious document. Davis says Longstreet will soon attack Sheridan and then move north as far as practicable, toward unprotected points.

(Note—This was done last Wednesday, but instead of moving north, the enemy was compelled to retreat south.)

Davis adds that a blow will soon be struck near Richmond on Grant's army, that it is not quite time.[1]

The movement by the enemy promised by Davis was at first successful, our army being forced back, losing many guns, with "Sheridan twenty miles away," on his return from a visit to Washington. A special train hurried him to the front, and he then made that John Gilpin ride celebrated by T. Buchanan Read in his stirring poem, and the reorganized Union forces routed the enemy, commanded by Jubal Early.

As stated in my diary, these two cipher-despatches were promptly translated by the War Department cipher-operators, and their contents proved of much interest to Lincoln, who always kept close tally on the movements, to and fro, of this messenger, who must have been possessed of great courage, intelligence, and ability, to have secured and held such a responsible and confidential position with both governments.

One of the later Confederate cipher-despatches was from Clement C. Clay, one of

[1] Copies verbatim of the two despatches referred to may be found on page 42 of the "Trial of the Conspirators," compiled by Pitman.

Thompson's associates in Canada, and the accommodating messenger, as usual, allowed us to take a copy. It was addressed to Judah P. Benjamin, Secretary of State, Richmond, and was promptly translated by us. It showed clearly that the Confederate agents were using Canada as a rendezvous for raids into border towns and that the Canadian government officials were favoring these movements; at least secretly. Secretary Stanton directed the spy to be brought, and asked him one question only. Major Johnson, Stanton's confidential secretary, says he did not hear what that question was, but it was short, and when the man answered, in as brief a manner, the Secretary dismissed him, and turning to President Lincoln, said we should by all means retain the original document signed by Clay, for use as evidence in support of our demand upon Great Britain for heavy damages sustained by us, in consequence of the ready asylum that country was affording our enemies.

This occurred on a Sunday, and the President had come direct from Dr. Gurley's Presbyterian Church, where he had a pew, to the War Department, for conference over the matter. Stanton was for taking instant action and withholding

Clay's despatch; but Assistant Secretary Dana said we had better not break this important line of communication, as we should do if we failed to allow the spy to carry the despatch to Richmond.

Lincoln, however, suggested a plan whereby two birds might be killed with one stone. He said: "Why not allow the messenger to depart as usual, and then capture him in Virginia somewhere, take the despatch from him, clap him in prison, and afterward let him escape?" This simple plan was adopted, and General Augur was directed to look out for a Confederate messenger on a certain road that night. The man was captured, his papers were seized, and he was put in old Capitol Prison, from which he soon escaped after being fired on and wounded by the guard. A reward for his recapture was widely advertised in the newspapers, and when he reported back to Clay and Thompson, glibly telling his story and showing his wounds, his word was credited, and he resumed his double service, trusted even more fully than before.

The identity of this messenger was disclosed to the public on the trial of Mrs. Surratt, in May, 1865, when a certain witness gave evidence against the conspirators, serving to show the great value placed by the Richmond government upon the services of Clay and Thompson in Canada, who were concerned in the scheme for setting fire to certain Northern cities, and also, it was believed, in the conspiracy to kidnap Lincoln.

Apropos of secret despatches carried through the lines, John H. Surratt, then about twenty years old, acted as a Confederate spy traveling between Washington and the enemy's boats on the lower Potomac, carrying his despatches "sometimes in the heel of his boots and sometimes between the planks of a buggy."

In the waistcoat pocket of John Wilkes Booth, when his body was searched after he was shot, was found a copy of an alphabet square exactly like the one used by Johnston and other Southern generals, and another copy was found in his trunk at the National Hotel, Washington, where he last roomed before the tragedy. In my war diary is this entry:

May 20, 1865.

I was subpœnaed to-day as a witness in the trial of Mrs. Surratt, Payne, Atzerodt, and other conspirators, but did not testify. Presume I will be called next week. My testimony is for the purpose of identifying the Cipher Code found on Booth's body with that used by Jeff Davis and the rebel generals.

In this connection let us refer to the official report of the "Trial of the Conspirators" in May and June, 1865, compiled by Pitman. On pages 41 and 42 is given the testimony of Lieut. W. H. Terry, Wm. Eaton, Charles Duell, Colonel Jos. H. Taylor, Charles A. Dana, and General Eckert, which, taken altogether, prove that the alphabet square cipher, at least three copies of which were in the possession of Booth and his co-conspirators,[1] was identical with one of the two cipher-keys found by Mr. Dana in the office of Judah P. Benjamin, Confederate Secretary of State at Richmond, on April 6, 1865, three days after

---

[1] Duell identified at the trial a cipher-letter dated Washington, D. C., April 15, written by one of Booth's band to another one in North Carolina, to whom, apparently, had been assigned the task of assassinating General Sherman. Duell testified that he had found this letter at Moorehead City, North Carolina, and that with the help of a friend he had deciphered it by means of the alphabet square.

The following is a copy of Duell's translation of the above-mentioned letter, with unimportant parts omitted:

Washington, D. C., April the 15, '65.

John W. Wise.

DEAR JOHN: I am happy to inform you that Pet has done his work well. He is safe and old Abe is in hell. Now sir, all eyes are on you. You must bring Sherman—Grant is in the hands of old Gray ere this. Red Shoes showed lack of nerve in Seward's case but fell back in good order. *Johnson* must come. Old Crook has him in charge . . . Old ——— always behind, lost the pop at City Point . . . No. Two will give you this . . . (signed) *No. FIVE.*

84

the evacuation of that city. That evidence also shows that the same cipher-code was used in 1864 (and no doubt at other times) for official despatches between President Davis and Secretary of State Benjamin at Richmond, and the Confederate agents, Thompson, Clay, Holcombe, and Saunders in Canada. It is inconceivable that Booth was not supplied with this cipher-code by the Confederate government, although it does not follow that President Davis or any of his cabinet had any previous knowledge of the assassination plot.[1]

[1] A more detailed reference to this secret agency will be made in a subsequent chapter on "The Attempt to Burn New York."

VI

MY first assignment to duty was at the Navy Yard under Captain, afterward Admiral, Dahlgren, who directed the sergeant of the guard to keep a sentry in front of the door leading to the telegraph room, and to allow no one to enter or leave. These orders were obeyed literally, and for four days I was virtually a prisoner, my frugal meals being sent to my room. The confinement became so irksome that on one occasion I locked the door and climbed out of the window; but on my return by the same route, the sentry overheard the noise I made, and when I opened the door he warned me that the manœuver could be repeated only at the risk of a shot from his gun.

Early in May I was transferred to Annapolis Junction, where on the night of the 10th I was roused from bed by General Butler, who ordered me to open the telegraph office and keep the railroad track clear to Annapolis for the train carrying Ross Winans, whom he had that day arrested in Baltimore for treason. I continued to call the Annapolis office for several hours, but finally concluded that General Butler's train had safely reached its destination or else had encountered obstacles which I could not hope to remove. I returned to the War Department on May 24, and remained there on continuous duty until a year after the close of the war, excepting for two weeks in June, 1864, when I served as cipher-operator for General Grant at City Point, Virginia.

In May, 1861, the telegraph office was moved from the chief clerk's room to the entresol, or first landing, of the stairway leading to the second story of the War Department building, a railing having been erected to inclose the telegraph-instruments and secure some measure of seclusion. The inner space was small and, during the disastrous days of Bull Run, when Lincoln came to the office, remaining for hours at a time with General Scott and one or more members of his cabinet, the place was so crowded that the operators found it difficult to attend properly to their work.

On Sunday, July 21, when the battle of Bull Run was fought, the military telegraph-line had reached Fairfax Court-house, and an improvised office had been opened at that point. Communication with General McDowell's headquarters at the front was maintained by means of a corps of mounted couriers, organized by Andrew Carnegie, under the immediate direction of William B. Wilson, who then served as our manager. These couriers passed back and forth all day long between Fairfax and the front. Lincoln hardly left his seat in our office and waited with deep anxiety for each succeeding despatch. At times during the awful day, General Scott would confer with the President or Secretary Cameron for a short period, and then depart to put into effect some urgent measures for protecting the capital.

Wilson says of these events:[1]

The group was composed on President Lincoln, Secretaries Seward, Cameron, Chase, Welles, Attorney-General Bates, General Mansfield, Colonels Townsend, Van Rensselaer, Hamilton and Wright of Lieutenant-General Scott's staff, and Colonel Thomas A. Scott. With maps of the field before them they watched, as it were, the conflict of arms as it progressed, at the same time keeping up a running desultory conversation.

[1] "Acts and Actors in the Civil War." By William Bender Wilson, p. 48.

From a photograph by Brady

Colonel Thomas A. Scott, Assistant Secretary of War, 1861

All the morning and well along into the afternoon, McDowell's telegrams were more or less encouraging, and Lincoln and his advisers waited with eager hope, believing that Beauregard was being pushed back to Manassas Junction; but all at once the despatches ceased coming. At first this was taken to mean that McDowell was moving farther away from the telegraph, and then, as the silence became prolonged, a strange fear seized upon the assembled watchers that perhaps all was not well. Suddenly the telegraph-instrument became alive again, and the short sentence, "Our army is retreating," was spelled out in the Morse characters. This brief announcement was followed by meager details concerning the first great disaster that had befallen our troops and the panic that followed.

The crowded telegraph office was quickly deserted by all except the operators, but Lincoln returned at intervals until after midnight, and shortly afterward the outlying office at Fairfax Court-house was abandoned. When morning dawned, our demoralized troops began to straggle, and then to pour, in an ever-increasing stream of frightened humanity over Long Bridge into

Washington, the immediate capture of which seemed then to be, and really was, within the power of the Confederate army, if only they had pressed their advantage. Consternation reigned supreme, and all realized that a great crisis of the war, the next after Sumter, was upon us.

The dark clouds that settled at that time upon Lincoln's already wrinkled brow were destined never to lift their heavy weight, except for that all too brief period of exaltation, just before his tragic ending, when Grant had pushed Lee to Appomattox, and Richmond was at last in our hands.

On March 28, 1907, a Reunion Dinner was given at the Hotel Manhattan in New York, which was attended by about fifty of the survivors of the United States Military Telegraph Corps. Mr. Andrew Carnegie, one of the members, in his address said that "not a single telegraph operator was among the frightened mob that crowded the railroad trains for Alexandria, when the stampede occurred at the first battle of Bull Run." Charles W. Jaques, now of Ashtabula, Ohio, also present at that dinner, afterward said in a letter to the writer:

IN THE FIRST MONTHS OF THE WAR

I was a boy of sixteen when that battle occurred, and was stationed at Springfield, Virginia, not far from the scene of action. I told the War Department office of the retreat of the Union Army, saying that those who passed my office first, were wounded soldiers, a few at a time, then squads of soldiers, followed later by companies and regiments. I added that I was going to close my office, and go with the crowd. The following telegram came back at once: "War Department, Washington, to Jaques, operator, Springfield, If you keep your office open until you have permission to close it, you will be rewarded. If you close it without such permission, you will be shot. Thos. A. Scott." So I remained, giving the War Department all the information obtainable until the entire army, including wounded and stragglers had passed by. It was 8 A.M. Monday, July 22, when my office was closed and I left for Washington. My reward was a leave of absence for two weeks to visit my home in Ohio, with free transportation and three months' pay, all in twenty-dollar gold pieces.

Our Bull Run experience in the telegraph office showed the necessity for more room and a location where the operators would be free from outside observation; so we were transferred to a large room on the first floor.

Lincoln visited us frequently in this room, and from its windows, in September, 1861, watched his friend Colonel E. D. Baker, with his brigade, including the so-called California regiment (71st Pennsylvania Volunteers) marching out on his way to Ball's Bluff and death. Lincoln also

6

made daily visits during this period to McClellan's headquarters on Fifteenth Street, to which wires had been run and the telegraph placed in charge of Thomas T. Eckert, who had been appointed captain and assistant aide-de-camp. Eckert's written instructions from Secretary Cameron (possibly at McClellan's request) were to deliver all military telegrams received at Washington to the commanding general; and this order, in at least one case, caused Eckert to keep from Lincoln's knowledge a despatch of great importance, as will be explained below.

On October 21, 1861, a message from General Stone, near Poolsville, was received at army headquarters over the hastily constructed telegraph-line, stating that his troops had moved across the Potomac at Edward's Ferry, and after an encounter with the enemy had been repulsed with considerable loss including Colonel E. D. Baker, who was killed. McClellan not being in his office Eckert started out to find him, taking from the stable the sole remaining horse, an ugly-tempered mare, dubbed the "man-killer." He rode over to Fitz-John Porter's headquarters across the Potomac, where he learned that McClellan had returned to the city. Eckert came back and finding that McClellan had gone to the White House, dismounted, walked across Lafayette Square and, in Lincoln's presence, delivered the message to McClellan, who did not tell the President what it contained.

It must be borne in mind that in the early part of the war, before Lincoln's unique personality and masterly qualities became known to the members of his cabinet, heads of departments, and others, his freedom of intercourse with the public ánd the readiness with which he gave out military information had been taken advantage of by newspaper correspondents and others.

From McClellan's "Own Story" we learn that he had no confidence in Lincoln's military ability or discretion, and that he believed information communicated to him would be divulged to congressmen and others, and he therefore thought it best to give him as little news as possible.

Soon after the delivery of Stone's despatch to McClellan, Lincoln came to headquarters and asked Eckert if he had any late despatches from the front. Eckert was in a quandary. He recalled the peculiar wording of his order of appointment, and as McClellan had not seen fit to disclose the contents of Stone's despatch, he did not feel that he was warranted in doing so. Accordingly he gave the evasive answer that there was nothing on file. Lincoln then went into McClellan's room and there saw the despatch for the first time. On his way out, passing Eckert's desk, he asked him why he had withheld the information. Eckert thereupon told the President what his written orders on the subject were, and explained that when he saw Mr. Lincoln enter the office he had deftly placed the copy of the despatch under the blotter, so that when he made his reply to the President he had told the truth, but not all the truth. Thereafter, when told there was no news, Lincoln would sometimes slyly remark: "Is there not something under the blotter?"

Eckert says that when Lincoln heard of the death of his old friend, Colonel Baker, he seemed greatly depressed.

Charles Carlton Coffin, a newspaper writer of note, said of this incident:[1]

I doubt if any other of the many tragic events of Lincoln's life ever stunned him so much as that unheralded message, which came over the wires while he was beside the instrument on that mournful day, October 21, 1861.[2]

[1] "Reminiscences of Lincoln," compiled by Allan Thorndike Rice.
[2] It will be observed from Eckert's account that Lincoln was not in the telegraph office at the precise moment when General Stone's message was received.

Colonel Baker had succeeded Lincoln in Congress, and between the two there had always been a close friendship, which was formed during the years in which they had practised law in Illinois. Lincoln's second son, who died in 1853, had been named Edward Baker Lincoln. The President, no doubt, keenly felt the death of his friend as a great personal loss; and, besides, it must have helped to make him realize that the terrible struggle in which the country was engaged would demand the sacrifice of many more such useful lives.

Reverting again to Eckert's explanation regarding the withholding of Stone's message from Lincoln, he says the President made no criticism of his action; but upon more careful reflection Eckert concluded he had made a mistake because as Commander-in-Chief of the Army, Lincoln outranked both the Secretary of War and the commanding general.

On November 1, 1861, the President issued an order placing Lieutenant-General Winfield Scott upon the retired list, and appointing Major-General George B. McClellan to the command of the army of the United States in his place.

On November 8, 1861, Captain Charles Wilkes,

commanding the United States war-ship, *San Jacinto,* overhauled the English mail steamer *Trent,* which had sailed from Havana the day before, having as passengers Mason and Slidell, Confederate commissioners, sent to seek from England and France recognition of the Confederacy. By a show of force Captain Wilkes compelled the English captain to surrender the two envoys. The seizure was not warranted by international law, but it seemed right and proper to the zealous sailor, who carried his prisoners to Boston, arriving there November 24. The entire North indorsed the seizure, and Congress, immediately on assembling in December, unanimously passed a resolution of thanks to Captain Wilkes for "his brave, adroit and patriotic conduct," and requested the President to place the two envoys in solitary confinement.

When the despatch announcing the arrival at Boston of the *San Jacinto,* and giving an account of the boarding of the British vessel and the capture of Mason and Slidell, reached the War Department, a conference was at once held in the telegraph office, Lincoln being present with his cabinet and several senators. I have read somewhere that a prominent senator or member of the cabinet, whose identity does not appear, was for hanging the two men, and then apologizing to Great Britain afterward. Each of the company present, with the exception of the President and one other, whose name is not recorded, expressed the opinion that Captain Wilkes did a brave and right thing in overhauling the British vessel and seizing the two emissaries.

Lincoln, however, was wise enough to realize that we were in the fault, and that we could not hope to hold the envoys, when England should demand their release, which it was certain she would do. His longer vision also enabled him to see that by yielding up our prisoners, with an apology to Great Britain, we should place her in such a position that she must keep her hands off our domestic affairs. After a brief correspondence between Secretary Seward and the British government, we released Mason and Slidell, confessed that the act was wrong, or, rather, that it was an inadvertence, and at one stroke brought England to acknowledge the rights of neutrals, her failure to do which, had caused the War of 1812.

This was one of many occasions when the War Department telegraph office was the scene of a historic conference. One reason why this was so, aside from the fact that news of many important and controlling events first reached the Government by telegraph through the medium of that office, was that the War Department building adjoined the Navy Department and the headquarters of the commanding general, all three locations being nearer the White House than the Treasury or other departments. It was therefore easier for the President to bring a majority of his cabinet together in the War Department than anywhere else, not even excepting the White House.

VII

McCLELLAN'S DISAGREEMENTS WITH THE ADMINISTRATION

IT is not within the scope of this work, nor would it appear advisable otherwise, to add anything to the great mass of testimony in favor of or against General McClellan in the wordy contest between his friends and critics; but it may be worth while to cast a few side-lights upon the controversy from the sources of information available to the telegraph staff at the War Department; bearing in mind the reasonable presumption that the slight amount of testimony here produced is from one who may be considered a prejudiced witness.

In the previous chapter reference has been made to McClellan's "Own Story," in which he gives his version of the innumerable and in fact almost continual differences with Lincoln and Stanton.

It is trite to say that McClellan began his military career in the Civil War period under extraordinarily favorable conditions, and that Lincoln had so high an opinion of his abilities as to raise him—a man only thirty-five years of age —to the position of Commanding General of the United States Army to succeed General Winfield Scott, whose first laurels were gained at Lundy's Lane in 1812. And yet, within less than six months, the relations between the Administration and McClellan had become so strained that the good President was forced to write him a conciliatory letter, the opening words of which are these:

Washington, April 9, 1862.

Major-General McClellan.

My Dear Sir: Your despatches, complaining that you are not properly sustained, while they do not offend me, do pain me very much.

The entire letter seems to show very clearly the extreme tension that existed; but the cause of the tension was elsewhere than in the President, who in closing says:

I beg to assure you that I have never written you or spoken to you in greater kindness of feeling than now, nor with a fuller purpose to sustain you, so far as in my most anxious judgment I consistently can; but you must act.

Yours very truly,

A. Lincoln.

So far as may be judged from telegraphic data the estrangement—if it may be so termed—first showed itself when McClellan decided upon his Richmond campaign by way of the Peninsula instead of the direct land route, and when he proposed to take McDowell's army with him, thus, in the opinion of the President and Secretary of War, leaving Washington inadequately protected. The gap widened when McClellan's independent course of action drew to his side political allies, who took advantage of the situation by tendering their partizan advice to the young "Napoleon"—as he was called by ardent admirers—and by offering him support.

In the latter part of April, 1862, Eckert was ordered by Stanton to go to Fort Monroe to look after telegraph matters, and while there several long messages were received from New York City, addressed to McClellan, whose headquarters were at White House on the Pamunkey, about twenty miles from Richmond. These messages were signed by a prominent New Yorker, who was then chairman of the National Democratic Committee, and were of such an extraordinary character that Eckert, on his own responsibility, concluded not to forward them over the headquarters line, but to hold them until he could deliver them in person. In effect, they advised McClellan to disregard interference by the Administration with army matters, and to act on his own judgment. In that case, his adviser said, he would be sustained by the people of the North, who were becoming weary of having military affairs directed by civilians at Washington.

Before Eckert could go to McClellan's headquarters, the President and Secretary of War, with Assistant Secretary Fox of the Navy, came to Fort Monroe, in order to be on hand when the movement against Norfolk should be made. That movement resulted (on May 10) in the capture of Norfolk by the Union forces, and the blowing up of the Confederate ram *Merrimac*. Eckert showed the messages to Stanton, who asked if any answers had been sent. Eckert said no, because the messages had not yet been delivered to McClellan.

Stanton then called Lincoln's attention to the matter, and, after a long discussion, it was decided to have Eckert go to White House Landing, and deliver the delayed messages to McClellan. This was done, and when the General read them, he asked whether they had been withheld by order of Stanton. Eckert said no; that Stanton had not seen them, nor had he known anything about them until that very morning.

McClellan said: "Thank God, Major, that Stanton had a man in your position who not only had the good sense, but the courage to suppress these messages!" McClellan added, that if he had received them promptly, he would have felt compelled to make some reply that would probably have placed him in a false position. McClellan then sat down and wrote a letter to Stanton, stating that he was glad that Eckert had withheld the messages, and that he had not received any others of a similar kind.

McClellan not only suffered from the injudicious suggestions and the adulation of his political admirers, but also from the indiscretions of his father-in-law, General Marcy, Inspector-General of the Army of the Potomac, who was naturally ambitious for the success of his son-in-law. About the end of May, 1862, when our army was moving toward Richmond, a considerable skirmish took place, at first resulting in our favor. McClellan being at the front, Marcy, at headquarters, wrote a glowing and exaggerated account of the incipient battle, and sent it to Washington over McClellan's name.

Shortly afterward other despatches, also over McClellan's signature, were received stating that our troops had been defeated with considerable loss, no allusion being made to the previous favorable news.

It was just at this time that the question of McClellan's removal from command of the army was being considered by Lincoln and Stanton. The latter sent for the President and showed him the two contrary despatches, and urged that the removal should be ordered at once. Eckert, who was present, ventured the opinion that the wording of the first despatch was unlike McClellan's usual diction and that perhaps he had not written or authorized it. Lincoln said he thought so too, and that it would be well to find out the facts before further judgment was passed upon McClellan. He added that Eckert had better go in person to McClellan's headquarters and learn all the facts on the ground. Stanton thereupon directed Eckert to apply to Colonel Rucker, Assistant-Quartermaster, for a boat to carry him that afternoon to the Pamunkey. Eckert arrived at Mc-

Clellan's headquarters about two o'clock the following morning and found Colonel Colburn, one of McClellan's aides-de-camp, who took him directly to McClellan's tent. The General, clad only in a red flannel shirt and drawers, awoke, and rubbing his eyes, asked what was up. Eckert showed him a copy of the two telegrams received at the War Department, and told McClellan that it was believed the first one was a forgery, and that Secretary Stanton had sent him down to find out the facts.

McClellan said he had not sent the first telegram, and could offer no explanation at the moment. He asked Eckert to get the original at the telegraph office. Eckert found Caldwell, the cipher-operator, asleep on a cot, who, when shown the troublesome despatch, said that it had been handed in the day before by General Marcy, and as it was signed "Geo. B. McClellan," he had every reason to believe it was duly authorized. Eckert asked Caldwell to indorse these facts upon the back of the copy, and then returned to McClellan, who for the second time within a month acknowledged his obligation to the Military Telegraph Corps for protecting him against his friends, whose indiscretions had already caused

107

more or less trouble and friction between the War Department and himself.

One must believe that McClellan at that time was sincere in this expression of friendly feeling toward the Administration, although we know that after the bloody Seven Days' fighting, and when his nearly demoralized army had been brought to the banks of the James at Harrison's Landing, he had drifted into an attitude of open hostility to the Administration, and had brought railing accusations against the Washington authorities.[1]

On February 25, 1862, Secretary Stanton, because of the premature publication in the newspapers of important military movements, appointed Edwards S. Sanford, president of the American Telegraph Company, to the position of military supervisor of telegrams.

Sanford's relations with the newspapers were always cordial and pleasant, notwithstanding the delicate and sometimes trying position of military censor. What his blue pencil erased from press reports had to be left out, and reporters frequently spent hours

---

[1] See his telegram of June 28, 1862, on page 424 of his "Own Story" of this campaign, referred to on the following page.

in procuring some choice bit of news which was never transmitted over the wires. Sanford even took liberties with an official telegram from General McClellan addressed to Secretary Stanton announcing the retreat of the Army of the Potomac to the banks of the James.

The following is a copy, in part, of this remarkable despatch, taken from the official report of General McClellan.

Savage's Station,

June 28, 1862, 12:20 A.M.

HON. EDWIN M. STANTON,
          Secretary of War:

I now know the full history of the day . . . I feel too earnestly to-night. I have seen too many dead and wounded comrades to feel otherwise than that the Government has not sustained this army. If you do not do so now the game is lost. If I save this army now, I tell you plainly that I owe no thanks to you or to any other persons in Washington. You have done your best to sacrifice this army.   G. B. McCLELLAN.

Such language was insubordinate, and might fairly be held to be treasonable. When it reached the War Department, Major Johnson sent for Sanford, who at once said that the charge made by McClellan was false, and that he, as military supervisor of telegrams, would not allow it to go before the Secretary of War. He therefore directed the despatch to be recopied, omitting the last paragraph, and the copy, so revised, was delivered to Stanton.

McClellan's biographer, William C. Prime, referring to this incident, charges Stanton with having received McClellan's scathing condemnation without denial or comment; but neither Stanton nor Lincoln ever knew that Sanford had suppressed an important part of an official despatch, or, at least, not until after the event.

The mutilated copy, so delivered, is contained in the report of the Committee on the Conduct of the War, Vol. I, p. 340.[1] The fact of the omission, so far as it means anything, supports Major Johnson's statement that Sanford took upon himself the grave responsibility of mutilating an official communication from the general commanding the Army of the Potomac addressed to the Secretary of War. In other countries, under strict military rules (which might well have applied to this case if the facts had been known at the time), officers could be court-martialed and shot for a lesser offense.

[1] See note at end of chapter.

In McClellan's official report, dated August 4, 1863, of his military service between July, 1861, and November, 1862, the despatch is given just as it was written by him and telegraphed to Washington, including the paragraph excised by Sanford, and consequently it was by his own act that the expunged lines were first made public.

It was in consequence of McClellan's defeats, the unsatisfactory character of his correspondence and the imminent danger of the capture of Washington by the enemy, that the President decided to transfer the Army of the Potomac to Alexandria, and to put General John Pope in immediate command; and to Eckert was assigned the delicate task of carrying to McClellan the order for his release from the supreme command of the Army of the Potomac, and for its transfer to the vicinity of Washington.

So, for the third time, Eckert visited McClellan as the confidential medium of communication from the Administration; but naturally he was not so welcome on this occasion as in the other cases, for McClellan yielded to the inevitable most unwillingly and even ungraciously, using language which Eckert deemed it wise not to report at Washington. There were unexplained delays in the transfer of the army to Alexandria, and after McClellan had reached that place, his troops did not promptly support Pope. However, his "Own Story" offers some facts and arguments in his favor which should be considered by those wishing to be fair and just to him.

NOTE. Major A. E. H. Johnson, Custodian of Military Telegrams during the Civil War, supplies the following authentic information in regard to McClellan's much discussed despatch of June 28, 1862.

"McClellan's historian—W. C. Prime—states that this despatch in its mutilated condition was laid before Congress by Stanton, who thus stood accused, not only of having suppressed the two paragraphs with which it closed, but also by that omission of admitting the truth of the accusation. I declare that the telegram as delivered to Stanton by the telegraph staff did not contain the words which McClellan's historian says were suppressed by Stanton. General E. A. Hitchcock testified, in the McDowell Court of Inquiry, in 1863, that he had access to all the records, and that the despatch in question (without the two paragraphs at the end) was an exact transcript of the official copy in the War Department files."

VIII

FROM the time that Edwin M. Stanton entered Lincoln's cabinet, January 15, 1862, the President visited the War Department telegraph office more frequently than during Secretary Cameron's incumbency, and his visits grew more and more prolonged.

It was in the telegraph office that I recall having first heard one of his humorous remarks. General Robert C. Schenck, who after the war became minister to England (but who is perhaps better remembered as the author of a treatise on the gentle art of playing poker, of which game the English public became greatly enamoured about that time), was in command of our forces near Alexandria. One evening he sent a telegram from Drainsville, Virginia, announcing a slight skirmish with the enemy, resulting in the capture of thirty or forty prisoners, all armed with Colt's revolvers. As Lincoln read the message, he turned to the operator, who had handed

113

it to him, and said, with a twinkle in his eye, that the newspapers were given to such exaggeration in publishing army news that we might be sure when General Schenck's despatch appeared in print the next day all the little Colt's revolvers would have grown into horse-pistols.

Many years afterward an Englishman supplied me with a sequel to this story. On March 17, 1905, while crossing the Atlantic on the Cunard liner *Caronia,* I addressed to the cabin audience some "Recollections of Lincoln," which were listened to by passengers of many nationalities. Reference was made to Lincoln's typical English patronymic, and also, it being St. Patrick's Day, to his reputed Irish ancestry, and I repeated the Lincoln story above quoted. On the following day an Englishman accosted me on the promenade deck, and said, "Oh, I was very much amused last evening by your anecdotes of President Lincoln, and particularly by that one about the Colt's revolvers growing into horse-pistols. That was quite funny, don't you know —but tell me, Mr. Bates, did the newspapers actually print horse-pistols, as Mr. Lincoln said they would?" I was compelled to tell my questioner that so long a time had elapsed I had really forgotten how the despatch read when published.

Another incident connected with the apparently futile operations of General Schenck led the President to give us a further bit of humor. Upon receiving a despatch one day which, like many others about that time, told of petty skirmishes, with no definite results, Lincoln remarked that the whole business of backing and filling on the part of Schenck's forces and those of the enemy reminded him of two snappy dogs, separated by a rail fence and barking at each other like fury, until, as they ran along the fence, they came to an open gate, whereupon they suddenly stopped barking, and after looking at each other for a moment, turned tail, and trotted off in opposite directions.

On March 9, 1862, the telegraph office was the scene of great excitement, when the startling news came by wire from Cherrystone Point, on the Virginia eastern shore, opposite Fort Monroe, that the Confederate iron-clad ram *Virginia* (usually called by her former name, the *Merrimac*) had come out of the Elizabeth River from Portsmouth, and after a short fight had sunk the *Cumberland,* burned the *Congress,* and run the

Minnesota aground, and might be looked for up the Potomac within forty-eight hours. In Nicolay and Hay's "Lincoln"[1] this incident is referred to thus:

Telegraphic news of these events reached Washington the next morning, Sunday, and the hasty meeting of the Cabinet . . . was perhaps the most excited and impressive of the whole war. . . . Lincoln was, as usual in trying moments, composed but eagerly inquisitive, critically scanning the despatches . . . joining scrap to scrap of information, applying his searching analysis and clear logic to read the danger and find the remedy.

Lincoln alone seemed hopeful that better news would soon be received, and his hopes were fulfilled. While the Sunday quiet of that day was being disturbed by the hurried preparations of the army and navy to block the Potomac channel by obstructions sunk at one or more points for the purpose of preventing the ram and her consorts from reaching Washington, the following telegram, dated the day before, but delayed by a break in the cable, was received:

Fort Monroe, March 8, 1862.

Secretary of War: The iron-clad Ericsson battery *Monitor* has arrived, and will proceed to take care of the *Merrimac* in the morning.

John E. Wool, *Major-Gen'l Com'd'g.*

[1] Vol. V, p. 226.

These were hopeful words from the brave old Mexican veteran, and when Lincoln and his cabinet were assembled that evening in the telegraph office, eager and anxious for news of the promised battle, we received the joyful news flashed over a new cable, laid during the day between Cherrystone Point and Fort Monroe, that Ericsson's little cheese-box *Monitor,* under command of Captain John L. Worden, had tackled the iron-clad giant, and sent her back to shelter, which, in fact, she never again forsook except for an occasional reconnaissance.[1]   These glorious tidings brought instant relief to all, and especially to the President, who could not refrain from showing his joy by every word and look.   Two months later (May 10), when Norfolk was captured, President Lincoln, Secretary Stanton, and another member of the cabinet being at Fort Monroe, and directing the movement, the enemy blew up the *Merrimac,* which drew too much water to permit

---

[1] In Church's "Life of John Ericsson," Vol. I, p. 287, appears a letter from Assistant Secretary Fox to Ericsson reading as follows: "I wrote the order forbidding the *Monitor* going into the Upper Roads to meet the *Merrimac.* Why? Because I had pledged McClellan that the *Merrimac* should not disturb his military maneuvres. . . . We fulfilled our duty and kept her in until she committed hari-kari."

her to retreat up the James River to Richmond.[1]

It is reasonable to suppose that when the model of the *Monitor* was first shown to Lincoln, his early experience with shallow river boats (out of which grew his invention of an "Improved Method of Lifting Vessels over Shoals") enabled him to perceive the inherent advantages possessed by Ericsson's proposed light-draft vessel, in its facility for rapid handling in shallow water. It was largely through this very facility that the little *Monitor* was enabled to vanquish her big opponent.

There were many times when Lincoln remained in the telegraph office till late at night, and occasionally all night long. One of these occasions was during Pope's short but disastrous campaign, ending in the second battle of Bull Run. Lincoln came to the War Department office several times on August 26, the first of those strenuous, anxious days, and after supper he came again, prepared to stay all night, if neces-

[1] On my request the Navy Department has supplied the following data:

"The *Monitor's* lower hull was 122 feet; her upper hull 172 feet long; her draft 10½ feet. The *Merrimac* was 280 feet long, her draft 23½ feet."

sary, in order to receive the latest news from Pope, who was at the front, and from McClellan, who was at Alexandria.

Hour after hour of the long night passed with no news from the front until just before dawn, when the following was received:[1]

August 27, 1862, 4:25 A.M.

A. LINCOLN, President: Intelligence received within twenty minutes informs me that the enemy are advancing and have crossed Bull Run bridge; if it is not destroyed, it probably will be. The forces sent by us last night held it until that time.

H. HAUPT.

Lincoln, who was still keeping vigil with the telegraph operators, at once penned this answer:

August 27, 1862.

COLONEL HAUPT: What became of our forces which held the bridge till twenty minutes ago, as you say?

A. LINCOLN.

Receiving no reply immediately, Lincoln telegraphed again:

War Department, August 27, 1862.

COLONEL HAUPT: Is the railroad bridge over Bull Run destroyed?

A. LINCOLN.

[1] Haupt's "Reminiscences," p. 100.

To this Colonel Haupt replied, the following day:

August 28, 1862.

PRESIDENT LINCOLN:

. . . Colonel Scammon held Bull Run Bridge a long time against a very superior force, retired at last in perfect order. . . .   H. HAUPT.

During the next few days, Lincoln sent other brief messages of inquiry to Colonel Haupt, upon whom he, as well as Secretary Stanton and General Halleck, seemed to depend for early information far more than upon Pope or McClellan, as shown by the following additional telegrams (taken from Haupt's "Reminiscences," p. 107 et seq).

War Department, Aug. 28, 1862, 2:40 P.M.

COL. HAUPT: Yours received. How do you learn that the rebel forces at Manassas are large and commanded by several of their best generals?   A. LINCOLN.

August 28, 1862.

PRESIDENT LINCOLN: One of Colonel Scammon's surgeons was captured and released; he communicated the information. One of our firemen was captured and escaped; he confirms it and gives important details. General McClellan has just seen him. . . .   H. HAUPT.

August 29, 1862.

COLONEL HAUPT: What news from direction of Manassas Junction? What generally?   A. LINCOLN.

LINCOLN IN TOUCH WITH ARMY

August 29, 1862.

PRESIDENT LINCOLN and GENERAL HALLECK: General Pope was at Centreville this morning at six o'clock. Seemed to be in good spirits. . . .   H. HAUPT.

August 30, 1862, 9:00 A.M.

COLONEL: What news?   A. LINCOLN.

August 30, 1862, 8:50 P.M.

COLONEL HAUPT: Please send me the latest news.
A. LINCOLN.

August 30, 1862.

A. LINCOLN, President: Our operator has reached Manassas. Hears no firing of importance. . . . We have reëstablished telegraphic communication with Manassas. . . .

. . . Our telegraph operators and railway employees are entitled to great credit. They have been advanced pioneers, occupying the posts of danger; and the exploit of penetrating to Fairfax and bringing off the wounded when they supposed that 20,000 rebels were on their front and flanks, was one of the boldest performances I have ever heard of.   H. HAUPT.

August 31, 1862, 7:10 A.M.

COLONEL HAUPT: What news? Did you hear any firing this morning?   A. LINCOLN.

August 31, 1862.

PRESIDENT LINCOLN: No news received as yet this morning. Firing heard distinctly in direction of Bristoe at six o'clock.   H. HAUPT.

And so the anxious hours passed, with "Lincoln in the Telegraph Office" on the watch until it was known that for the second time our army had met defeat on the fatal field of Bull Run.

General Haupt, in his "Reminiscences," makes this reference to Lincoln's anxiety: "During this protracted engagement, August 24 to September 2, 1862, the President was in a state of extreme anxiety and could have slept but little. Inquiries came from him at all hours of the night asking for the latest news from the front." The cipher-operators could confirm this statement even if Lincoln's messages here quoted did not establish the fact. They also clearly show that for a man who never had a day's military experience (if strictly speaking, we may except the farcical episode in his career in the Black Hawk Indian Campaign in 1832), Lincoln, who by virtue of the presidential office, was Commander-in-Chief of the Army and Navy of the United States, possessed an almost intuitive perception of the practical requirements of that responsible office, and that in his usual common-sense way of doing things, he was performing the duties of that position in the most intelligent and effective manner.

During the entire war, the files of the War Department telegraph office were punctuated with short, pithy despatches from Lincoln. For instance, on May 24, 1862, he sent ten or twelve to various generals; on May 25, as many more; and from one to a dozen on nearly every succeeding day for months. It is also worthy of remark that Lincoln's numerous telegrams, even those sent by him during his busy two weeks' visit to City Point in March and April, 1865, and the less than half a dozen after his return to Washington, were almost without exception in his own handwriting, his copy being remarkably neat and legible, with seldom an erasure or correction.

While Lincoln was sometimes critical and even sarcastic when events moved slowly, or when satisfactory results that seemed to be demanded by the immediate conditions were lacking, yet he never failed to commend when good news came, as in the following:

August 17, 1864, 10:30 A.M.

LIEUTENANT-GENERAL GRANT, City Point, Va.: I have seen your despatch expressing your unwillingness to break your hold where you are. Neither am I willing. Hold on with a bull-dog grip, and chew and choke as much as possible. A. LINCOLN.

IX

THE most prominent figure in the War Department telegraph office, was Major Thomas Thompson Eckert, our chief. Born in Ohio in 1821, he was just forty years old at the outbreak of the Civil War. He first became interested in the telegraph through reading "The National Intelligencer," for which his father subscribed, and which contained the proceedings of Congress relating to Professor Morse's invention, and the various steps which led up to the appropriation by Congress in 1843 of $30,000 for the construction of an experimental line. After the trial had proved successful and lines had been built from Washington to New York, young Eckert eagerly followed Morse's doings, and finally, in 1847, against the will of his father and the appeal of his mother, he started from Wooster, Ohio, with thirty dollars in his pocket,

124

traveling by stage, steamboat, horseback, and railroad, working his way nearly the entire journey to New York City, for the sole purpose of seeing the Morse telegraph in operation, which he did at the office in the old Astor House, then said to be the largest hotel under one roof in the world. Returning to his home he soon learned to telegraph, and with Jeptha H. Wade, and Isaac R. Ellwood, as partners, he built the first telegraph-line on the Fort Wayne railroad in the early '50's.

He was its superintendent until a few years before the war, when he went to North Carolina to take charge of a gold-mine, controlled by Baltimore capitalists, after one of whom— Steele—the mine was named. In June, 1861, Eckert came North, ostensibly to procure additional machinery for his mine, but really for the purpose of diagnosing the political situation, which he found to be so alarming that he determined to return to North Carolina and bring his family, consisting of his wife, her sister, and his three young children, to Ohio. Reaching Atlanta in July, the day after news had been received of the battle of Rich Mountain, in West Virginia, and the death of the Confederate general Garnett, he found the old railway-station

8   **125**

filled with an excited crowd of people. Upon inquiring the cause of the tumult, he was told that a Northern man had been hanged just outside the depot an hour before. Pressing his inquiries, he learned the name of the victim, who had been employed in a mine not far from the one he had been superintending. Meantime, upon looking over the hotel register, he had observed the name of Alexander H. Stephens, Vice-President of the Confederacy, who, when a member of Congress in Washington some years before, had been a room-mate of Eckert's cousin, George Eckert, both being bachelors. He sent his card to the room of the vice-president, who told the colored bell-boy to bring Eckert to him, and when this was done, a cordial greeting was extended to the cousin of Stephens's old friend.

While they were talking there was a loud knocking at the door. When it was opened three men entered, one of whom, pointing to Eckert, said they wanted that man down-stairs. Stephens interposed his slight frame between Eckert and the delegation, and said: "This man is my guest and friend, and I will be responsible for him. He is all right." The men thereupon withdrew,

From a war-time photograph

Major Thomas T. Eckert

and Eckert, having the patronage of so influential a Southerner got safely out of Atlanta, taking with him a letter from Stephens addressed to Governor Pickens of South Carolina, in which the suggestion was made that Eckert with his knowledge of mining would probably be useful to the Confederacy in supplying saltpeter for the manufacture of gunpowder.[1]

Eckert went to Charleston to meet Governor Pickens, and, after discussing the saltpeter question, proceeded on his journey to the Steele mine, Montgomery County, North Carolina, not far from Salisbury. At Branchville, he heard the news of Beauregard's victory over the Union forces at the first battle of Bull Run, and at Columbia he witnessed the landing of a balloon in which Professor Lowe, the aëronaut, had started from Cincinnati intending to land at Louisville, but which had been carried by high winds far out of its course.

When Eckert arrived at the mines he learned that, owing to his Northern birth and sentiments, and because of his visit to Baltimore, a warrant for his arrest as a spy had been issued. When

---

[1] The next time Eckert met Stephens was in February, 1865, at City Point. See chap. XXIV.

haled before the judge, however, he was advised by the latter not to employ a lawyer, and not to answer questions, but to trust him—the judge. There being no affirmative proof Eckert was released, and influential friends, including his family physician, Dr. Verdin, assisted in arrangements for his escape to the North. His party left the place one night in August, 1861, in an old covered wagon driven by a friendly negro. Their route was up the French Broad river and over the mountains into Tennessee. At Greenville he saw the sign of "Andrew Johnson, Tailor." From Greenville they went by train to Louisville. The entire journey was an anxious one, as they were held up and closely questioned at several points, and when they finally reached Louisville, they were penniless. Eckert was forced to ask help from his old friends in the railroad and telegraph service. He at last reached his former home in Cleveland, and Amasa Stone (for whom Eckert had rendered a service of some importance before the war) telegraphed to Colonel Scott, Assistant Secretary of War, that Eckert's services could be had. Scott had met Eckert previously, and he was ordered to Washington, arriving there early in

September. He was at once assigned to McClellan's staff as captain and aide-de-camp in charge of the military telegraph. Eckert was then a perfect specimen of physical manhood, erect and fine-looking, as, indeed, he still is at the age of eighty-six.

I recall an incident which occurred in 1862, in the room of John Potts, chief clerk of the War Department, where a supply of soft-iron pokers had just been received for use at the open fires by which the building was then heated. Eckert chaffed the chief clerk about his purchase, and to prove his statement that the pokers were of poor quality, he took one of them in his right hand and with a smart blow struck it across the tense muscles of his left forearm, bending the poker quite noticeably. On a later occasion Potts bought a lot of pokers which turned out to be cast-iron of poor quality, four or five of which Eckert actually broke over his arm in the presence of President Lincoln, who remarked to the chief clerk: "Mr. Potts, you will have to buy a better quality of iron in future if you expect your pokers to stand the test of this young man's arm."

The story of how Eckert was promoted to be major and became chief of the War Department

Telegraph Staff, touches Lincoln at several points. In a previous chapter reference was made to the peculiar wording of Eckert's appointment as manager of military telegraphs at army headquarters which required him to deliver all despatches to the commanding general. These instructions also caused him to refrain from sending military news to the Secretary of War himself, and when Stanton entered the cabinet (January 15, 1862), he soon found that he was being kept in ignorance of army news, which, however, in some cases was printed in the newspapers and affected the financial markets. It seemed evident to Stanton that there was a leak somewhere, and naturally the telegraph department was suspected. Stanton directed Assistant Secretary Watson to investigate the matter, and the latter devoted a part of his time for a week or so to this inquiry. His report to Stanton, while not locating the leak in the news, was to the effect that Eckert was not giving close attention to his duties, and particularly that he had withheld important military despatches from the knowledge of the President and the Secretary of War. An order was thereupon made out for his dismissal. Stanton telegraphed for Edwards S.

Sanford, President of the American Telegraph Company, to come from New York and take charge of the telegraph. This was early in February, 1862. Sanford had a high opinion of Eckert's abilities, faithfulness, and honesty, and so reported to Stanton, who, however, preferred to trust his assistant's report. At once, upon learning from Sanford that there was dissatisfaction with his service, Eckert wrote out his resignation, and sent it by messenger to the War Department. This was on a Saturday afternoon. Stanton was surprised and indignant that an officer under charges, and whose order of dismissal had been prepared, should have received an inkling of the facts, and sent in his resignation before the dismissal could be served on him. This placed Sanford in an unpleasant situation, and he went to Stanton's house early Sunday morning to intercede for Eckert, and finally obtained Stanton's consent to an interview.

Eckert, accompanied by Sanford, went to the War Department that afternoon, and was ushered into the Secretary's presence, and, as he has recently told me, he and Sanford stood for at least ten minutes while Stanton continued to write at his desk, without looking up to see who his callers were. Finally Stanton turned, and asked Eckert what he wanted. The latter replied, "Mr. Sanford tells me that you sent for me, and I am here."

Then Stanton, in a loud voice, said he understood that Captain Eckert had been neglecting his duties, and was absent from his office much of the time, and allowed newspaper men to have access to the telegraph office; also that he was an unfit person for the important position he occupied. Pointing to a large pile of telegrams, all of which were in Eckert's handwriting, he demanded to know why copies had not been regularly delivered to the Secretary of War at the time of receipt.

Eckert replied that his order of assignment from Secretary Cameron expressly required all military telegrams to be delivered to the commanding general and to no one else.

"Well," Stanton retorted, "why have you neglected your duties by absenting yourself from your office so frequently?"

Eckert replied that he had not neglected his duties; that he had attended to them strictly and faithfully; that any statements to the contrary were false; that for over three months he had been at his post of duty almost constantly, and had hardly taken off his clothes during that time except to change his linen; that he had remained in his office many times all night long, and that he seldom slept in his bed at his hotel; and finally, inasmuch as it appeared that his services were not acceptable, he insisted upon his resignation being accepted.

Just then Eckert felt an arm placed on his shoulder, and supposing it to be that of Sanford, who had all this time remained standing with him, turned round, and was surprised to find that, instead, it was the hand of the President, who had entered the room while the discussion was going on.

Lincoln, still with his hand on the captain's shoulder, said to Stanton: "Mr. Secretary, I think you must be mistaken about this young man neglecting his duties, for I have been a daily caller at General McClellan's headquarters for the last three or four months, and I have always found Eckert at his post. I have been there often before breakfast, and in the evening as well, and frequently late at night, and several times before daylight, to get the latest news from the army. Eckert was always there, and I never observed any reporters or outsiders in the office."

Governor Brough of Ohio, who had known Eckert before, in connection with a telegraph-line on Brough's (Bellefontaine) railroad in Ohio, which Eckert had inspected and rebuilt about 1857, happened to be in the Secretary's room while Eckert was uttering his denial of the charges against him, and after Lincoln had finished his statement, Brough went up to Eckert, took his hand, and addressed him in a most cordial manner. Then turning to Stanton, he told him that he would vouch for anything that Eckert would say or do; that he believed him to be the ablest and most loyal man who could be selected for the place.

Stanton was so impressed by the intercession of Lincoln, Sanford, and Brough that he quietly took from his desk a package of papers, and opening one said, "I believe this is your resignation, is it not, sir?"

Captain Eckert said it was; whereupon Stanton tore it up and dropped the pieces on the floor. He then opened another paper and said, "This is the order dismissing you from the army, which I had already signed, but it will not be executed." He then tore up the order of dismissal, and said: "I owe you an apology, Captain, for not having gone to General McClellan's office and seen for myself the situation of affairs. You are no longer Captain Eckert; I shall appoint you major as soon as the commission can be made out, and I shall make you a further acknowledgment in another manner."

So, from that Sunday afternoon, in February, 1862, until just before the close of the war, Eckert's military title and the one by which he was best known was "Major." The additional acknowledgment referred to by Secretary Stanton, consisted of a horse and carriage, purchased for Eckert's use in the performance of his official duties.

The day after the interview described above, Stanton detached Eckert from McClellan's staff, and ordered him to make his office in the War Department, and to connect all wires with that building, leaving only enough instruments at army headquarters to handle the separate business of the commanding general. This order naturally offended McClellan, and it was doubtless one of the influences which operated to create or increase the bad feeling between him and Stanton, which was never allayed.

X

THE FIRST DRAFT OF THE EMANCIPATION PROCLAMATION

UNTIL very recently it has not been known, except by a few persons, that Lincoln wrote the first draft of the Emancipation Proclamation while seated at Eckert's desk in the cipher-room of the War Department telegraph office. Some of the incidents connected with the writing of that immortal document have now been recorded by Eckert, as follows:

"As you know, the President came to the office every day and invariably sat at my desk while there. Upon his arrival early one morning in June, 1862, shortly after McClellan's 'Seven Days' Fight,' he asked me for some paper, as he wanted to write something special. I procured some foolscap and handed it to him. He then sat down and began to write. I do not recall whether the sheets were loose or had been made into a pad. There must have been at least a quire. He would look out of the window a while and then put his pen to paper, but he did not write much at once. He would study between times and when he had made up his mind he would put down a line or two, and then sit quiet for a few minutes. After a time he would resume his writing, only to stop again at intervals to make some remark to me or to one of the cipher-operators as a fresh despatch from the front was handed to him.

"Once his eye was arrested by the sight of a large spider-web stretched from the lintel of the portico to the side of the outer window-sill. This spider-web was an institution of the cipher-room and harbored a large colony of exceptionally big ones. We frequently watched their antics, and Assistant Secretary Watson dubbed them 'Major Eckert's lieutenants.' Lincoln commented on the web, and I told him that my lieutenants would soon report and pay their respects to the President. Not long after a big spider appeared at the cross-roads and tapped several times on the strands, whereupon five or six others came out from different directions. Then what seemed to be a great confab took place, after which they separated, each on a different strand of the web.

189

Lincoln was much interested in the performance and thereafter, while working at the desk, would often watch for the appearance of his visitors.

"On the first day Lincoln did not cover one sheet of his special writing paper (nor indeed on any subsequent day). When ready to leave, he asked me to take charge of what he had written and not allow any one to see it. I told him I would do this with pleasure and would not read it myself. 'Well,' he said, 'I should be glad to know that no one will see it, although there is no objection to your looking at it; but please keep it locked up until I call for it to-morrow.' I said his wishes would be strictly complied with.

"When he came to the office on the following day he asked for the papers, and I unlocked my desk and handed them to him and he again sat down to write. This he did nearly every day for several weeks, always handing me what he had written when ready to leave the office each day. Sometimes he would not write more than a line or two, and once I observed that he had put question-marks on the margin of what he had written. He would read over each day all the matter he had previously written and revise it, studying carefully each sentence.

"On one occasion he took the papers away with him, but he brought them back a day or two later. I became much interested in the matter and was impressed with the idea that he was engaged upon something of great importance, but did not know what it was until he had finished the document and then for the first time he told me that he had been writing an order giving freedom to the slaves in the South, for the purpose of hastening the end of the war. He said he had been able to work at my desk more quietly and command his thoughts better than at the White House, where he was frequently interrupted. I still have in my possession the ink-stand which he used at that time and which, as you know, stood on my desk until after Lee's surrender. The pen he used was a small barrel-pen made by Gillott— such as were supplied to the cipher-operators." [1]

On July 1, 1862, a call for three hundred thou-

[1] Frank B. Carpenter in his "Six Months at the White House," p. 20 *et seq.*, quotes from Lincoln's own account thus: " . . . I now determined upon the adoption of the emancipation policy; and, without consultation with, or the knowledge of, the cabinet, I prepared the original draft of the proclamation, and, after much anxious thought, called a cabinet meeting upon the subject, . . . The result was that I put the draft of the proclamation aside as you do your sketch for a picture, waiting for victory . . . From time to time I added or changed a line, touching it up here and there . . ."

sand additional troops had been issued, but there was more or less anxiety as to the result of the call. On July 12, Lincoln convened the Representatives from the border states and discussed with them his second "Appeal to favor compensated emancipation." On July 14, twenty of the delegation signed their reply. On July 22, the draft of the proclamation was laid before the cabinet for the first time. On September 13, Lincoln, in an address to a committee from the churches of Chicago, who urged him to issue a proclamation of emancipation, said ". . . I can assure you that the subject is on my mind by day and night more than any other. Whatever shall appear to be God's will, I will do . . ."

At this time Antietam had just been fought and won and Lee's army was escaping across the Potomac, much to the disappointment of Lincoln, who telegraphed McClellan, on September 15, to "destroy the rebel army if possible." The failure to do that when the chances seemed so favorable may, therefore, be considered as the immediate cause of Lincoln's sudden decision to lay the Emancipation Proclamation before his cabinet, for the second time, which was done on September 22.

Chase's diary of that date says that Lincoln read to the cabinet from Artemus Ward's humorous account of the "High-handed Outrage at Utica," and enjoyed it very much as did the others "except Stanton, of course."

The text of the Proclamation was given to the press that night, and was published throughout the country the following day. Of course there was wide-spread comment and criticism, most of it favorable, but some unfavorable; and the subject was very freely discussed between that time and January 1, 1863, when the Emancipation Proclamation became effective.

Tinker tells of an occurrence on the evening of that day when, after a long, tiresome public reception at the White House, at which the President was obliged to stand for hours shaking hands with all sorts of people, he came over to the telegraph office, settled himself in his accustomed place at Eckert's desk, and, placing his feet on a near-by table, relaxed from the strain and fatigue of the day. General Halleck and Assistant Secretary Fox of the navy were present, with a number of others who had dropped in to learn if there was any news from Rosecrans, who was then engaged in what at that time seemed almost a death struggle with Bragg. Tinker says that he was engaged in translating a long cipher-despatch from General Grant, who was then between Memphis and Milliken's Bend, and also one from Rose-

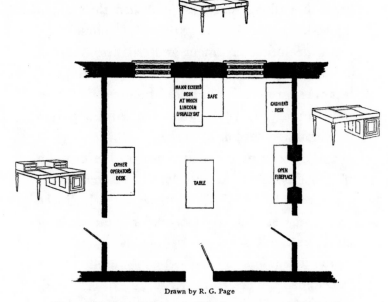

Drawn by R. G. Page

Plan of the cipher-room in the War Department telegraph office

Made from data supplied by General Thomas T. Eckert

crans in Tennessee, when Lincoln came in. For a while Tinker paid no attention to the conversation in the room. Presently, however, Lincoln began to tell of an occurrence in Pekin, Illi-

nois, before his election; but after a while he hesitated at a name he was trying to recall, but could
not, which, however, Tinker well knew, having
been employed as telegraph operator in Pekin at
the very time of which Lincoln was speaking.
The President resumed his story, but again
stopped, remarking, as he ran his long fingers
through his disheveled hair to awaken thought,
"I wish I could remember that name." Whereupon Tinker, with some trepidation, suggested,
"Mr. President, permit me to ask if it is not
Judge Puterbaugh?" Tinker then adds, in his
account of the incident: "Lincoln turned upon
me in great surprise and fairly shouted, 'Why,
yes, that's the name. Did you know him?' Gaining confidence, I replied, 'Yes, sir, down in Pekin,
where I once had the honor of explaining to the
future President of the United States the working of the Morse telegraph, in the telegraph office
in the Tazewell House.' Lincoln, his face full of
pleased surprise, then turned to his audience, and
exclaimed, 'Well, isn't it funny that Mr. Tinker
and I should have met 'way out in Illinois before
the war, and now again here in the War Department telegraph office?' He then proceeded to tell
how and when we had first met, and that, being at

that time specially interested in the telegraph, which was comparatively new and still a subject of wonder to the great majority of people, he had asked me how it worked and that I had given him a full explanation of its mysteries. After this interruption Lincoln resumed his story and I returned to my translation of Grant's and Rosecrans's cipher-messages. As this was the day on which the final decree of the Emancipation Proclamation was issued I recall with the utmost pleasure the incident above referred to."

No one would have supposed from Lincoln's perfectly composed manner at the time that he had that day given to the world a document of imperishable human interest, which meant so

[1] The site of this building was Pennsylvania Avenue at the corner of 17th Street. It was erected about 1820 and was torn down in 1879 to make way for the new State, War, and Navy Building. The two windows, one on each side of the Maltese cross, afforded an outlook on Pennsylvania Avenue from the room occupied by the cipher-operators during the Civil War. Next to the right-hand window stood Major Eckert's desk, at which Mr. Lincoln almost always sat when at the Telegraph Office and on which he wrote the first draft of the Emancipation Proclamation. He spent more time in this room during the last four years of his life than in any other place, the White House only excepted. The room to the left of the cipher-operators' room was occupied by Major Johnson, custodian of military telegrams. The corner room was Secretary Stanton's own office. The five windows under the portico to the right of the cipher-operators' room belonged to the old library room of the War Department, in which was the Telegraph Office proper, where all Government messages were sent and received.

The old War Department building [1]

much to the country, and especially to four millions of slaves, whose shackles were forever loosed.

The effect upon the public mind of the Emancipation Proclamation was, of course, not the same in all sections. By the radicals it was welcomed as one of the most important acts of the President since the war began, while the conservative element feared it would prove ineffective in the North, and would lead to reprisals on the part of the enemy. In New York City the draft riots, culminating on July 15, 1863, had a curious relation to the color question, the wrath of the malcontents being to a large extent vented upon the negro race, whose members were in an unreasoning way apparently held responsible in the last analysis for the draft.

In the border states the lines were sharply drawn between the military and the loyalists on the one hand, and Southern sympathizers and former slave owners on the other.

In the summer of 1863, Mr. Richard O'Brien, one of the three operators who went to Washington with me in April, 1861, was stationed at Norfolk, Virginia, as chief operator. There still remained in that city, which had fallen into our hands a year previously, a number of persons whose sympathies were naturally with the South, and so, on July 11, 1863, when colored troops first arrived in the city, its members were cheered by no outburst of welcome but were met by the cold, repellent gaze of men, women and children who crowded the streets to witness the unwelcome sight. Dr. David M. Wright, a leading and reputable citizen, in some way or other got into an altercation with one of the white officers, Lieutenant Anson L. Sanborn, from New England. Suddenly the sound of a shot broke the silence, and Sanborn, a lad in years, fell to the ground, killed by a shot fired by Dr. Wright, who was arrested with the still smoking revolver in his hands. The following telegram gives the bare facts:

Norfolk, July 11, 1863.

MAJOR-GENERAL JOHN A. DIX: Lieut. Anson L. Sanborn of the 1st Colored Regiment was shot at the head of his Company in Main Street this P.M., by Dr. Wright and died immediately. Dr. Wright is in jail, heavily ironed.

A. E. BOVAY,
Major and Provost Marshal.

Dr. Wright was promptly tried by court-martial, convicted, and sentenced to be hanged. Richard O'Brien's younger brother, John Emmet

O'Brien, was also employed as operator at Norfolk, and Dr. Wright had once attended him for a slight injury. He was therefore specially interested in the case. Dr. O'Brien (now and for many years a prominent physician of Scranton) says that Dr. Wright's brave and devoted daughter visited her father one evening and exchanged clothes with him, so that he walked out of prison past the guards, and might have escaped, had not an officer in the street, who had observed the masculine stride of the supposed woman, stopped him and sent him back to his cell.

Knowing Lincoln's merciful nature, numerous petitions were soon on their way to Washington, asking for the pardon or reprieve of Dr. Wright. One was signed by ninety-five "Citizens of Norfolk," upon the receipt of which Lincoln sent the following telegram:

Washington, D. C., Aug. 3, 1863.

MAJOR GENERAL FOSTER, Fort Monroe: If Dr. Wright, on trial at Norfolk, has been or shall be convicted, send me a transcript of his trial and conviction, and do not let execution be done until my further order.   A. LINCOLN.

General Foster answered, stating that the trial had been concluded and that the proceedings had been forwarded to the President.

Meantime other petitions were received urging that Dr. Wright be "restored to his home and family," and protesting that he was insane when he committed the deed. Dr. John P. Gray of Utica, a celebrated alienist, was selected to make an examination of Dr. Wright's mental condition, and on September 10, the President had a long interview with Dr. Gray, who left at once for Norfolk, with Lincoln's autograph letter of instructions in his pocket. Upon Dr. Gray's return with a report that he found no evidence of insanity, the President, having considered all the testimony, approved the sentence of the court and telegraphed General Foster as follows:

October 15, 1863.

Postpone the execution of Dr. Wright to Friday October 23rd inst. This is intended for his preparation and is final.

A. LINCOLN.

Still the friends of Dr. Wright did not give up hope of executive clemency, but bombarded the President with telegrams and letters. The Confederate government was also besieged by some of the doctor's friends in the South, who presented an application dated Edenton, N. C., August 7, 1863, addressed to President Davis, signed by Mrs. Starke A. Righton, asking that efforts be made to secure clemency for Dr. Wright. This communication was indorsed by Secretary of War James A. Seddon, expressing deep sympathy and referring to the "natural indignation of Dr. Wright at the shameful spectacle, and his prompt vindication of his honor." On September 1, 1863, President Davis wrote the Hon. Thomas Bragg, at Raleigh, "I would gladly do anything in my power to rescue him from an enemy regardless alike of the laws and customs of civilized people."

On October 22, the day before the time fixed for the execution, my comrade, Richard O'Brien, was approached by a man who said that if he would anticipate a telegram which was hourly expected from President Lincoln granting a reprieve, he would be paid $20,000 in gold, and would be given a free passage to England on a blockade runner. O'Brien indignantly refused the bribe.

October 23 dawned, and still no telegram from the President, and at 11:20 A.M., General Foster telegraphed to General Halleck, "Dr. Wright was executed this morning."

XI

THE GETTYSBURG AND VICKSBURG YEAR

THE year 1863, which began with the issue
of the final draft of the Proclamation giving freedom to four million slaves, and the welcome news of Rosecrans's victory over Bragg
at Stone's River, did not long continue to supply
favorable incidents, for Hooker's defeat at Chancellorsville at the beginning of May, and the
raids of the enemy down the Shenandoah Valley
into Maryland and Pennsylvania, with Grant
still held at bay by Pemberton at Vicksburg, led to a loss of confidence. In some
quarters there was actual discouragement.
Louis Napoleon was causing anxiety to the
administration by his efforts to keep the Arch-
duke Maximilian on his newly erected Mexican
throne.

On March 30, Lincoln for the second time appointed a day of fasting and prayer (for April
30).[1] On June 15 he found it necessary to call
for 100,000 additional troops, the drafting of

[1] Lincoln's first proclamation of a fast day was dated August 12,
1861 (for September 5).

the quota from New York City causing bloody riots.

But meantime, a glimmer of hope had been kindled by the false news received on May 24, of the capture of Vicksburg. Tinker's diary of that date, says:

I have just finished copying, and have delivered to the Secretary of War, the despatch telling us of the capture of Vicksburg. The President, Secretary Seward, Senator Doolittle, and Judge Whiting have just come in and are all talking so loudly I can hardly write.

Lee's invasion of Maryland in June had greatly increased the anxiety felt by the President, especially as communication with our army was frequently interrupted. All the news we received dribbled over a single line of wire via Hagerstown; and when Meade's headquarters were pushed beyond that place through the necessity of following Lee's advance, we lost telegraphic connection altogether, only regaining it by the Hanover Junction route, a day or two later. From that point to Hanover there was a railroad wire. Thence to Gettysburg the line was on the turnpike, and the service was poor and desultory. Lincoln was in the telegraph office hour after hour during those anxious days and nights, until, on the morning of July 4, he penned his welcome announcement to the country that Meade had won a notable victory.

However, as further news from the scene of action reached him Lincoln began to realize that Meade was likely to lose much of the fruit of his hard-earned victory by allowing Lee's army to escape across the Potomac. So he still kept close to the telegraph instrument during the succeeding days. But even after leaving the office his thoughts returned to it lest something should be left undone to insure decisive success, for at 7 P.M. on July 6 he sent a telegram from the Soldiers Home to General Halleck saying:

I left the telegraph office a good deal dissatisfied. . . . These things all appear to me to be connected with a purpose to . . . get the enemy across the river again without a further collision. . . .

When Lincoln came to the office the next morning, he received Grant's despatch announcing the capture of Vicksburg with many thousand prisoners, and this welcome news coming so soon after Meade's victory at Gettysburg revived his spirits and led him eight days later to issue his second thanksgiving proclamation, naming August 6 as a "day for national thanksgiving, praise and prayer."

Nevertheless, Lincoln's thoughts were still with Meade, and in his note to General Halleck stating that Vicksburg had surrendered he said:

. . . Now, if General Meade can complete his work so gloriously prosecuted thus far, by the literal or substantial destruction of Lee's army, the rebellion will be over.

Notwithstanding the urgency of the telegrams from Lincoln and Halleck, Meade did not seem disposed to hurry, but, finally, on July 12, his despatch reached the War Department stating his "intention to attack the enemy to-morrow, unless something intervenes." My colleague, Chandler, relates that when this message was received by Lincoln, he paced the room wringing his hands and saying: "They will be ready to fight a magnificent battle when there is no enemy there to fight." Lee recrossed the Potomac that night, and Meade did not attack him, and on July 15, the very day on which the thanksgiving proclamation was issued, Lincoln wrote his historic despatch to ex-Secretary Cameron, then at Meade's headquarters (see page 55), saying:

. . . Please tell me, if you know, who was the one Corps Commander who was for fighting, in the council of war on Sunday night.[1]

[1] This was the night of the second day's fighting at Gettysburg.

XII

LINCOLN'S TENDER TREATMENT OF ROSECRANS

IN August, 1863, while Rosecrans was engaged in the preliminary movements leading up to the battle of Chickamauga, and after the fighting was known to be in progress, Lincoln, as at other critical periods, remained in the telegraph office, sometimes for hours, waiting for the latest news respecting what was then felt to be one of the most serious crises of the war. For three or four days the tension was very great, the President, Secretary Stanton and General Halleck conferring together almost constantly. Prior to this period, Rosecrans seems to have reached the conclusion that he did not possess the full confidence of the Administration, and in fact he did not, but he fancied the situation was worse than it really was, this impression being deepened by Halleck's censorious letters. In reply to a communication from Rosecrans, Lincoln wrote him a most encouraging letter on August 31, 1863, in which he said:

> . . . I repeat that my appreciation of you has not abated. I can never forget, whilst I remember anything, that about the end of last year and beginning of this, you gave us a hard earned victory, which, had there been a defeat instead, the nation could scarcely have lived over. Neither can I forget the check you so opportunely gave to a dangerous sentiment which was spreading in the North.

The significance of this reference to Rosecrans's success eight months before at Stone's River, after two days of fierce fighting, with heavy losses on both sides, lay in the belief on the part of the Administration, that certain European governments, notably France and Great Britain, had virtually promised to recognize the Confederacy, if it should win one more substantial victory before the end of 1862. The result of the Stone's River battle shattered that hope and explains Lincoln's strong words to Rosecrans.

One authority for the above statement regarding European recognition of the Confederate States, is Lieut-Col. Horace N. Fisher, in his historical paper printed in the proceedings of the Society of the Army of the Cumberland, held at Indianapolis, September 20, 1904. Colonel Fisher says, "According to an eminent Confederate general,[1] who was promoted to a confidential position at Richmond after losing a leg at Stone's River, that battle was fatal to the hope held out by European governments of the recognition of the Confederate independence, if they should win one big battle before the end of 1862."

Lincoln's closing sentence in his telegram to Rosecrans, about "a dangerous sentiment which was spreading in the North," also needs a word of explanation, which is supplied by an officer who was frequently at Rosecrans's headquarters during the period referred to.

An effort was being made by the Democrats to nominate prominent military men for office throughout the country, so as to take them from the field and tempt them to forget their loyalty to the Government and thus make it easier to recognize the South and let the erring brethren go. A delegation of prominent Ohio Democrats called on General Rosecrans at Murfreesboro' in the spring of 1863 and made a tremendous onslaught on him to secure his consent to become a candidate for Governor of Ohio, with the expectation that if successful there he might go a step higher later on. The delegation was very secretive at first with Rosecrans, and he finally broke out in his impulsive way and demanded their plans. When they were uncovered, he gave them a most vigorous tirade and in language stronger than polite, suggested their leaving the camp and returning to a more

---

[1] The Lieut.-Governor of Tenn.—A. S. Marks—so stated in his speech at the Reunion of the Society of the Army of the Cumberland at Chattanooga in 1889. He was the officer referred to.

congenial clime. Garfield, as Rosecrans's chief of staff, was informed of the whole transaction, although the delegation tried to pledge Rosecrans in advance against communicating with Garfield or any others of his staff.

A part of the Democratic plan seemed to have been to run General McClellan as a popular military man for the presidency (which was in fact done in 1864), and to make as many as possible of the successful general officers Democratic candidates for governors in the Northern States, such as Indiana, Ohio and New York, by which means they hoped it would be possible to divide and weaken the patriotic sentiment then existing.

Three weeks after the President's encouraging message to Rosecrans, and after the sanguinary battle of Chickamauga (in which the losses were in two days proportionately larger than in the three days' fighting at Gettysburg), when Rosecrans left the field for Chattanooga in utter despondency, supposing the day to be lost, Assistant Secretary of War Dana, to whom had been assigned the task of keeping the Administration fully posted on military matters in the West, telegraphed to the War Department (September 20, 1863) doleful accounts of the situation of affairs. Rosecrans later on the same day telegraphed the President, "We have no certainty of holding our position." Lincoln thereupon sent these further words of encouragement:

10   161

September 21, 1863.

Be of good cheer, we have unabated confidence in you
, . . We shall do our utmost to assist you. . . .

But while thus trying to put backbone into
Rosecrans, the President himself was worried
and anxious. He had been sending message
after message to Burnside at Knoxville, urging him to go to the relief of Rosecrans. Although Burnside in each case answered that he
would comply with the order, he still dallied, and
on the very day when Rosecrans sent his despair-
ing message, Burnside telegraphed the President
that he had gone to Jonesboro to clear out a force
of the enemy that had been annoying him in that
direction.

Meantime the distressing reports from both
Rosecrans and Dana were not fully confirmed,
because George H. Thomas, upon whom the
general command devolved when Rosecrans
personally retired from the front to Chattanooga,
had rallied his troops, reformed his broken lines,
and after six or seven hours of desperate fighting,
had compelled Bragg to assume the defensive,
thus preventing him from following up his early
advantages. Thomas withdrew our almost defeated army in good order to Rossville and finally

reached a position of natural safety for the time being at Chattanooga. The President's anxiety, however, continued to be very great, for on September 22, he telegraphed Rosecrans that no word had been received from him for thirty-six hours, adding: "Please relieve my anxiety as to position and condition of your army up to the latest moment."

On the following day, still not hearing from Rosecrans, and wishing to encourage him, he telegraphed a copy of Bragg's despatch to the Richmond authorities, which Grant had culled from a Richmond newspaper, the President adding: "You see he (Bragg) does not claim as many prisoners or captured guns as you were inclined to concede. He also confesses to heavy loss."

Then, on September 24, he telegraphed Mrs. Lincoln, who was in New York City visiting friends, a pretty full summing-up of the battle of Chickamauga, mentioning that among six Confederate generals killed was her brother-in-law, Helms of Kentucky. So the anxious days passed, rivaling those of a year before, when Pope's Virginia campaign had ended so disastrously, for while Rosecrans's army was safe, it was only so for the time being. Bragg was being rapidly reinforced from Virginia and it became evident that prompt relief must be given to our army at Chattanooga or it would be cut off by the enemy. That relief was given in the remarkable manner set forth in chapter XIII by the transfer of 23,000 men. under Hooker, from Virginia to Tennessee.

The heavy reinforcement rendered our position at Chattanooga entirely secure. In fact it was soon discovered that the battle of Chickamauga in its final results was more of a victory for the Union cause than a defeat as first supposed; for the enemy suffered greater losses than we did, and reaped no ultimate advantage; while our reinforced army, soon to be placed under the command of Grant (who, two weeks later, was appointed to succeed Rosecrans), took the offensive, and in November whipped Bragg almost to a finish.

Meantime, the general military situation being more satisfactory, the President, on October 3, 1863, issued his proclamation setting apart the last Thursday of November as a day of thanksgiving and praise. This is memorable, because it was the second occasion within three months when a national thanksgiving was appointed by presidential proclamation, to be observed, as the historic document is worded: "by my fellow citizens in every part of the United States and also those who are at sea and those sojourning in foreign lands."

This proclamation is remarkable not only as exhibiting his implicit reliance upon an "ever-watchful God," but for beauty of phrase, and logical belief in an overruling Providence. For instance, after reciting the blessings of fruitful fields, healthful skies, bountiful harvests, untold wealth in our mines and productive industries, harmonious foreign relations, and the success attending our armies in the field, he says in the spirit of an old scriptural herald and seer: "No human counsel hath devised, nor hath any mortal hand worked out these great things. They are the gracious gifts of the most high God, who, while dealing with us in anger for our sins, hath nevertheless remembered mercy." He then commends to the tender care of our beneficent Father who dwelleth in the heavens, "all those who have become widows, orphans, mourners, or sufferers in the lamentable civil strife."

No ruler of millions, since King David the Psalmist, has clothed great thoughts in sublimer language.

The great victories of the combined armies under Grant, in and about Chattanooga, including the capture of Orchard Knob by the Army of the Cumberland, November 23, 1863; the capture of Lookout Mountain by troops of the armies of the Potomac and Cumberland, under Hooker, on the 24th, and the wonderful assault and capture of Missionary Ridge by the Army of the Cumberland under Thomas on the 25th, came in time to make Lincoln's third national thanksgiving the greatest day of rejoicing the people had experienced since the war began.

The first national thanksgiving proclamation ever issued in the United States was dated April 10, 1862. The second was dated July 15, 1863, setting apart August 6, as a day of thanksgiving for recent victories, particularly those of Vicksburg and Gettysburg. Thanksgiving Day, prior to that time, had been generally observed in the New England and Middle States only, but since 1863 the custom inaugurated by President Lincoln has been followed, of having the last Thursday in November of each year set apart as a national day of thanksgiving in all the States of the Union.

On many occasions, telegrams from irresponsible persons were received at the War Department, generally addressed to the President, criticizing the Administration, or some of the generals in the army, and volunteering advice concerning political and military matters. One of these free-lance advisers, named Maxwell, lived in Philadelphia, and scarcely a month passed in which he did not telegraph direct to the President. My memory recalls several of these telegrams. I will quote two only as fair samples of many others.

During Burnside's unsuccessful campaign before Fredericksburg late in 1862, there was a great deal of newspaper talk about certain of his generals, formerly under McClellan, being out of sympathy with and jealous of Burnside; and the court-martial of Fitz-John Porter then in progress had as a basis for its charges the contention that Porter failed to promptly support Pope in August, 1862, because of his partizan friendship for McClellan. The President showed no surprise when he received the following telegram from his unknown adviser:

Philadelphia, December 19, 1862.

HIS EXCELLENCY A. LINCOLN, President.

Richmond campaign, Franklin remaining, foregone conclusion.   ROBERT A. MAXWELL.

No reply was made to this foolish despatch, nor to several others which were afterward received from Maxwell. But at the time of the New York draft riots these despatches were exchanged:

Philadelphia, July 15, 1863.

A. LINCOLN, President.

Albert Gallatin Thorp, informed me that Seymour is well controlled beyond safe limits. Why hesitate?

ROBERT A. MAXWELL.

Washington, D. C., July 15, 1863.

ROBT. A. MAXWELL, Philadelphia:

Your despatch of to-day is received, but I do not understand it.   A. LINCOLN.

Maxwell's despatch no doubt had reference to Governor Seymour of New York, who at that time—during the progress of the draft riots, which culminated on that day, July 15, 1863,— was supposed, at least by the War Department officials, to be in sympathy with the Confederate government, and particularly with the efforts of their Northern agents, Jacob Thompson and

168

others in Canada, to incite opposition in the North to the Administration, and to hinder the draft, then being enforced under Lincoln's proclamation of June 15, 1863, for one hundred thousand men, for six months' service.

The next Maxwell telegram of record was as follows:

New York City, 1:30 P.M., September 23, 1863.
His EXCELLENCY A. LINCOLN, President: Will Buell's testamentary executor George Thomas ever let Rosecrans succeed? Is Bragg dumb enough to punish Thomas severely and disgracingly? ROBERT A. MAXWELL.

The President held this impertinent telegram until his evening visit to the War Department. Meantime, no doubt thinking that some defense of General Thomas by the Administration might serve to allay the already evidently wide-spread distrust and anxiety, he wrote the following despatch at the White House and brought it to the telegraph office and handed it to Tinker for transmission:

"Cypher"
Executive Mansion, Washington, Sep., 23, 1863.
ROBERT A. MAXWELL, New York: I hasten to say that in the state of information we have here, nothing could be more ungracious than to indulge any suspicion towards Gen.

169

Thomas. It is doubtful whether his heroism and skill exhibited last Sunday afternoon, has ever been surpassed in the world.   A. LINCOLN.

But the message had been in Tinker's hands only a few minutes, when Lincoln came over to the ci-

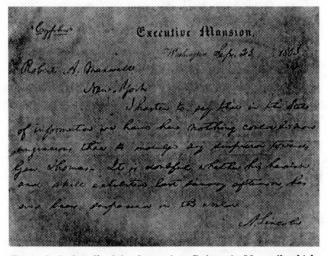

Facsimile (reduced) of the despatch to Robert A. Maxwell, which Lincoln wrote for transmission, but soon after countermanded

The original is in the possession of Mrs. Frances Breckenridge Kellogg, widow of Colonel Sanford Cobb Kellogg (formerly of General Thomas's staff). Mrs. Kellogg has kindly consented to its publication in this history

pher-desk and said, "I guess I will not send this; I can't afford to answer every crazy question asked me."

Thereafter, adopting Lincoln's description, we always referred to these officious despatches as "crazygrams." Tinker, of course, did not send the message which Lincoln had written, and deeming it of curious interest as a memento, preserved it carefully with a copy of the message from Maxwell. Several years afterward, he met General Thomas in Washington, and thinking he would be especially gratified to see and possess the documents, he had the pleasure of delivering them into Thomas's hands at Willard's Hotel, Washington, with a letter, of which the following is a copy:

May 27, 1867.

Major-General George H. Thomas,

GENERAL: I have had in my possession since the day it was written, a telegram penned by our late beloved President. Its history is this. Robert Maxwell, a quixotic individual, residing in Philadelphia, has during the war, and since, humored a propensity for addressing dictatorial and sensational despatches to the President, his cabinet and prominent officials of the Government. By those who were familiar with his character, no consideration was accorded them. On receipt of one of these, a copy of which I enclose, the President wrote a reply, which he handed to me for transmission, but afterwards concluded not to send. I have preserved this precious autographic document, hoping some time to be honored with an opportunity to present it to you in person, to whom it justly belongs—a priceless tribute to a noble hero, whose dauntless courage on that fateful day saved the Army of the Cumberland.

Very Respectfully Yours,

CHARLES A. TINKER, Cipher Operator,
War Dept. Telegraph Office.

171

XIII

A REMARKABLE FEAT IN RAILROAD TRANSPORTA-
TION

AS stated in the previous chapter, Rosecrans's
army had succeeded in reaching Chattanooga, a place of natural safety, but with deci-
mated numbers and an extended line of communication with its base of supplies. Bragg's
army, amply reinforced, resumed the offensive, and Rosecrans became greatly alarmed
lest he should be besieged by Bragg and starved
out. Charles A. Dana, who was with Rosecrans,
also became demoralized and his letters and telegrams to Washington were gloomy and disheart-
ening.[1]   Lincoln and Stanton were both greatly

[1] The following extract is from an article by Charles A. Dana on
Chickamauga, which appeared in "McClure's Magazine" for
December, 1897, p. 353.

"I had not sent him [Stanton] any telegrams in the morning
[Sept. 20, 1863], for I had been on the field at Rossville with Rosecrans and part of the time at some distance from the Widow
Glenn's where the operators were at work. The boys kept at their
post there until the Confederates swept them out of the house.
When they had to run they went instruments and tools in hand,
and as soon as out of reach of the enemy set up shop on a stump.

impressed with the gravity of the situation, but hoped that things were not so bad as represented. Instead they grew worse, until, on September 23, after Lincoln's encouraging message to Rosecrans, several particularly pessimistic cipher-despatches were received from Rosecrans and Dana, which led Stanton to decide that heroic action was needed; so he sent a messenger to Lincoln, at the Soldiers Home, with copies of the alarming despatches, asking that a cabinet meeting be called immediately to consider the steps necessary to prevent a great disaster to our army.

Mr. Carnegie, in his Kenyon College address on "Stanton, the Patriot," (April 26, 1906,) referring to this incident, says that, "startled by the summons, the President mounted his horse and rode to Washington in the moonlight to preside over the cabinet."

It was not long before they were driven out of this. They next attempted to establish an office on the Rossville road, but before they had succeeded in making connections a battle was raging around them and they had to retreat to Granger's Headquarters at Rossville. . . .

"Having been swept bodily off the battlefield and having made my way into Chattanooga through a panic-stricken rabble, the first telegram I sent to Mr. Stanton was naturally colored by what I had seen and experienced. I remember that I began the despatch by saying, 'My report to-day is of deplorable importance. Chickamauga is as fatal a name in our history as Bull Run.'"

When Lincoln reached the War Department,[1] Halleck, who had been called in conference, was asked how long it would take to move two army corps from Virginia to Tennessee. Halleck replied that, in his opinion, it would take nearly three months to complete the transfer. This was a great disappointment to Lincoln and Stanton, especially as both Rosecrans and Dana had meantime sent further appeals for help, repeating the expression of their fear that unless relief came quickly, the enemy might cut off our communications.

When Eckert brought in the later despatches he was asked by Stanton what he knew of railroad routes to Chattanooga. His former railroad experience enabled him to supply important data, and when told of Halleck's three months' estimate, he promptly demurred and said it was much too long; that sixty days or perhaps even forty would be sufficient. Eckert was thereupon instructed to submit a written report that night. Naturally such an order placed him in an embarrassing position with relation to Halleck, but he was on his mettle, and

[1] John C. Hatter the messenger, now of Brooklyn, returned with the President.

while the cabinet was discussing the grave contingency, the cipher-operators and their chief were busy examining railroad schedules and maps.

It was found that from Washington to Nashville, seven days were required for the movement of fast freight traffic, passenger trains, of course, taking much less time.

Tinker's diary says:

September 23, 1863. Long despatches from Dana and Rosecrans. Reinforcements to be sent from Army of Potomac. Left Office 11:30 P.M., Eckert and Bates still at work.

Sept. 24. Eckert and Bates in office all night. President and cabinet are there arranging to reinforce Rosecrans. Hooker going with 19,000 men.

Lincoln and Stanton waited in the building until after daybreak, and at 2:30 A.M., September 24, Meade was ordered by telegraph to prepare two army corps, the 11th and 12th, under Hooker, to be sent to Washington immediately, with five days' cooked provisions; their baggage to go with them; artillery ammunition, horses, etc., to follow quickly. At 10:45 A.M. Meade answered that "every effort will be made to have the troops designated ready to move." By 8 A.M. Eckert had his report ready, and, after discussing it with Assistant Secretary Watson, took it to Stanton's room. When the latter read it and learned that Eckert allowed only fifteen days, instead of his previous hastily expressed opinion of "sixty and perhaps forty," he jumped for joy and began eagerly to ask for details. His first inquiry was, "How do you propose to get so large a number of men, with batteries and horses, across the river at Louisville safely and quickly?" Eckert replied that at that season the Ohio River was full of coal barges, loaded and empty, and that a pontoon bridge could be got ready in twenty-four hours. The next question was, "How will you feed the hosts without losing time?" Answer was made that the Quartermaster's Department could establish a force of cooks and waiters every fifty miles or so along the route and at each eating station a supply of hot coffee, bread, etc., with waiters, could be put on the train and be carried to the next eating-place, and the waiters could then come back to their starting-point on regular trains. The plan was so well laid and withal so sensible, that Lincoln and Stanton both indorsed it, subject to the approval of the railroad authorities and military officials.

Meantime, urgent telegrams had been sent the

night before to Garrett and Smith of the Baltimore & Ohio, Felton of the Philadelphia, Wilmington & Baltimore, and Scott of the Pennsylvania railroads, to come to Washington by first train. McCallum, general manager of military railroads, and Whiton, his assistant, were brought into conference.

McCallum, while approving the general plan, would not bind himself to the low estimate of fifteen days, but agreed to exert every effort to approximate that limit, and thereupon the formal order was given by Stanton, with Lincoln's approval, to begin the movement in accordance with the telegram to Meade a few hours earlier.

An essential part of the plan was to have the Government take military control of all railroads on the route, so that every required facility would be subject to the orders of the War Department. This was, of course, accepted by the railroad authorities, and from the moment the orders were given for the great movement, every one involved in it was kept busy day and night.

At 9 A.M., September 24, General Meigs, Quartermaster-General, telegraphed from Nashville that he would look after matters from that end and coöperate with the railroad people. At

10 A.M., Garrett and Smith of the Baltimore & Ohio railroad, reached the War Department. McCallum went by special train to Meade's headquarters and telegraphed the following: "Will commence loading 17,000 men at Bristow (thirty-seven miles south of Washington) to-morrow morning" (September 25).

Scott, of the Pennsylvania Railroad, received Stanton's telegram at night somewhere on the road, and started by special train for Washington, where he arrived about 1 P.M., September 24, with Felton of the Wilmington road, and hurried to the War Department. After reading Eckert's report and learning what had already been done, and listening to Stanton's impassioned appeals for haste, Scott quietly remarked, in his quick decisive manner, that Eckert's time could be met and the transfer effected—perhaps sooner than fifteen days. To those now living who knew Thomas A. Scott in his prime, such a statement will convey a world of meaning. It was most welcome to the President and Secretary of War, and especially gratifying to Eckert. Scott remained at the War Department not more than an hour, returning to his special train which had been kept ready at the station and which took him at fast speed to Louisville. While en route, he kept the wires hot with brief, imperative messages to his subordinates and officials of connecting roads, ordering cars to be hurried to Washington for the transportation of men, baggage, ammunition, cannon and horses to Tennessee. Reaching Louisville, he sent this message:

Louisville, September 26, 1863, 2:30 P.M.

SECRETARY OF WAR,
         Washington, D. C.

Arrangements for ferriage of troops across Ohio River completed.   THOS. A. SCOTT.

To make a long story short, the entire movement, counting from the hour when the first train-load left Bristow Station, Thursday, September 25, until the last train arrived at Chattanooga, October 6, was completed in eleven and a half days, or three and a half less than Eckert's low estimate, and two and a half months less than Halleck's figures. The distance by rail from Bealeton, Virginia—below Bristow Station—to Chattanooga, Tennessee, is 1233 miles.

In Carnegie's Kenyon College address he gives the time as seven days, but this is obviously an error if we consider the movement from start to finish.

On October 1, this telegram was sent:

Col. Thomas A. Scott,
                    Louisville.

Tell me how things have advanced, as far as you know.
                                        A. Lincoln.

Scott's reply was satisfactory, and while the great movement was in progress, and when it was seen that it would be a success, the following despatch was sent:

Colonel Thomas A. Scott,
                    Louisville.

Your work is most brilliant.   A thousand thanks.   It is a great achievement.   Edwin M. Stanton.

Similar messages of congratulation and thanks were sent to all the other railroad officials concerned.   The records show that the total number of men in the two army corps was 23,000, instead of 19,000, as at first estimated.

The reinforcements thus given to Rosecrans were ample and timely, and served to place his army in an impregnable position.   Such a feat was unprecedented and will long be referred to by railroad men as the record of marvelous accomplishment in the way of transportation of large bodies over single track railroads.

Meantime, the Confederates were kept informed of the proposed movement by means of secret agents in Washington, as shown by the following despatches:

Signal Office, Richmond, Va., Sept. 30, 1863.

HON. JAS. A. SEDDON, *Sec. of War*, Richmond, Va.

SIR: —I have the honor to inclose copy of despatch just received at this office from Washington from a source which may be considered reliable. Very respectfully,

WM. NORRIS,

Maj. & Chf. Sig. Corps.

Sept. 25, 1863. The 11th Army Corps, 30,000 strong is at Alexandria; is to be forwarded at once to the relief of Rosecrans. General Meade, if circumstances demand it, will fall back on Washington. The President has telegraphed Railroad Presidents to meet here and it is said they are already here. The troops are to be hurried through on shortest time. There is immense trepidation here with the "powers that be" in regard to Rosecrans. General Meade is already, it is said, at Warrenton. Recent information shows that two of Meade's Army Corps are on the move. Large numbers of troops are at the cars now loaded with cannon. There is no doubt as to the destination of these troops, part for Rosecrans and perhaps for Burnside. Eleventh Army Corps commanded by General Howard—the Dutch Corps.   A. HOWELL.

LINCOLN IN THE TELEGRAPH OFFICE

Sept. 27, 1863. It is reported that Joe Hooker is in command of these troops and their destination is the White House.[1] The troops are at the Relay House this evening.

Orange Court House, Va., Sept. 28, 1863.

HON. JEFFERSON DAVIS, *President,* Richmond, Va.

A report was sent to me yesterday from Shenandoah Valley, which if true furnishes additional reason for prompt action on the part of General Bragg. It is stated that General Slocum's and Howard's Corps, under General Hooker, are to reinforce General Rosecrans. They were to move over the Baltimore & Ohio Railroad and to commence on the night of the 25th. . . .   R. E. LEE, General.

Orange Court House, Va., Oct. 3, 1863.

HON. JEFFERSON DAVIS, *President,* Richmond, Va.

A despatch from Major Gilmor last night states that reinforcements for Rosecrans have all passed over the Baltimore & Ohio Railroad. The force composed of Slocum's and Hooker's Corps, estimated at between 20 and 25,000 men. He states he made several attempts to break the railroad but could accomplish nothing. . . .

R. E. LEE, General.

[1] NOTE. This is evidently an error. AUTHOR.

XIV

THERE were many angles in Lincoln's character. That which he showed in the telegraph office was the personal, homely side as distinguished from the business, political, or literary side. The cipher-operators saw him at close range, and in his most anxious hours, amid the excitement of great military movements, with their attendant horrors: the clash of arms, the carnage of the battle-field, the groans of the dying and the tears of loved ones. We also met him in the calmer but no less trying hours of patient waiting for the slow development of wide-reaching plans for the preservation of the Union.

I do not presume to speak of Lincoln as a politician, as a statesman, or as a born and trained leader of men, although he was preëminent in each of these rôles; nor as a story-teller, with all that such a term meant in his day; but I do wish to emphasize that personal trait of his which has impressed itself upon me more forcibly than any other, namely, his kindly, charitable disposition, which was especially shown toward his political opponents and his country's enemies.

In his second inaugural, March 4, 1865—that remarkable address, which Carl Schurz likens to a "sacred poem"—he made use of words which in their beautiful setting are immortal: "With malice toward none; with charity for all." This simple phrase is probably quoted more frequently than any other from Lincoln's writings, just as General Grant is referred to so often in his sententious remark, "Let us have peace," which is graven on the portal of his tomb.

Reference being made by some one in the telegraph office to Lincoln's inveterate habit of story-telling, he said that he really could not break himself of it; that it had been formed in his younger days, and later he found it difficult to refrain from clinching an argument or emphasizing a good point by means of a story. He said his case was like that of the old colored man on the plantation, who neglected his work in order to preach to the other slaves, who often idled their time away listening to the old man's discourses. His master admonished him, but all to no purpose, for the good old man had the spirit of the gospel in him and kept on preaching, even when he knew the lash awaited him; but finally he was ordered to report at the "big house," and was berated soundly by his master and told that he would be punished severely the very next time he was caught in the act of preaching. The old man, with tears in his eyes, spoke up and said, "But, marsa, I jest cain't help it; I allus has to draw infrunces from de Bible textes when dey comes into my haid. Does n't you, marsa?" This reply interested his master, who was a religious man, and who said, "Well, uncle, I suspect I do something of that kind myself at times, but there is one text I never could understand, and if you can draw the right inference from it, I will cancel my order and let you preach to your heart's content." "What is de tex', marsa?" " 'The ass snuffeth up the east wind.' Now, uncle, what inference do you draw from such a text?" "Well, marsa, I 's neber heered dat tex' befo', but I 'spect de infrunce is she gotter snuff a long time befo' she git fat."

During some of Lincoln's daily visits to the War Department, there were many spare moments while he waited for fresh news from the front or for the translation of cipher-messages, and when he did not fill up the otherwise idle time by telling stories, he would read aloud some humorous article from a newspaper, as, for instance, Orpheus C. Kerr's droll reports from Mackerelville, or Petroleum V. Nasby's letters in sarcastic vein; at other times Artemus Ward's inimitable lectures. Some of Nasby's letters were irresistibly funny, especially those relating to the continuous struggle for the post-office at "Confedrit Cross Roads," and to the backwardness of some of our generals. Others referred to the great excitement caused by the discovery of flowing oil-wells in Pennsylvania, whereby great and sudden wealth had come to many formerly poor farmers and others in that region. One catch phrase which Lincoln especially enjoyed repeating was, "Oil 's well that ends well." He was particularly fond of David R. Locke (Nasby), whom he first met in 1858 in Quincy, Illinois. In 1863 he wrote a letter to Locke in appreciation of one of Nasby's humorous articles, and ended the letter with this inquiry: "Why don't you come to Washington and see me?" Locke accepted the invitation and spent a delightful hour with the President, during which we may imagine the two humorists "swapped stories" to their hearts' content.

Beckwith, Grant's cipher-operator, says that on April 6, 1865, the day after Lincoln's return from Richmond, Lincoln was in Colonel Bowers's tent at City Point in happy humor over Grant's successes, and that he quoted from memory Artemus Ward's account of the escape of the *Polly Ann* on the Erie Canal when being chased by pirates. The part of the story to which Lincoln called special attention was where one of the crew of the *Polly Ann,* carrying a bag of oats, ordered the pilot to "heave to" and when the vessel "huv to" the sailor went ashore and scattered the oats liberally along the tow-path. After this was done the vessel went on her way and when the mules of the pirates' craft reached the oats, no amount of persuasion could induce them to proceed until the oats had all been consumed; and so the *Polly Ann* escaped. Lincoln was interrupted at this point of the recital by the entrance of Secretary Harlan but immediately resumed, saying, "Now, gentlemen, that was true strategy because the enemy was diverted from his real purpose."

He then, without waiting for comments, began

again the study of the map of Virginia in connection with several despatches that Beckwith had just brought in from Grant's pursuing columns.

Orpheus C. Kerr's effusions were on a different line from either Ward's or Nasby's, but were equally laughable; for instance, when at the close of an exciting campaign in which the Mackerelville army had bravely marched several miles one day and had been engaged in an impossible battle, it was gravely stated that "Victory has once again perched upon the banners of the conqueror." Lincoln would stop his reading to laugh with us at these foolish expressions. He greatly enjoyed this sort of humor, especially when it was directed against the faults of our generals, or even when in the form of criticisms upon his own public acts or those of his cabinet. In fact, he dearly loved to twit some of his official family by calling attention to newspaper references of a humorous character reflecting upon their administration or personal peculiarities, and to those of us who watched him day after day it was clear that the telling of stories and the reading of droll articles gave him needed relaxation from the severe strain and heavy burden resting upon him, leading his mind away from the awful incidents of the war that were ever present—the bloody battles and loss of life, the execution of deserters, the mistakes and jealousies of his generals, and the criticisms of the daily press, often unjust and sometimes disloyal.

On the night of November 8, 1864, while Lincoln with a number of his cabinet-officers and others were in the telegraph office awaiting the presidential election returns, he took from his inside pocket a small pamphlet containing some of Nasby's effusions, and at intervals read aloud to the company various extracts. Charles A. Dana, in his "Reminiscences," says that Secretary Stanton was indignant that the President should give attention to such trifling subjects at important moments when, as it appeared to him, the destinies of the country hung in the balance, but Lincoln had a method in this apparent foolishness. Frank B. Carpenter, the artist who painted the Emancipation Proclamation group, says that Lincoln remarked, in reply to a criticism similar to Stanton's, "that if it were not for this occasional vent I should die." After the bloody battle of Fredericksburg, where 11,000 of our men were killed and wounded, he said, "If there is a man out of perdition who suffers more than I do, I pity him." [1]

So we may now look back over the stretch of years and better realize than we did then the relief which the repetition of humorous and even frivolous stories brought to his tired body and harassed brain. Oftentimes indeed in those days of stress he would lean back in his chair, with his feet upon a near-by table, and relapse into a serious mood, idly gazing out of the window upon Pennsylvania Avenue, that great thoroughfare over which he had seen so many brave soldiers march to the front never to return. In these intervals of repose Lincoln's face was a study; the inherent sadness of his features was evident even to us youngsters. Indeed, it was sometimes pathetic. We often wondered of what he was thinking; but he would not long remain idly pensive. Soon he would come out of the clouds, his expressive face would light up, and he would make some humorous remark as Stanton entered the room, or as he observed one of the cipher-operators make a movement toward the little drawer in which the incoming despatches were filed.

[1] See also "Lincoln on His Own Story-Telling," by Silas W. Burt, in "The Century Magazine" for February, 1907.

Lincoln's stories were never long, but they were always funny and laughter-provoking, and usually effective in their purpose of proving a point or answering an objection. They were homely and old-fashioned, which terms well express their general character. This is only natural and to be expected, in view of his rude surroundings in early life, before the telegraph had done more than thread its slender way through the forests and over the prairies of our broad land, bringing in its later development the current news of the world for the enlightenment of the masses, and calling for attention with each successive edition of the daily press. In those almost primitive days of our nation's history, the post-office, the country store, and the court-house, were the rendezvous, especially of the young men who, ten or twenty years later, would be the leaders of public opinion; and around the blazing fire in these places of resort during the winter days and nights, or on the street or sidewalk close by in the summer-time, were congregated the talkers and listeners of the town, and the man who could hold his own in argument, or command the attention of the crowd, whether politics, religion, or gossip was the topic of discussion, was the one most ready with a story to illustrate a point or parallel some other story that had just commanded a general laugh. In these trials of wit and humor, Lincoln, from all accounts, must have been easily first. The habits thus formed held their grip upon him even to the end; for in his last public address, on the evening of April 11, 1865, which he delivered from the porch of the White House, and which I had the pleasure of listening to on my way home from the War Department, he made this remark concerning the progress of reconstruction measures in Louisiana:

Concede that the new government of Louisiana is only to what it should be as the egg is to the fowl, we shall sooner have the fowl by hatching the egg than by smashing it.

This form of argument left no sting behind it; and the opponents of his Louisiana reconstruction plan, at least those of his own political party, must have admitted later that his policy of "malice toward none; with charity for all," was superior to theirs.

A great many anecdotes and stories have been attributed to Lincoln. It is certain that not all so called were his; indeed, it is probable that most of them were not. As the years go by, it is be-

coming more and more difficult to decide which
are genuine; that is to say, those which originated
with Lincoln or were known to have been repeated by him. Many stories said to be Lincoln's
were no doubt his own by right of first telling,
others may also be called his because of his apt
selection and manner of telling, with his own
unique wording and application; but it is probable that by far the larger number of such stories
now current are associated with his name merely
because he happened to be present when they
were told by some one else.

It is natural also that in the re-telling of some
really genuine stories, even by those who heard
them from his own lips, there will be numerous
variations, one instance being the Cave of Adullam incident told by Nicolay and Hay (Vol. IX.
p. 40). Their version is not the same as mine,
which is given below.

On May 30, 1864, the Cleveland Independent
Convention met, and on the following day nominated Frémont and Cochrane for president and
vice-president respectively. This was an unconstitutional selection, because both candidates were
from the same State—New York. The convention was organized and controlled by a lot of

ultra patriots, sore-heads and cranks, who held the most divergent opinions on political and military affairs; but they were all agreed in condemning Lincoln's conduct of the war and his administration generally, and they all professed to believe that there was no hope for the country save through an entire change of policy. Even "The New York Herald," of May 31, the morning after the convention assembled, used this language in an editorial:

As for Lincoln, we do not conceive it possible that he can be reëlected after his remarkable blunders of the past three or more years.

The Northern press generally, however, was favorable to Lincoln, and a great deal of ridicule was cast upon the convention and its heterogeneous and discordant elements by the newspapers and the public.

On June 1, the "Herald's" report of the proceedings of the day before began thus:

The Cleveland Convention opened to-day with some 350 to 400 delegates in attendance.

My record shows that in the evening, at the War Department, the "Herald's" report above referred to, just received from New York, was read aloud, and Lincoln at once asked for a Bible. Mr. Stanton's private secretary, Major Johnson, went to get a copy, and not finding one immediately, came back to apologize for the delay, and then went out again in further search of the desired volume. Presently he returned with an open Bible in his hands, and presented it to the President in his most polite manner.

Lincoln then opened the Bible at I Samuel xxii, 2, and, referring to the "Herald's" report of the number of delegates in the convention (350 to 400), read aloud to us this verse:

And every one that was in distress, and every one that was in debt, and every one that was discontented, gathered themselves unto him; and he became a captain over them: and there were with him about four hundred men.

Nicolay and Hay say that the incident occurred in the White House on the morning after the convention, when a friend who called on the President remarked upon the fact that instead of thousands, who had been expected, there were in fact at no time more than 400 present, and that Lincoln, being struck by the number mentioned, reached for the Bible that usually lay on his desk, and turned to the verse above quoted in order to verify the number composing King David's band,

and then read it aloud. Nicolay and Hay make no reference to the "Herald" report. Which version is the correct one may never be certainly known. Perhaps both may be. My account makes no mention of Nicolay or Hay, and, in fact, those gentlemen seldom came to the War Department with Lincoln. It may well be that Lincoln looked up the verse in the Bible in the White House, as well as in the telegraph office.

The well known Cave of Adullam reference by John Bright in the British Parliament was in 1866 and had no relation to Lincoln's particular application of the Scriptural incident *i.e.*, to the number (400) composing the band of discontents.

Some of Lincoln's stories here recorded were told by him in my hearing, others were repeated to me shortly after the telling, and some at a later period by my comrades in the telegraph office, who claimed to have heard them from Lincoln himself, and I believe therefore that, subject to these qualifications, they are all genuine; although I have heard it stated that all current standard jokes can be traced back to antiquity, one leading type for instance furnishing the basis for innumerable variations in successive periods of time. This theory was propounded by Solomon long ago, when he said, "There is no new thing under the sun. Is there any thing whereof it may be said, See, this is new? it hath been already of old time, which was before us." So it seems probable that some of Lincoln's stories, genuine though we may believe them to be, were current before his time; for instance, the one with the Kentucky flavor referring to the brand of whisky which General Grant's enemies protested he used with too much freedom. Lincoln disclaimed this story in my hearing, stating that King George III of England was said to have remarked, when he was told that General Wolfe, then in command of the English army in Canada, was mad, that he wished Wolfe would bite some of his other generals.

Many of Lincoln's stories were in couples, like man and wife, one complementing the other; for instance, some one spoke of Tom Hood's spoiled child, which, as I recall, was represented in a series of pictures. First, the nurse places baby in an arm-chair before the fire and covers it with a shawl to shield it from the heat; next the fussy aunt comes into the room and, being near-sighted, fails to observe the sleeping baby and flops into the easy chair when, of course, there is a scream; then the nurse enters and rescues the baby from the heavy weight of the aunt and holds it in her arms edgeways so that when the father of the now *spoiled child* comes in the baby is mashed so flat that he does not perceive it. A reference being made to Hood's story, Lincoln produced its counterpart as follows:

Scene, a theater; curtain just lifted; enter a man with a high silk hat in his hand. He becomes so interested in the movements on the stage that involuntarily he places his hat, open side up, on the adjoining seat without seeing the approach of a fat dowager who, near-sighted, like the fat aunt of the spoiled child, does not observe the open door of the hat. She sits down, and there is a crunching noise, and the owner of the spoiled hat reaches out to rescue his property as the fat woman rises, and holding the hat in front of him says: "Madam, I could have told you that my hat would not fit before you tried it on."

IN connection with the observance of the first national fast day, September 5, 1861, Col. Wm.

Bender Wilson, in his "Acts and Actors of the Civil War," page 111, gives an account of the President's visit to the telegraph office that morning. As he entered the room he saw George Low, one of the junior operators, at work cleaning a blue vitriol battery. "Well, sonny, mixing the juices, eh?" the President inquired. Then sitting down and adjusting his spectacles, which were specially made with short spring ends to clasp the sides of his head just back of his eyes, he became aware that all the operators were busy, and a smile broke over his countenance as he remarked: "Gentlemen, this is fast day, and I am pleased to observe that you are working as fast as you can; the proclamation was mine, and that is my interpretation of its bearing upon you. Now, we will have a little talk with Governor Morton, at Indianapolis. I want to give him a lesson in geography. Bowling Green affair I set him all right upon; now I will tell him something about Muldraugh Hill. Morton is a good fellow, but at times he is the skeeredest man I know of." This talk with Governor Morton was in consequence of the latter's telegram expressing great anxiety concerning the Confederate general, Zollicoffer's reported movement toward Louisville.

Lincoln told Morton over the wire that he hoped the report was true, as in such event our troops would be able to advance and occupy Cumberland Gap, which Lincoln claimed was a very important strategical position.

Earlier in the same month Lincoln, accompanied by Mr. Seward, dropped into the office with a pleasant "Good morning. What news?" Wilson replied, "Good news, because none." Whereupon Lincoln rejoined, "Ah, my young friend, that rule does not always hold good, for a fisherman does not consider it good luck when he can't get a bite."

On another occasion Lincoln came to the office after dark and asked for the latest news. He was told that McClellan was on his way from Arlington to Fort Corcoran and that our pickets still held Ball's Cross-roads and that no firing had been heard since sunset. The President inquired if any firing had been heard *before sunset,* and upon being answered in the negative, laughingly replied: "That reminds me of the man who, speaking of a supposed freak of nature, said, 'The child was black from his hips down,' and upon being asked the color from the hips up, replied, 'Why, black, of course.' "

Another humorous remark by Lincoln about this period—late in 1861—was recorded by my comrade Wilson, who has answered my inquiry as follows:

The unvarnished incident was simply this. You, Flesher, and I were the three operators regularly on duty at "W D" (the office call at that time—a few months later when we moved up-stairs into the large "Library" room the call was changed to "D I"). We always set apart a large chair for the President. One day he came in alone, sat down in his chair, and after a few moments arose and walked over to the instrument table, and took possession of a vacant chair and began writing. Almost immediately there was a call on the instrument, and Flesher hurried to answer it and in doing so had to lean over Lincoln's shoulder. The President turned and said,"My young friend, have I hunkered you out of your chair?" Having heard the word "hunkered" used in the sense of elbowing one out of his place, I made a note of the incident as I had previously done in the case of his frequent use of the phrase "By jings."

On one occasion Lincoln, when entering the telegraph office, was heard to remark to Secretary Seward, "By jings! Governor, we are here at last." Turning to him in a reproving manner, Mr. Seward said, "Mr. President, where did you learn that inelegant expression?" Without replying to the Secretary, Lincoln addressed the operators, saying: "Young gentlemen, excuse me for swearing before you. 'By jings' is swearing, for my good old mother taught me that anything that had a 'by' before it was swearing." The only time, however, that Lincoln was ever heard really to swear in the telegraph office was on the occasion of his receiving a telegram from Burnside, who had been ordered a week before to go to the relief of Rosecrans, at Chattanooga, then in great danger of an attack from Bragg. On that day Burnside telegraphed from Jonesboro, farther away from Rosecrans than he was when he received the order to hurry toward him. When Burnside's telegram was placed in Lincoln's hands he said, "Damn Jonesboro!" He then telegraphed Burnside:

September 21, 1863.

If you are to do any good to Rosecrans it will not do to waste time with Jonesboro. . . .

There was popular, many years ago, a pictorial book of nonsense to which Lincoln once referred in my presence. He said he had seen such a book, and recited from it this rime as illustrating his idea that the best method of allaying anger was to adopt a conciliatory attitude. The picture shown, he said, was that of a maiden seated on a stile smiling at an angry cow near-by in the field, and saying:

> I will sit on this stile
> And continue to smile,
> Which may soften the heart of that cow.

A few months later, after Lincoln's death and the capture of Jefferson Davis, the latter and some of his party, including his private secretary, Col. Burton N. Harrison, were brought to Fort Monroe, their baggage and official papers being forwarded to Washington. Secretary Stanton ordered this material stored in one of the library alcoves in the telegraph room, and the cipher-operators were directed to make an inventory. My father, Francis Bates, a townsman of Mr. Stanton and belonging to the same masonic lodge, was placed in charge of the property, which, by the way, became the nucleus of the Confederate Archives Bureau, first presided over by Francis Lieber, the historian. In examining the satchel of Colonel Harrison, I came across a copy of the old book of nonsense above mentioned. Years afterward, having business relations with Harrison, I told him of the coincidence, and he explained that the volume had been put into his satchel by the captain of the gunboat on which he was brought to Fort Monroe, and that it had served to while away many idle hours.

Tinker records that one day Secretary Seward, who was not renowned as a joker, said he had been told that a short time before, on a street crossing, Lincoln had been seen to turn out in the mud to give a colored woman a chance to pass. "Yes," said Lincoln, "it has been a rule of my life that if people would not turn out for me, I would turn out for them. Then you avoid collisions."

In 1863 Assistant Secretary of War Dana was detailed to visit Grant's army in Mississippi, and make full reports to the War Department of military conditions, which were not satisfactory to the Administration. After remaining with Grant for a while, Dana went to Tennessee to make similar reports regarding affairs in Rosecrans's army. Dana's reports by telegraph were generally full, and the cipher-operators during that period had occasion to consult the dictionary many times for the meaning of words new and strange to our ears.

It was an education for us, particularly when errors occurred in transmission and words like "truculent" and "hibernating" had to be dug out of telegraphic chaos. Dana's strong, virile manner of expressing himself on salient questions became better known to the reading public in the last quarter of the nineteenth century.

While Dana's long despatches, ruthlessly criticizing or commending our generals, were being deciphered, Lincoln waited eagerly for the completed translations which he would usually read aloud with running comments, harsh criticisms being softened in the reading. In this way he brought his hearers into the current of his thoughts. In our cipher-codes there were arbitrary words representing proper names; for instance, for Jefferson Davis, *Hosanna* and *Husband;* for Robert E. Lee, *Hunter* and *Happy.* Whenever Lincoln would reach these names in a despatch he was reading he would invariably say "Jeffy D" or "Bobby Lee," thus indicating at once his kindness of heart and love of humor. He would seldom or never pronounce their full names.[1]

---

[1] It is well right here to refer to Davis's remark in 1875 concerning Lincoln. In "Our Presidents and How We Make Them," Colonel A. K. McClure tells of his visit to Davis in that year. He says Davis paid a beautiful tribute to Lincoln. After listening closely to what McClure said of Lincoln and his character, Davis remarked with earnestness and pathos: "Next to the destruction of the Confederacy, the death of Abraham Lincoln was the darkest day the South has ever known."

LINCOLN IN THE TELEGRAPH OFFICE

At the annual banquet of the Military Telegraph Corps at the Arlington Hotel, Washington, on the evening of October 11, 1906, Mr. Tinker said:

I think I had the pleasure of hearing what in all probability was the last anecdote ever told by Mr. Lincoln in the telegraph office. Early on the morning of April 13, 1865, the day before his assassination, he came into the telegraph office while I was copying a despatch that conveyed important information on two subjects and that was couched in very laconic terms. He read over the despatch, and after taking in the meaning of the terse phrases, turned to me and, with his accustomed smile, said: "Mr. Tinker, that reminds me of the old story of the Scotch country girl on her way to market with a basket of eggs for sale. She was fording a small stream in scant costume, when a wagoner approached from the opposite bank and called: 'Good morning, my lassie; how deep 's the brook, and what 's the price of eggs?' " 'Knee deep and a sixpence,' answered the little maid, who gave no further attention to her questioner."

Mr. Tinker, continuing his recital, said that the President, with a smile still on his sunny face, left the office to go into Secretary Stanton's room adjoining.

On one occasion an official letter was received from John Wintrup, the operator at Wilmington, Delaware, on the route of the military line from Washington to Fort Monroe. Wintrup is still living in Philadelphia. His signature was written in a rather bold hand with the final letter quite large, almost like a capital, and ending in flourishes which partly obscured the name itself. Lincoln's eye dropped on this letter as it lay on the

A duplicate of Wintrup's signature

In 1907 the writer received a letter from his friend Wintrup in the ordinary course of business, from which the facsimile signature here shown was taken

cipher-desk, and after satisfying his curiosity as to the peculiar signature he said: "That reminds me of a short-legged man in a big overcoat, the tail of which was so long that it wiped out his footprints in the snow."

XV

LINCOLN at all times showed a most tender regard for Mrs. Lincoln and great affection for his sons (of whom he had four), especially for the youngest (born 1853), familiarly called "Tad," who was christened Thomas, after his paternal grandfather.

One son, Edward Baker (born 1846), died before the war, and William Wallace (born 1850), died in 1862.

The writer recalls many telegrams written by Mr. Lincoln during the war, some signed in Mrs. Lincoln's name, others addressed to her, the wording of which indicated that between husband and wife there was deep affection and close confidence. One of many cases will serve to illustrate this fact.

As recorded elsewhere, the President's family occupied a small cottage at the Soldiers Home, on the outskirts of Washington during the summer and autumn months. In the latter part of

1862, Mrs. Lincoln went to Boston to visit some friends, and while there Mr. Lincoln sent this message:

Washington, November 9, 1862.

MRS. A. LINCOLN, Boston: Mrs. Cuthbert and Aunt Mary want to move to the White House because it has grown so cold at the Soldiers' Home. Shall they? A. LINCOLN.

This deference to Mrs. Lincoln's wishes was habitual with him.

William Wallace Lincoln, always called "Willie," was next older than Tad, and I well remember his quiet manner and interesting personality from having seen him frequently during the summer and autumn of 1861, when he was about eleven. He died of typhoid fever, February 20, 1862; and Lincoln's deep sorrow over the loss of a second son was evident for months afterward. In my war diary, under date of February 11, 1864, is this entry:

Last night, when leaving the telegraph office I discovered that the White House stables were on fire, and running back to the War Department, where there was a call wire, I sent an alarm to the fire-engine house above 17th Street. The engine responded quickly, but the fire had gained too much headway, and the stable and contents were destroyed, including the President's three spans of carriage horses and Willie's little pony.

13

This was two years after the boy's death, but his winning ways had made him such a great favorite that his pony was still identified with his name. In Bishop Simpson's funeral oration, when Lincoln's body was brought to Springfield in 1865, he made this reference:

"In his domestic life Lincoln was exceedingly kind and affectionate. . . . To an officer of the army he said not long since, 'Do you ever find yourself talking with the dead?' and then added, 'Since Willie's death, I catch myself every day involuntarily talking with him as if he were with me.'"

No other record of this incident has been discovered by me, but Frank B. Carpenter, the artist, in his "Six Months at the White House," p. 293, says that on April 14, 1865, the day of the assassination, and more than three years subsequent to Willie's death, Lincoln said to Mrs. Lincoln: "We must both be more cheerful in the future. Between the war and the loss of our darling Willie we have been very miserable."

Here are two telegrams out of a large number in which Lincoln referred to his children in an affectionate manner.

LINCOLN'S LOVE FOR HIS CHILDREN

August 31, 1864.

Mrs. A. Lincoln, Manchester, Vermont:

All reasonably well. Bob not here yet. How is dear
Tad? A. Lincoln.

September 8, 1864.

Mrs. A. Lincoln, Manchester, Vermont:

All well, including Tad's pony and the goats.

A. Lincoln.

On another occasion Lincoln wrote to Mrs.
Lincoln as follows:

. . . Tell dear Tad poor Nanny goat is lost. . . . The
day you left, Nanny was found resting herself and chewing
her little cud on the middle of Tad's bed, but now she 's
gone. . . .

The President's affection for his youngest boy
was such that they were together much of the
time, even while the father was receiving callers
or attending to official business in the White
House, and nearly always when visiting the army
at the front or in the defenses around Washington. They came to the War Department together very often.

Many stories are told of Tad's mischievous
pranks, and of his father's close companionship
with his favorite boy. Tinker records that on
one occasion Lincoln came into the telegraph of-

fice chuckling to himself over a fairy story-book that some one had given to Tad, who was holding his father's hand as he entered the room. He thereupon repeated the story to the cipher-operators. It told how a mother hen tried to raise a brood of chicks, but was much disturbed over the conduct of a sly old fox who ate several of the youngsters while still professing to be an honest fox; so the anxious mother had a serious talk with the old reynard about his wickedness. "Well, what was the result?" one of us asked, when it appeared that Lincoln did not intend to continue his narrative. "The fox reformed," said Lincoln, his eyes twinkling, "and became a highly respected paymaster in the army, and now I am wondering which one he is." The significance of this reference is in the fact that about that time there were rumors of fraud in the Paymaster's Department.

My comrade, Madison Buell of Buffalo, New York, has given an account of a visit of Lincoln to the War Department, accompanied as usual by Tad, who wandered through the cipher-office into the adjoining room, where the telegraph instruments were located, each set (relay, sounder, and key) resting on a marble-topped table. In pure mischief Tad thrust his fingers into an ink-well and wiped them across several of the white tops, making a horrible mess. Buell seized the boy by the collar and marched him at arm's length into the cipher-room, where his father was seated looking over the latest despatches which he had taken from the little drawer of the cipher-desk. Each one of the trio was surprised and a little embarrassed, Buell perhaps more so than the other two. Tad held up his inky fingers, while Buell, with a look of disgust on his face, pointed through the open door to the row of marble tops smeared with ink. Lincoln took in the situation at once, and without asking for further explanation, lifted his boy in his arms and left the office, saying in a pleasant tone, "Come, Tad; Buell is abusing you."

Lincoln went to City Point in March, 1865, and, as usual, Tad went with him and remained with his father after Mrs. Lincoln returned to Washington a week later. Tad became a 'great pet among the officers and men. Each afternoon, during their two weeks' stay, the headquarters' band marched up to the open space near the President's tent, and played popular airs for an hour or so. Tad enjoyed the music of the brass band very greatly, and was on the lookout each afternoon when the appointed hour approached. As soon as he heard the strains of music in the distance he would jump up and down and shout: "There comes our band! there comes our band!"

Robert Todd Lincoln, the President's eldest son (born 1843), was even more quiet and reserved in his manner than Willie; and came to the War Department with his father very seldom. He was absent from Washington, at college, part of the time during the war, and just before its close received the appointment of captain, and was assigned to Grant's staff, remaining with him until Lee's surrender. After the war he entered the legal profession. During President Arthur's administration he was Secretary of War and in Harrison's administration Minister to England, performing the duties of both high offices with signal ability.

Much has been said about Lincoln being influenced by his dreams. For instance, it has been stated by good authorities, including members of his cabinet, that before each of the great battles of the war, and also before the occurrence of some other specially notable event in his life, he had a vivid dream which led him to look forward at such a time with great anxiety for the announcement of some disaster, or other incident, of a particularly important character. It is related that on the night before his assassination he had an unusually exciting dream, which he thought was a portent of impending danger of some sort. That he did have this habit of being deeply affected and influenced by these visions of the night, is clearly shown by the following telegram:

Washington, D. C., June 9, 1863.

Mrs. A. Lincoln, Philadelphia:

Think you had better put Tad's pistol away. I had an ugly dream about him.   A. Lincoln.

During the war I was frequently asked by my friends and casual acquaintances whether Lincoln was a Christian and a member of church. The same question has been asked many times since his death. My reply has always been that he had a regular pew in Dr. Gurley's Presbyterian Church on New York Avenue in Washington and that he attended service there frequently, but that I could not vouch for his creed, nor did I know that he was an enrolled member of any church. Now, after my daily contact with him for four years, and having studied his personality and character, as revealed in his speeches and writings, and in the innumerable biographies issued since the war ended, I am of the opinion that if love be the fulfilling of the law of Christ, Abraham Lincoln, in his day and generation, was the nearly perfect human example of the operation of that law. I do not refer directly to his belief in a divine Being, nor in orthodox creeds, although his manifold utterances on the subject of slavery and his published writings must ever proclaim to the thinking world the fact that at the very root of his spiritual being he held sacred the teachings of the Bible, and his official acts while in the presidential office, as well as all his utterances, oral and written, when shorn of a certain rudeness incident to his homely surroundings in early life, exemplified those teachings.

Bishop Simpson, one of Lincoln's closest personal friends, said in his funeral oration at Oakwood Cemetery, Springfield, Illinois, May 11, 1865:

He believed in Christ, the Saviour of sinners, and I think he was sincerely trying to bring his life into the principles of revealed religion. Certainly, if there ever was a man who illustrated some of the principles of pure religion, that man was our departed President. I doubt if any President has ever shown such trust in God, or, in public documents, so frequently referred to divine aid.

The four years of the Civil War comprised that fateful period of his wonderful career, in which the inborn kindliness of his nature was taxed to the utmost by the treason of some of his former political friends, by the perfidy and malice of Northern disloyalists, and by the impatience of certain would-be saviors of the Union, who thought the war should be carried on in accordance with their narrow ideas; and whatever may have been his inmost feelings respecting his country's enemies, and his political foes and their repeated efforts to sting and crush him, his noble heart in its outward expressions, during those trying, strenuous days, exhibited only faith, hope and charity, and the last most prominently of all.

The crystallized opinion of the generation since Lincoln's death is that his official papers, as well as his letters and speeches, are models of clear, undefiled English. Some of them, notably his Gettysburg speech and second Inaugural Address, are recognized classics, to which coming generations may turn for patriotic inspiration and education in the best forms of expression for great thoughts. But beyond all beauty of form, cogent words and irresistible logic, inherent in the body of all his utterances, whether oral or written, there was something more; there was the spirit of a simple, great man, the throb of a human heart, that had malice for none, and charity for all, and loving all, sought to protect them from injustice and wrong. He never allowed force of logic or beauty of diction in choice or arrangement of words to obscure his one great purpose to lead men always to hate tyranny and love freedom.

On one occasion when in the office with Lincoln alone, he began to talk of the functions of the eye and brain when one was reading aloud from a printed page. He said that in his boyhood days he had come across a book in which it was stated that as each letter of the alphabet and each word or sentence appeared before the eye, it was pictured upon the retina so that each particular word could be spoken aloud at the exact moment when its printed form in the volume was reflected upon the eye. He discoursed at some length upon this marvel, remarking upon the curious fact that the eye is capable of receiving simultaneously several distinct impressions or a series of impressions constantly changing as one continues to read across

Half-tone plate engraved by H. Davidson

Secretary of War 1862–1868

Mr. C. P. Filson, son of the photographer, writes that this portrait is from the last negative of Stanton, which was taken by his father, Davidson Filson, while Stanton was stumping Ohio for General Grant in the presidential canvass of 1868

the page, and that these numerous and sometimes radically different impressions are communicated from eye to brain and then back to the vocal organs by means of the most delicate nerves; for instance, said he, the eye may rest at the same instant not only upon a single letter of the alphabet, but upon a series of letters forming a given word, and upon a moving procession of words in a sentence, and not only that, but the resultant record of all these numerous and different impressions is translated by the brain into thought and sent back; telegraphed as it were, to the organs of speech, each organ selecting its own particular message, the whole sentence then being spoken aloud even while the eye is still resting upon the printed page. The skilled accountant casts up a long column of figures as fast as his eye moves down the page, and at the instant he reaches the end of his column his ready fingers jot down the total. In other words, he added, communications are being transmitted continuously and simultaneously in both directions between the outer and inner senses. He likened this mysterious, instantaneous and two-fold operation to the telegraph, although as regards the dual process it should be remembered that the invention of duplex telegraphy was not brought into use until more than ten years after this interesting discourse of Lincoln in the presence of his solitary auditor.

Over thirty years after this incident was recorded in my diary, I found in his "Complete Works" (Vol. I, pp. 522–526), a lecture on "Discoveries and Inventions," which he delivered at various towns in Illinois in 1859, and which contained several of the analytical ideas which he had mentioned in his talk with me; for instance, in his lecture he says, "Run your eye over the printed list of numbers from one to one hundred . . . it is evident that every separate letter, amounting to eight hundred and sixty-four, has been recognized and reported to the mind within the incredibly short space of twenty seconds or one third of a minute."

That entire lecture of Mr. Lincoln's is full of interesting ideas, expressed with great clearness, and appears to have been the result of a considerable amount of close study on his part. It could well be made a text-book for lyceums and schools, its perusal and study suggesting new lines of thought and aiding in the formation of habits of analysis and logical reasoning from every-day facts, that could not fail to be of great service to each growing generation.

I am led to mention Lincoln's love of Shakspere because in the winter of 1865, a few months before his death, he went a number of times to see James H. Hackett play *Falstaff*, and for a week or more he carried in his pocket a well-worn copy in small compass of "Macbeth," and one of "The Merry Wives of Windsor," selections from both of which he read aloud to us in the telegraph office. On one occasion I was his only auditor, and he recited several passages to me with as much interest apparently as if there had been a full house. He was very fond of Hackett personally, and of the character of *Falstaff*, and frequently repeated some of the latter's quaint sallies. I recall that in his recitation for my benefit he criticized some of Hackett's renderings. He wrote a letter to that gentleman on August 17, 1863, in which he said:

For one of my age I have seen very little of the drama. The first presentation of *Falstaff* I ever saw was yours, here last winter or spring. Perhaps the best compliment I can pay is to say as I truly can, I am very anxious to see it again . . . I think nothing equals "Macbeth." It is wonderful. . . .

A. K. McClure, in his "Life of Lincoln,"

speaks of the latter's love of the great master and mentions an interview between Lincoln, Judge Kelley, and an actor named McDonough, during which Lincoln took from a shelf a well-thumbed copy of Shakspere and turning to "Henry IV" read with discrimination an extended passage, which he said was not surpassed in wit and humor by anything else in literature. The omission from the acted play of the passage in question was remarked upon by Lincoln as curious.

All these incidents show an intimate acquaintance with the text of Shakspere's writings and not only so, but a keen and discriminating appreciation of their depth and meaning. While on this subject I am reminded of an incident occurring early in 1864.

James E. Murdoch of Cincinnati, an actor of repute before the war, upon learning that his son had enlisted and was in camp at Lancaster, Pennsylvania, went there to say good-by to his boy. He whiled away some of his otherwise idle time in camp in making patriotic speeches and giving recitations, to the great delight of the officers and men of the regiment. Afterward he visited other regiments and companies at enlistment points and also at the front, devoting a large part of his time for several years to the task of contributing to the comfort of the soldiers in the army through the medium of the United States Sanitary Commission. Murdoch's favorite recitations were the stirring poems of George H. Boker, Julia Ward Howe, Francis de Haes Janvier, and T. Buchanan Read. In 1863, a relative or friend of Murdoch was court-martialed for sleeping on post, or for some other serious violation of military duty, and Murdoch's married sister Adelaide visited Washington to intercede for the boy's life. A Mrs. Guthrie of Wheeling, having known Major Eckert when both were children, asked him to secure an interview with the President for Mrs. Murdoch. This was done, and the appeal was so effective that the President pardoned the soldier. Whether this man was named William Scott (from Vermont), whose pardon by Lincoln inspired Janvier to write his beautiful poem entitled "The Sleeping Sentinel," is not recorded. Murdoch, in his volume, "Patriotism in Poetry and Prose," says of this poem:

I had the pleasure of reading this beautiful and touching poem for the first time to Mr. and Mrs. Lincoln and a select party of their friends at the White House, by invitation of Senator Foote of Vermont. . . . Its second reading was in the Senate Chamber, the proceeds being for the aid of our sick and wounded soldiers.

Soon after the relative (or friend) of Murdoch had been pardoned, the latter visited Washington and went with Eckert to the White House to thank the President in person for his merciful act. During the interview Lincoln told Murdoch how much he appreciated his splendid work for the Union cause, and added that if agreeable he would like him to recite something from Shakspere. Murdoch said he would prefer to do that on another occasion so that he might select something suitable and prepare himself, but that if the President would allow him he would then recite a poem entitled "Mustered Out," by W. E. Miller. The words are put into the mouth of a dying soldier, who in one of the verses says:

> I am no saint;
> But, boys, say a prayer. There 's one that begins
> "Our Father," and then says "Forgive us our sins."
> Don't forget that part, say that strongly, and then
> I 'll try to repeat it, and you 'll say "Amen."

When the poem was finished Murdoch asked permission to continue the theme by giving in full the Lord's Prayer, and the President, who was visibly affected by Murdoch's fine rendering of the beautiful poem, nodded his assent; Murdoch then began, "Our Father, who art in heaven," and in a most reverent and devout manner repeated the whole prayer, Mr. Lincoln audibly joining in the closing petitions. When he had concluded, all three of the group were in tears. Eckert says that on the following day Murdoch, accompanied by the late Mr. Philp (of Philp and Solomons), visited Mr. Lincoln and gave some readings from Shakspere. On a later occasion (Feb. 15, 1864), Mr. Nicolay, private secretary, wrote Murdoch thus:

MY DEAR SIR: The President directs me to send you the enclosed little poem and to request that if entirely convenient you will please to read it at the Senate Chamber this evening.

The printed inclosure read thus:

"The following patriotic lines were written by one of the most distinguished statesmen of the United States in answer to a lady's inquiry whether he was for peace."

Note by Author, there were in all eight stanzas, the first of which only is here quoted, as follows:

"Am I for Peace? Yes!
  For the peace which rings out from the cannon's throat,
    And the suasion of shot and shell,
  Till rebellion's spirit is trampled down
    To the depths of its kindred hell."

XVI

A BOGUS PROCLAMATION

ON May 18, 1864, there appeared in two New York papers—the "World" and "Journal of Commerce"—what purported to be an official proclamation, signed "Abraham Lincoln, President," and attested by William H. Seward, Secretary of State, calling for a levy of 400,000 men for the army, and appointing May 26 as a day of fasting, humiliation, and prayer for the nation. The author of the forgery, for such it proved to be, in some of his phrases and wording had copied Lincoln's peculiar and forceful style of writing so closely, that it is remarkable no more than two New York morning papers (to all of whom copies were sent) fell into the trap. Without burdening this account with the full text of the document, it will be sufficient to quote the first two paragraphs.

Executive Mansion, Washington, D. C., May 17, 1864.
FELLOW CITIZENS OF THE UNITED STATES:

In all exigencies it becomes a Nation carefully to scrutinize its line of conduct, humbly to approach the Throne of Grace and meekly to implore forgiveness, wisdom and guidance.

A BOGUS PROCLAMATION

For reasons known only to Him, it has been decreed that this country should be the scene of unparalleled outrage, and this Nation the monumental sufferer of the nineteenth century. With a heavy heart but an undiminished confidence in our cause, I approach the performance of duty, rendered imperative by sense of weakness before the Almighty, and of justice to the people . . .

Then, after a reference to Grant's Wilderness Campaign, the Red River disaster and other military movements, there followed a recommendation that the "26th day of May, 1864, be set apart as a day of fasting and prayer." The document closed with a call for 400,000 men to be raised by draft, if not furnished by volunteering before June 15, 1864.

It was well known to the Northern public that Grant's "Wilderness" campaign in Virginia had caused an immense loss of life, and that Lee's stubborn resistance to the repeated and terrific onslaughts of Grant's army indicated a further protracted struggle "on that line, if it took all summer," so that in a measure the country was prepared for an additional call for troops, if the President should deem it necessary. But the false news had only a transient effect, even upon Wall Street, in depressing security values. In fact, owing to the alertness of the New York and

Washington commercial telegraph staff, official denial from the authorities at Washington was made public so promptly that there was no apparent effect on the financial markets. Gold rose 5 or 6 per cent. on that day, but fell again as soon as the forgery was exposed.[1] The author of the bogus proclamation must therefore have been disappointed at the failure of his scheme in its market effect; for his sole purpose, as he afterward confessed, was to cause such fluctuations in the prices of stocks, bonds and gold, as to enable him and his single confederate to make money.

The news of the publication of the bogus proclamation was promptly telegraphed to the War Department by the manager of the New York telegraph office (Mr. M. S. Roberts), and was soon followed by a telegram from General Dix:

New York, May 18, 1864.

Hon. W. H. Seward, Secretary of State, Washington, D. C.: A proclamation by the President, countersigned by you and believed to be spurious, has appeared in some of our morning papers, calling for 400,000 men, and appointing the 26th inst. as a day of fasting, humiliation, and prayer. Please answer immediately for steamer.

John A. Dix, Major General.

---

[1] Later gold reached a much higher figure; on October 31, 1864, it was 227 and on November 9, the day after the presidential election, it rose to 260.

At that time there were no transatlantic ocean cables.[1] News to Europe must therefore be sent by steamer, ten days being the usual time occupied by the passage. The next day, May 19, was steamer day, and this explains the closing paragraph in General Dix's telegram.

A conference was at once held in the War Department, President Lincoln having sent for Secretary Seward, who drew up an address to the public, which was telegraphed to General Dix and distributed to all newspapers, as follows:

Department of State, Washington, D. C., May 18, 1864.

To THE PUBLIC: A paper purporting to be a proclamation of the President, countersigned by the Secretary of State, and bearing date the 17th day of May, is reported to this Department as having appeared in the New York "World" of this date. The paper is an absolute forgery. No proclamation of that kind or any other has been made or proposed to be made by the President, or issued or proposed to be issued by the State Department, or any other Department of the Government.

WILLIAM H. SEWARD, Secretary of State.

Copy to be sent to the New York press and to Charles Francis Adams, U. S. Minister, London; and William L. Dayton, U. S. Minister, Paris, by outgoing steamer.

Secretary Stanton also telegraphed General Dix that "the spurious proclamation was a base

[1] The first cable opened for actual business July 27, 1866.

and treasonable forgery." Stanton never minced matters in his reference to anything savoring of disloyalty to the Government.

Lincoln wrote a despatch over his own signature, extracts from which are given below:

Executive Mansion, Washington, D. C., May 18, 1864.

MAJOR GENERAL JNO. A. DIX, Commanding, New York. Whereas there has been wickedly and traitorously printed and published this morning in the New York "World" and New York "Journal of Commerce" . . . a false and spurious proclamation, purporting to be signed by the President, and to be countersigned by the Secretary of State, which publication is of a treasonable nature, designed to give aid and comfort to the enemies of the United States and to rebels now at war against the Government . . . you are therefore hereby commanded forthwith to arrest and imprison . . . the editors, proprietors and publishers of the aforesaid newspapers . . .   A. LINCOLN.

General Dix had meantime telegraphed the result of his preliminary investigation into the fraud as follows:

New York, May 18, 1864.

HON. E. M. STANTON, Secretary of War: I am investigating the gross fraud of this morning. The paper purporting to be a proclamation of the President was handed in to the offices of the city newspapers at 4 o'clock (A.M.), written on thin manifold paper of foolscap size like the despatches of the Associated Press. In handwriting and every other respect it was admirably calculated to deceive.

A BOGUS PROCLAMATION

It was published in the "World" and "Journal of Commerce." None of the responsible Editors of either of the papers was present . . . It was printed by the "Herald," but none of the copies was issued, the fraud having been discovered before they left the office. . . . I think the authors will be detected, and I need not add that I shall in that case arrest and imprison them for trifling in so infamous a manner with the authority of the Government, and the feelings of the community at this important juncture in our public affairs. . . .

JOHN A. DIX, Major General.

In addition to Seward's address "To the Public," a copy of which was to be sent by steamer to our ministers abroad, he sent the following by the same means of communication:

Department of State, Washington, D. C., May 18, 1864.

CHARLES FRANCIS ADAMS, U. S. Minister Plenipotentiary, London, England.

WILLIAM L. DAYTON, U. S. Minister Plenipotentiary, Paris, France.

Orders have been given for the arrest and punishment of the fabricators and publishers of the spurious proclamation.

WILLIAM H. SEWARD, Secretary of State.

Colonel E. S. Sanford, Military Supervisor of Telegrams, was in New York at the time, and attended in person to this part of the business, as shown by the following telegram:

233

LINCOLN IN THE TELEGRAPH OFFICE

New York, May 19, 1864.

HON. E. M. STANTON, . . .

I have the honor to report that the Secretary of State's despatch to Ministers Adams and Dayton was delivered to the Purser of the *Scotia*[1] and that he was ordered by Mr. Cunard to telegraph it from Queenstown. Slips were issued by some of the morning papers exposing the forgery and circulated among the passengers before the vessel sailed.

Although it was made evident to General Dix early in the day that the editors of the "World" and "Journal of Commerce" were innocent of the fraud, Secretary Stanton forbade their release until the real culprit was found. Meantime the publication of the fraudulent document had created great excitement throughout the country. The editors of four other New York papers— the "Herald," the "Times," the "Tribune," and the "Sun"—joined in a strong appeal to the President for the release of the two editors who had been arrested and sent to Fort Lafayette, and for the restoration to them of their newspaper offices. Governor Seymour of New York fiercely resented Secretary Stanton's alleged tyrannical orders for the seizure of the two news-

[1] The mails for the *Scotia* closed at 10:30 A.M., and Colonel Sanford sent the Government despatches for Europe by the despatch-boat down the bay.

paper offices, and the arrest of the editors, claiming that they were an unwarranted interference with the public press; and he even called upon the Grand Jury to indict Stanton for his "illegal" acts. This request, however, was not complied with. It was not until May 22 that Stanton ordered the editors to be released and their establishments restored to them.

For some reason, never made public, it was at first believed by the authorities that the author of the forgery had concocted his scheme in Washington, and caused the bogus call for additional troops to be telegraphed over the wires of the Independent Telegraph Company, a new concern and a rival of the American Telegraph Company. The wires of the latter ran into the War Department and were directly under the control of the Government, while those of the Independent Company were not under such direct supervision. Major Eckert, under orders from Secretary Stanton, went personally to the Independent Company's office on Twelfth Street, Washington, and ordered the superintendent, Mr. James N. Worl (who is still living in Philadelphia, now over eighty years old) to deliver up all messages and news reports in his custody. Worl at first refused, claiming they were confidential and privileged communications, but Eckert's demand was backed up by General Wiswell, who called in a file of soldiers from the outside to act as a guard while Eckert actually took possession of the office and its contents, as shown by this report:

Ninth Street Office, Washington, D. C., May 18, 1864.

Hon. Edwin M. Stanton, Secretary of War: I have the honor to report that the arrests have been made and the office closed. Thos. T. Eckert, Major, Supt., Military Telegraphs.

Mr. Worl in an interview published in March, 1905, in the "Telegraph Age," states that the writer was placed in charge of the captured office, but in this he is mistaken. Mr. Tinker is the one to whom was assigned that duty, while I remained in the War Department. I clearly recall Tinker's return and his oral report to Secretary Stanton that the entire staff of the office in question had started for Old Capitol Prison in a pouring rain, and that he had possession of all messages and news reports, but had not yet found the original of the bogus proclamation.

Meantime Secretary Stanton telegraphed General Dix to seize the New York offices of the

Independent Telegraph Company at Cedar and Nassau streets, and in the Gold Room in William Street, the Brokers Exchange, etc., arrest the superintendents, managers and operators, and confine them in Fort Lafayette. Similar orders were sent to General Lew Wallace at Baltimore, General Cadwallader at Philadelphia, and the commanding officers at Harrisburg and Pittsburg.[1]

Dix at New York, under Stanton's imperative orders, seized the offices of the Independent Company and arrested the manager—Wallace Leaming, and his staff of operators and clerks. The entire party were escorted, under guard, to Dix's headquarters. The charge preferred against them was "aiding and abetting in the transmission over the wires of the Independent Telegraph Company of a forged document purporting to be a proclamation by the President of

[1] In Pennsylvania the company was called the Inland Telegraph Company. The employees arrested at Baltimore, Philadelphia, Harrisburg and Pittsburg were sent under guard to Washington. Of the telegraph people who were thus arrested and imprisoned unjustly, as was soon found to be the case, only a few survive, among them Jesse H. Robinson of Washington, D. C., manager of the Weather Bureau Telegraph Department, James N. Worl of Philadelphia and Robert C. Edwards and George A. Hamilton of New York, the last two having held responsible positions with the Western Union Telegraph Company for many years.

the United States and by William H. Seward, Secretary of State, which had been . . . published in two New York newspapers."

Conjecture the feelings of Manager Leaming and his comrades when they faced this charge in the presence of the stern old warrior, the author of the sentiment that had thrilled every loyal heart at the beginning of the war, "If any one attempts to haul down the American flag, shoot him on the spot." [1] Perhaps they might be summarily tried and executed. Sadly they heard the order given that they were to be confined in Fort Lafayette, and they soon began their march under guard to the Battery, where the *Berdan* was waiting to carry them down the bay. The telegram was sent to the War Department:

May 18, 1864.

The manager, superintendent and operators of the telegraph line were arrested at 5 P.M., and will be sent to Fort Lafayette in an hour. JOHN A. DIX, Maj. Genl.

General Cadwallader at Philadelphia telegraphed to Stanton on May 18: "Lines seized, manager, operators and superintendent arrested and sent to Washington."

[1] The original of this famous despatch, dated January 29, 1861, is in the possession of the Lincoln Club of Brooklyn, N. Y.

Captain Foster, Provost Marshal, Pittsburg, telegraphed: "At 5:30 P.M. seized office of Inland Telegraph Company and will send manager and three other employees to Washington at 8:35."

Colonel Bomford at Harrisburg telegraphed: "At 7 P.M. seized Independent Telegraph line, (self-styled Inland and American line) papers and operators."

Two days later General Dix telegraphed to the Secretary of War:

I have arrested and am sending to Fort Lafayette, Joseph Howard, the author of the forged proclamation. He is a newspaper man and is known as Howard of the "Times." He has been very frank in his confession, says it was a stock-jobbing operation and that no person connected with the press had any agency in the transaction, except another reporter,[1] who took manifold and distributed the copies to the newspapers, and whose arrest I have ordered . . .

To the above Stanton replied at 9:10 P.M., May 20:

Your telegram respecting the arrest of Howard has been received and submitted to the President. He directs me to say that while in his opinion the editors, proprietors and publishers of the "World" and "Journal of Commerce" are responsible for what appears in their papers injurious to

[1] "The New York Times," May 22, 1864, gives the name as F. H. Mallison.

the public service and have no right to shield themselves behind a plea of ignorance or want of criminal intent, yet, he is not disposed to visit them with vindictive punishment, and, hoping they will exercise more caution and regard for the public welfare in future, he authorizes you to restore to them their respective establishments.

The next day, May 21, Dix reported that the "superintendent, manager and operators are completely exonerated from the charge of complicity in the publication of the proclamation fraud." Whereupon Stanton directed that the telegraph employees be released, but that the telegraph offices be still held. Similar action was taken in respect to the telegraph employees from Philadelphia, Harrisburg, Pittsburg, Baltimore and Washington, who had been put in Old Capitol Prison. Forty-eight hours later the telegraph offices were restored to the telegraph company, to whom a clean bill of health was given, together with an offer to allow their wires to be connected with the War Department, so that a share of the Government telegraph business might be given to them.

Howard, the author of the forged proclamation, was a newspaper correspondent of ability as a collector of news, and a fluent writer. He had formerly acted as Rev. Henry Ward

Beecher's secretary. Mr. Beecher had a strong liking for Howard, notwithstanding his action in this instance, and he made an urgent appeal to the President for his release. Howard's personality was pleasing, and for forty years he has maintained a position of prominence as a newspaper writer.

In considering Mr. Beecher's appeal, Lincoln could not have forgotten the valiant and useful service that distinguished man had rendered this country during the early part of the war, in his masterly speeches in support of the Union cause, delivered in many cities of England, when the tide of sentiment there seemed to be setting so strongly against us.

The following despatches passed with regard to the release of Howard:

Executive Mansion, Washington, August 22, 1864.

Hon. Secretary of War,

My Dear Sir: I very much wish to oblige Henry Ward Beecher by releasing Howard; but I wish you to be satisfied when it is done. What say you? Yours truly,

A. Lincoln.

I have no objection, if you think it right—and this is a proper time. E. M. S.

It will be observed that Stanton did not favor the release of Howard, but Lincoln had a more merciful nature and the next day issued the order:

Let Howard, imprisoned in regard to the bogus proclamation, be discharged. A. LINCOLN.
August 23, 1864.

While the search for the culprit was in full tide, Stanton extended his Briarean arms to the newspaper men in Washington. As his suspicion had fallen upon the telegraph company because of its newness, it also fell upon a news syndicate recently organized by Henry Villard, Adams Hill (afterward Professor of Rhetoric at Harvard) and Horace White, which had attracted attention to itself by some notable "scoops" in the way of army news. He caused Villard to be arrested and detained two days at the headquarters of the Provost Marshal General. Hill was kept "under observation" for the same period, and White, who had been one of Stanton's prime favorites, but who had recently resigned his position in the War Department to join the news syndicate, was summoned to Stanton's private office and subjected to sharp questioning. When the real culprit was discovered Villard was released, and

242

although no apologies were made to him or his colleagues, some choice scraps of news later found their way to the office of the syndicate, which supplied material for new "scoops," and had a soothing influence generally.

XVII

GRANT'S WILDERNESS CAMPAIGN

ON March 9, 1864, Grant received his commission as lieutenant-general and was placed in command of the armies of the United States, establishing his headquarters with the Army of the Potomac, then near Culpeper, Virginia, under the immediate command of Meade.

My war diary makes little mention of events at this time, but the Rev. H. E. Wing, now of South Norwalk, Connecticut, has recalled an incident in his experience that connects Lincoln with the telegraph office in an interesting manner. Grant had started his Wilderness Campaign by moving his army across the Rapidan, and advancing in strong force against Lee. It was an open secret which Lincoln himself shared, that Grant preferred to be cut off from Washington while making this movement. In Lincoln's letter to Grant of April 30, 1864,[1] he says:
. . . "The particulars of your plans I neither

[1] The original of this letter was sold at auction in New York City on May 19, 1902, to G. H. Richmond for $1050. See "New York Times," May 20, 1902.

know nor seek to know . . . " So, when the army advanced from Culpeper over the Rapidan, the telegraph did not follow immediately, and for nearly a week we were without any news from Grant except brief intimations that the two armies had been engaged and that Lee was being slowly pushed south. The tension became very great until, as Tinker's diary records:

May 6, 1864. A reporter arrived at Union Mills. Left the army near Chancellorsville at four o'clock this morning. Everything pushing along favorably. No news direct from Grant.

That reporter was H. E. Wing of "The New York Tribune," from whose account of his journey from our army through the enemy's lines to Union Mills, the following extract is taken:

I crawled out of a rebel camp at Manassas Junction at dusk Friday, May 6, 1864, and hustled down the railroad track to Bull Run, where I came into our lines and learned that our people had no news from the front. I realized that I was probably the only one of four or five newspaper men who had succeeded in getting through. As my paper would have no issue after the following morning until Monday, May 9, my news would be stale unless it went through that night. There was no train, I could not get a horse, so I offered $500 for a hand-car and two men to run it, but all to no avail. So I kept on until I reached a military telegraph office and asked the operator to let my report go through; but he refused, his orders being to send no newspaper reports over government wires. I then sent a despatch to my friend, Charles A. Dana, Assistant Secretary of War, to the effect that I had left Grant at four o'clock that morning. That waked up the Department in which there was the utmost anxiety. Instantly Secretary Stanton asked me where Grant was when I left him. This assured me I had a corner on the news from the front. I replied that my news belonged to the "Tribune," but if he would let one hundred words go through to my paper I would tell him all I knew. Stanton's response was a threat to arrest me as a spy unless I uncovered the news from the army. This made me very anxious, but still I refused. I was disgusted that after all my enterprise my paper would not get my important news. But just then Lincoln must have come into the War Office for I was asked if I would tell the President where Grant was. I repeated my previous offer and he accepted the terms at once. I did not have a scrap of paper about my person (discreet correspondents in the field never took anything of that sort through the lines), so I dictated to the operator while he transmitted my despatch, which Lincoln would not limit to one hundred words and which was telegraphed direct to New York and appeared in Saturday's "Tribune," May 7. Mr. Lincoln ordered a locomotive to be sent out on the road to bring me to Washington, about thirty miles; and at two o'clock in the morning I reached the White House travel-stained and weary, but delighted at my success in having brought the first news from Grant's army, and especially in being honored by the President's special favor. That early morning interview with Lincoln was the beginning of a strong friendship accorded to me, a mere boy, by that wonderful man, the memory of which is a precious treasure in my heart.[1] Mr. Lincoln told me that

[1]"The New York Tribune" of May 7, 1864, has a half column dated Union Mills, Va., Friday, May 6, 9 P.M., commencing: "The

to relieve the anxiety of the whole country regarding Grant's first contest with Lee he decided to let my despatch come through; also that he had arranged with Managing Editor Gay to give a summary to the Associated Press to appear in all the papers.

The issue of May 9, has a despatch stating that

No one has come in from the army since the "Tribune" correspondent. His account was published on Saturday morning, and no newspaper has any accounts from the field save those which he bore.

The "Tribune," May 10, says in a despatch from Washington:

The "Tribune" messenger who brought not only to the Government, but to the country, the first news of the recent great battles was Henry E. Wing of Connecticut. He footed half the distance in, and was frequently fired on by guerillas. He was a totally used up pedestrian when he reached the "Tribune" Bureau in this city—used up in everything but pluck. Mr. Bushnell of New Haven heard of his brave devotion to the paper that employed him, and got up a little purse of $50, which was given him with a presentation speech by Sam Wilkeson.

Then follows reference to another purse made up by newspaper men, including Whitelaw Reid, Uriah Painter, Puleston and Henry. The ac-

Grand Army of the Potomac crossed the Rapidan on Wednesday." Then follows an account of Grant's initial successes in the great movement. The despatch ended thus: "I am on my way to Washington with more complete reports that I will send to-morrow."

count says: "This purse would have been heavier if the newspaper men had been richer."

Lincoln's action in overruling Stanton's strict orders barring press reports from Government wires, in order to relieve the general anxiety, discloses once more his acute sympathy with and constant thoughtfulness for the common people.

General Eckert has recently told me the following incident which well illustrates Lincoln's kindly nature.

On his way to the telegraph office early one morning in April, 1864, just before Grant started on the Wilderness Campaign, Lincoln observed in the hall a young woman who seemed to be in great distress. She carried a baby in her arms and was pacing to and fro and crying. The President asked Eckert to go out and see the woman and learn the cause of her trouble. This was done, the major reporting that the woman had come to Washington thinking she could get a pass to the front to enable her to visit her husband, and let him see his child, who had been born since the father enlisted; but she had learned that she would not be allowed to go to the army. Lincoln said, "Major, let 's send her down." Eckert replied that strict orders had been given not to let women go to the front. Stanton, entering the office at the time and seeing the evident sympathy of Lincoln for the woman in her trouble, said, "Why not give her husband a leave of absence to allow him to see his wife in Washington?" The President replied: "Well, come, let's do that. Major, you write the message." But Eckert said the order must be given officially, and Lincoln replied: "All right, Major; let Colonel Hardie (Assistant Adjutant-General) write the order and send it by telegraph, so the man can come right up." Colonel Hardie wrote the message, which was telegraphed to the Army of the Potomac, and when the sorrowing woman was informed of what had been done, she came into the office to express her gratitude to the President. Lincoln then asked her where she was stopping. She said that she had not yet found a place, having come direct from the railroad station to the White House, and then to the War Department. Lincoln then directed Eckert to obtain an order from Colonel Hardie to allow the young mother and her baby to be taken care of in Carver Hospital until her husband arrived. This was done, and the soldier was allowed to remain with his wife and child for over a week before returning to his regiment.

XVIII

TOWARD the end of June, 1864, General Lee detached a body of 20,000 men, including a large cavalry force, from the army defending Richmond and sent them North under the command of General Early for the purpose of making a quick dash into Maryland and to Washington, if the capital were found to be insufficiently protected, as Lee had heard was the case. This condition of imminent danger[1] really existed, for it is well known that but for the brave and heroic action of Lew Wallace in attacking Early at the mouth of the Monocacy with a force much smaller in numbers than that of the enemy, thus delaying Early's movements twenty-four

---

[1] My war diary says:

July 10, 1864.—The enemy broke the railroad at Laurel to-day (11 miles out). Yesterday they seized a passenger train at Gunpowder Bridge, north of Baltimore, capturing General Franklin and staff, but they afterwards escaped.

July 11, 1864.—Great excitement in Washington. Department clerks are being armed and sent to the forts at the boundary.

hours, the latter might easily have reached and entered Washington before reinforcements could have arrived from Grant's army. Wallace's command consisted of 2700 troops, largely raw militia, and about 3300 veterans belonging to the 6th Corps under General Ricketts, the latter having reached Baltimore from City Point only two days before.

The Monocacy fight was waged all day Saturday, July 9, and ended in Wallace's defeat, leaving Early free to resume his march upon Washington. Wallace sent this telegram to the War Department on Sunday, July 10: "I have been defeated. The enemy are not pressing me, from which I infer they are marching on Washington." This was indeed the fact, for Early's advance reached the District boundary line on Monday morning, and later in the day the signal officer wigwagged this sentence: "The enemy is within twenty rods of Fort Stevens." Early at once began a reconnaissance to learn the strength and disposition of our defenses and for two days kept up an almost continuous firing which could be heard distinctly in Washington.

There was one considerable skirmish, witnessed by Lincoln, whose summer residence was only four miles from Fort Stevens, in a cottage at the Soldiers Home. Lincoln visited the fortifications on Monday and Tuesday, and on both occasions was in great danger, one of our men having been killed within a few feet of where the President stood. His tall form must have been a conspicuous target for the enemy's sharp-shooters, and it was a matter of remark at the time that he did not seem to realize the serious risk incurred in going to the front of our line while skirmishing was in progress. It is of historical importance to note that this was the first time (and up to the present the only time) when a President of the United States, although Commander-in-Chief of the army and navy, has been exposed to the fire of the enemy's guns in battle. The total number of killed and wounded on both sides in the two days' skirmishes at the boundary line of the District of Columbia was nearly 1000.

While Lincoln witnessed the spirited skirmish with Early's troops in front of Fort Stevens on July 11, he carefully observed the whole situation of affairs and upon his return to the city he came direct to the War Department and gave us a pretty full account, which has been recorded by my comrade Chandler, as follows:

"I have in my possession the diagram which Lincoln made in the telegraph office, immediately after his return from his tour of the fortifications to the north and west of the city. This diagram showed the relative positions of the two bodies of troops and where the skirmish took place, all of which he explained to Major Eckert, Tinker, Bates and myself, who were, of course, extremely interested in his picturesque description." My comrade, H. H. Atwater, now of Brooklyn, gives this account of Early's raid:

On Monday, July 11, 1864, I received orders from Major Eckert to take the telegraph ambulance at the War Department and go to Fort Reno, Tenallytown, as fast as possible, as they were expecting an engagement at any moment. It was one of the hottest days I ever experienced, and the dust rose in clouds blinding the vision. Beyond Georgetown we met a great number of people coming into Washington with their household effects, some driving cattle and leading horses. On each side of the road wherever a bush or tree cast any shade soldiers could be discerned prostrated by sunstroke. When half-way there my horses gave out and I started on foot, but the driver overtook me, the horses having had a few minutes' rest. The office at General M. D. Hardin's headquarters was in a building left standing between the two forts. This building was demolished the next day because it was in line with the guns of the forts. On the roof in the blazing sun, signal-men were wigwagging their despatches. To the northeast we could see the dust of the enemy as they moved back and forth. At 11 P.M. General

Hardin handed me a message reading as follows: "A scout just reports that the enemy are preparing to make a grand assault on this fort to-night. They are tearing down fences, and are moving to the right, their bands playing. Can't you hurry up the Sixth Corps?" General Hardin told me if we were attacked to run my wires inside Fort Reno and keep up continuous communication with the War Department.

The next day, July 12, the skirmish in front of Fort Stevens took place. I could see the fight from Fort Reno. It lasted until after dark. Operator Loucks at Fort Stevens said to me over the wire: "I am going out to take a shot at the rebels."

On Tuesday one of Early's men was captured, and after necessary pressure had been put upon him he confessed that Early had not made the grand attack Monday night because he learned of the arrival of the Sixth Corps. Had he done so it is probable he would have come into Washington. [1]

For forty-eight hours, therefore, the long-coveted prize had been within Early's grasp. Never before during the war had a Confederate army been so close to Washington as to be within sight of the glittering dome of the capitol, and Early must have gnashed his teeth when he thought of his one day's delay at the Monocacy, which had been just long enough to allow veteran troops from Grant's army to reach

[1] Early's official report says the weather was extremely hot, the roads very dusty, and his troops utterly worn out and unfit for an attack when they reached our defenses.

Washington, for neither he nor his men failed to recognize on the parapets of our forts the well-known flags of the famous 6th Corps, a part of which brave body of troops had fought him all day Saturday at the Monocacy. The remainder of this veteran corps, under General Wright, had landed at Seventh Street wharf, Washington, on Monday, at just about the hour at which Early's advance had come in sight of Fort Stevens.

Emory's division of the 19th Corps from New Orleans, had also landed at Washington on Monday, July 11, and followed the 6th Corps to the front.

With the dawn of Wednesday, however, it was discovered that Early had retreated, and Washington emerged from what is now known to have been one of its most serious crises during the whole war, for, as was said in an address in May, 1902, by Leslie M. Shaw (then Secretary of the Treasury), "with the national capital in the hands of the enemy it would have been impossible to prophesy the foreign complications, to say nothing of the demoralization of the people of the United States." Grant has said of this raid, "If Early had been one day earlier he might have entered the capital."

This was not the only time Early's fate belied his name, for three months later his army of raiders also lost one day's time in their calculations when Sheridan sent them whirling down the Valley of the Shenandoah after their initial victory during his temporary absence in Washington. [1]

[1] See pages 79, 80.

XIX

CABLES AND SIGNALS

IN his Annual Message to Congress, December, 1863, Lincoln, after referring to the arrangements with the Czar of Russia for the construction of a line of telegraph from our Pacific coast through the empire of Russia to connect with European systems, urged upon Congress favorable consideration of the subject of an international telegraph (cable) across the Atlantic and a cable connection between Washington and our forts and ports along the Atlantic coast and the Gulf of Mexico. In the latter scheme he took a deep personal interest, and he had a number of conferences with Cyrus W. Field, the chief exponent of ocean cables.

My war diary refers to one of Field's visits to Washington, when Stanton assigned to me the duty of transcribing from dictation a memorial to the Government, urging the laying of a coast cable which Field was engaged in preparing. The latter was intensely interested in the subject, and being of an excitable nature, his words flowed from his lips in a rapid, intermittent stream, while his thoughts outran his spoken words ten to one, so that it was not long before I, not being a shorthand writer, was engulfed, and the result was, judging from my notes, that Field's memorial, like an ocean cable, was discernible only at its two ends, with here and there indications of a struggle and a splash. Several weary hours were spent in this way, and when at last some sort of order had been evolved out of seeming chaos and the memorial finally completed and signed, Field shot out of the door and rushed over to Stanton's room, waving the document as if it were a danger-signal, leaving me alone and in a semi-collapse. Drawing long breaths of relief at the removal of the tension, I returned to my regular cipher-work, resolved never again to act as an amanuensis for Cyrus W. Field.

Probably because of the large expense involved and the fact that up to that time no very long cables had been successfully laid, and also because of the difficulty of maintenance in working order free from injury by Confederate blockade-runners, Lincoln's cherished plan of a coast cable from Fort Monroe to New Orleans, was not adopted. Had we then known what we do now about cables, their construction, maintenance, protection, and operation, without doubt Field's plan, which in its essentials was entirely feasible, would have been accepted and Lincoln's recommendation acted upon by Congress, and the war brought to a close much sooner. In this case Lincoln's "far sight," as in other important matters, is now seen to have been prophetic and his broad views were further in advance of and more comprehensive than those of others of his time.

It is not generally known that early in 1862 the War Department purchased about fifty miles of the abandoned Atlantic cable of 1858. A section of this cable was laid by the Military Telegraph Corps across Chesapeake Bay from Cape Charles to Fort Monroe, the work being finished and the cable connected up the first week in March of that year. It failed a few days before the Confederate ram *Merrimac* attacked our fleet, sinking the *Cumberland,* burning the *Congress,* and running the *Minnesota* aground in Hampton Roads. The cable was repaired, however, and General Wool's telegram of March 8, to the Secretary of War stating that Ericsson's iron-clad—*Monitor*—had arrived and would proceed to take care of the *Merrimac* the next day, was sent over it and reached Washington on March 9, the day of the fight between the *Monitor* and the *Merrimac*.

This cable—about twenty miles in length—is believed to have been the longest submarine cable successfully laid in this country up to that time. It was interrupted frequently, either because of faulty construction, or from being caught by dragging anchors.

In August, 1864, an additional section was laid in the James River between Jamestown Island, near Norfolk, and Fort Powhatan, below City Point, because the land line between those points, on the south side of the river, had been broken by the enemy several times, and the topography of the country was such that it could not be sufficiently well guarded.

As a matter of collateral interest it may here be noted that Cyrus W. Field obtained from the legislature of Newfoundland on March 10, 1854, an exclusive grant for fifty years for the establishment of a line of telegraph from the continent of America to Newfoundland and thence to Europe. The first cable was laid in 1857, but it did not work successfully. He made two attempts in 1858, the first of which was a failure. The third cable was laid the same year, and for a short time signals were exchanged slowly. Congratulatory messages between Queen Victoria and President Buchanan were sent, each message occupying in transmission over an hour. This third cable failed, however, after 732 messages had been successfully transmitted over it. In 1866 the fourth, and finally successful, attempt was made to lay an ocean cable, and on July 27 of that year it was opened for public business. It is believed that since that date cable communication between Europe and America has never been entirely interrupted. There are now sixteen transatlantic cables, all duplexed: nine to Ireland direct, one to Ireland via the Azores, two to England, two to France, and two to Germany via the Azores. The ocean cable mileage of the world at the close of 1906 has been given as 251,132 miles.

Fifty years ago one of the quack remedies in vogue, extensively advertised, was "Swaim's Panacea," the headquarters of which were in Philadelphia. The proprietor—James Swaim—was a character in his way. In his early days he was in the naval service, and became familiar with the somewhat crude methods of signaling by means of flags and lanterns. Swaim appeared in Washington in November, 1862, with his newly invented signal system, which was turned over to Tinker and myself for trial. The plan included a code-book of several thousand words and phrases, each represented by a combination of numerals, usually four. There were six separate signals which were transmitted thus: Number 1, by the flag or torch being held aloft to the right of the operator or suspended from a pole or standard; Number 2, straight out to the right; Number 3, to the right in a downward direction; Numbers 4–5–6 were represented by similar movements or positions to the left. Two numerals were needed for each letter of the alphabet, thus:

A	G	M	S	Y	5
11	21	31	41	51	61
B	H	N	T	Z	6
12	22	32	42	52	62
C	I	O	U	1	7
13	23	33	43	53	63
D	J	P	V	2	8
14	24	34	44	54	64
E	K	Q	W	3	9
15	25	35	45	55	65
F	L	R	X	4	0
16	26	36	46	56	66

For the next twenty-four hours Tinker and I devoted all our spare moments to the task of learning this code of signals.

Swaim at the outset suggested a novel plan by means of which he said any one could quickly learn his alphabet. By referring to the foregoing table, it will be observed that the letters A, G, M, S, and Y stand at the top of the respective columns. Now, quoting Swaim's words, "The first question one asks when the new system is proposed is, 'Who is the inventor?' The answer is given by repeating rapidly the four letters A G M S, so as to make them sound like 'A Jeems,'" Swaim's Christian name being James. Then, having that fact in mind, one is immediately led to ask "Y" (Why?); so there you have the key to the entire alphabet, and by following down the several columns in order, he said, the whole picture is before you, and each letter can be readily classed with its corresponding pair of numerals.

To tell the truth this curious method did really help to fasten in our minds the several features of Swaim's code, and on the morning of November 14 we went over to the White House grounds and practised for an hour, the President stopping on his way to the War Department to observe our strange antics.   On the third day—November 15 —Tinker and I went to the roof of the Soldiers Home and Swaim and Stager to the Smithsonian Institute, about four miles distant, and we exchanged signals for two hours, using palm-leaf fans covered with black muslin in lieu of flags. The wind was blowing so strongly that we found it difficult to move the fans properly and one of the messages sent by Tinker was "It is windy." Stager received this all right and signaled back to us, "Take peppermint."   Notwithstanding our successful experiments, the Government did not adopt Swaim's code.

Two years later some one proposed that we should make a test of signaling at night by means of a calcium light, which could be displayed and screened at will by the use of a button, operated by hand, in the same manner as a telegraph-key is manipulated; the alternate flashes of light, long or short, representing the dashes and dots of the Morse alphabet.

At that time Lincoln, with his family, lived in one of the cottages at the Soldiers Home, and so it was arranged that there should be an exhibition (for his special benefit) of Morse signaling to and from the Smithsonian, and on the evening of August 24, 1864, Major Eckert and I went to the Soldiers Home with suitable instruments, our comrades, Chandler and Dwight, having gone to the Smithsonian Institute, with a similar equipment. My diary records that there were present on the tower of the Soldiers Home, besides the operators the President, Rear-Admiral Davis of the Navy Department, Colonel Nicodemus of the Signal Corps and Colonel Dimmick of the army. We were able to send Morse signals to the roof of the Smithsonian and receive responses from Chandler and Dwight. Professor Joseph Henry was present and witnessed our experiments. Mr. Lincoln was greatly interested in this exhibition and expressed the opinion that the signal system of both the army and navy could and would be improved so as to become of immense value to the Government. This has, in fact been done, and our efforts of over forty years ago now appear rudimentary.

Comrade H. H. Atwater was stationed at the Washington Navy Yard much of the time during the war, and has given the following account of a visit which Lincoln made on one occasion when experiments were being made with rocket signals:

One evening a party of six or eight, including Mr. Lincoln, came to the Navy Yard and proceeded to the bulkhead, where they had arranged to demonstrate the workings of certain signalling rockets, several of which were sent up with good results. When the last one was tried each one in the party watched it as it soared aloft, leaving its streams of fire trailing behind, but when half-way up it exploded prematurely and fell to the water a miserable failure. "Well," remarked Lincoln, "small potatoes and few in a hill." I had never heard the expression before and it fastened itself in my mind.

Two weeks after the assassination Atwater saw Booth's body when it arrived from the lower Potomac and was transferred to a monitor, at the same pier where not very long before Lincoln had witnessed the experiments with signal rockets.

XX

LINCOLN'S FOREBODINGS OF DEFEAT AT THE POLLS

ON June 8, 1864, the Republican convention at Baltimore unanimously renominated Lincoln for President. Horace White, who had formerly been employed as a clerk in Secretary Stanton's office, was then engaged in newspaper work, and was in the convention, seated next to the operator who was working the wire leading to the War Department. White sent the first congratulatory message to Lincoln, and shortly afterward telegraphed that Andrew Johnson of Tennessee had been nominated for Vice-President. Lincoln's private secretary, Nicolay, had also meantime telegraphed the news, and when the President reached the telegraph office, my colleague, Mr. Tinker, offered his congratulations, but Lincoln said he had not yet seen the message announcing his renomination. When the copy was shown him he said: "Send it right over to the Madam. She will be more interested

than I am." [1] When the announcement of Johnson's nomination was handed to the President, he
looked at the telegram a moment and then said,
"Well, I thought possibly he might be the man;
perhaps he is the best man, but—" and rising
from his chair he walked out of the room. Mr.
Tinker has always contended from this incident
that Lincoln preferred that Hannibal Hamlin
should have been placed on the ticket a second
time, and expected that he would be.

In these peaceful days, more than forty years
after the close of the Civil War, when we read
of the fraternization of the Blue and the Gray at
army reunions, South and North, and of Republican Presidents being enthusiastically welcomed by
the people of the South, it is somewhat difficult
to recall clearly the troublous times of 1864, that
most critical and momentous year of the war, and
harder still to realize that there was so much of
doubt in the minds of the Northern people, and
even of our chosen leaders, as to the ultimate outcome of the struggle. Our great war President
himself, whose heroic faith voiced itself so often in

---

[1] My comrade, Mr. Chandler, says that Lincoln made exactly the
same remark on the night of November 8, when the news that came
over the wires was such as to make it certain that Lincoln had been
reëlected.

his public utterances, was in his heart more or less of a doubter at critical times, as the writer can bear certain witness. He seemed to recognize more clearly than some of his advisers the great anti-war feeling in the North and the underlying forces back of it, and the weight of this subtle and malign influence.

I consider 1864 the most critical and momentous year of the war from a military point of view, although in that year we had no Bull Run defeat as in 1861, nor Chickahominy disaster as in 1862, nor Gettysburg nor Vicksburg victories as in 1863. The year was remarkable also in political movements. The sorehead convention at Cleveland in May had nominated Frémont and Cochrane, both from New York, unmindful of the Constitutional provision against taking both the President and the Vice-President from the same State. At that nondescript gathering a letter from Wendell Phillips, the abolitionist leader, was read in which he said:

The administration therefore I regard as a civil and military failure and its avowed policy ruinous to the North in every point of view. If Mr. Lincoln is reëlected, I do not expect to see the Union reconstructed in my day unless on terms more disastrous to liberty than even disunion would be.

269

"The New York Herald" of May 31, 1864, commenting on the probable nomination of McClellan by the Democratic convention soon to meet, said editorially: "As for Lincoln, we do not think it possible that he can be reëlected after his remarkable blunders the past three or four years." Leonard Swett of Illinois, one of Lincoln's closest friends, wrote to his wife three months before the election: "Unless material changes can be wrought Lincoln's election is beyond any possible hope. It is probably clean gone now."[1]

The regular Democratic convention at Chicago, with Seymour as its chairman and Vallandigham, lately returned from enforced exile in the Confederacy, as chairman of the Committee on Resolutions, had nominated McClellan and Pendleton. General Grant made this reference to these nominations: "Their only hope (the South) is a divided North and the election of a peace candidate."

My friend, Mr. Edward A. Hall, has recently told me the following incident: He was in Abram S. Hewitt's office shortly before the election, when McClellan's chances were discussed, Ed-

[1] See Tarbell's "Lincoln," Vol. 3, p. 200.

ward Cooper and Wm. H. Osborn being present. Both Hewitt and Cooper expressed the opinion that McClellan would win, as McClellan had told them only a day or two before that he was sure of his election, and that he would resign his commission in the army on November 1. Osborn had formerly been president of the Illinois Central Railroad and at that time was chairman of its board of directors. In that connection he had known both Lincoln and McClellan, Lincoln having been employed by the road at various times in a legal capacity, and McClellan having held the position of chief engineer. Osborn, blunt spoken, as always, after hearing Hewitt and Cooper express their opinion, said, "No, Lincoln will beat McClellan, for he has the courage of his convictions and does things, but McClellan, while able and great in preparation, lacks confidence in himself at critical times. Even if elected, he would be a failure in the responsible position of President. He could, and did, build the best and strongest bridges on our road, but I always noticed that at the finish he hesitated to give the order to send over the first train."

George Francis Train, in one of his erratic and sparkling effusions in the form of an open letter to General McClellan in October, 1864, calls him the peace candidate on a war platform, adding that "as you are a railway man, General, you know that it is dangerous to stand on the platform."

As one straw showing how the wind of opinion then veered toward McClellan, it is noted that only two days before Lincoln recorded his remarkable estimate, hereinafter given, the soldiers and attendants at Carver Hospital, Washington, in a State election, had cast an unusually large vote—one in three—against the Administration. This otherwise trivial incident must have exerted a special influence on Lincoln, in view of the fact that he had frequently visited that hospital and mingled with its occupants. Nor must we forget that the exponents of peace-at-any-price were still firing their sputtering squibs at Lincoln, which irritated although they probably did not much hurt.

The general effect of these eccentric peace movements, however, was to foster among certain classes in the North a feeling of unrest and of dissatisfaction with the conduct of the war. Such persons no doubt believed they were patriots, but they had no backbone, and events not turning out as they wished, they were too ready to cast blame upon the Administration,—on the one hand upon Stanton, the Bismarck of our Civil War, who was the personification of zeal and implacable fury in his treatment of his country's enemies, whether North or South, and on the other hand, without logic or reason, upon Lincoln, who had "malice toward none; with charity for all," but who also had "firmness to do the right," no matter if his best friends and legal advisers were against him.

Lincoln, silent under the stings of criticism, but with sublime faith in the final success of the cause of liberty, of which he was the great exponent, appears in 1864, as we now see him in his environment, to have become imbued with the idea that perhaps, after all, the people of the North would declare themselves at the polls in November as being willing to end the war by putting McClellan in the presidential chair and thus pave the way for an amendment to the Constitution which would permit the Southern States to withdraw peacefully from the Union and set up a separate government, with negro slavery as its corner-stone. Lincoln, with his lofty ideas of eternal right and justice between man and man, whether white, black, red or yellow, had, it seemed, almost lost heart and his long-tried patience was nearly exhausted. He was, indeed, almost at the parting of the ways as he saw so many of his own political party and former supporters wavering or actually deserting the colors and opposing the Government in the very matters which to him were vital. They had turned back from their march up freedom's heights, the topmost peaks of which he had already scaled, and from which only, as he believed, could be had clear visions of the controlling questions of his day and generation. To him those visions and what they meant to his country were sublime verities, as indeed they later came to be to most or all of his countrymen.

Senator John T. Morgan of Alabama said in 1895: "The character of Lincoln is not yet known to this generation as it will be to those who shall live in later centuries. They will see, as we cannot yet perceive, the full maturity of his wisdom, in its actual effects upon the destinies of two great races of men."

But at this time—October, 1864—with the waves of civil war beating upon him, with the snarling tones of his political enemies sounding in his ears, with the nagging of those who professed to be his friends, but who criticized his words and actions from their lowly habitat in the slough of despond, with such meager disappointing results from the Emancipation Proclamation, the general features of which had been announced two years before, it is perhaps not to be wondered at that Lincoln feared defeat in the approaching November election.[1]

In his great anxiety Lincoln had sent John Hay, one of his secretaries, on a special mission to Hilton Head, South Carolina, with instructions to the commanding general, to coöperate in certain measures intended to aid in bringing Florida back into the Union, on the lines of his Reconstruction Proclamation of December 8, 1863, the program being to extend the Union lines as far as possible into that State and induce the loyal citizens to set up a reorganized

---

[1] On p. 568, Vol. II, of Lincoln's "Complete Works" appears this:

Memorandum

Executive Mansion, Washington, D. C., August 23, 1864.

This morning, as for some days past, it seems exceedingly probable that this administration will not be re-elected. Then it will be my duty to so coöperate with the President-elect as to save the Union between the election and the inauguration; as he will have secured his election on such ground that he cannot save it afterward.   A. LINCOLN.

See, also, Nicolay and Hay's "Lincoln," Vol. IX, p. 251.

State government to give its three electoral votes for the Administration at the November election. This plan, if under more fortunate conditions it could have succeeded, was rendered futile by the wholly unexpected defeat of General Truman Seymour at the battle of Olustee.

John G. Nicolay, his first secretary, was despatched to Missouri with a view to overcoming factional troubles in that State, kept alive by political leaders of strong contrary types, and thus to secure if possible her eleven electoral votes, which in Lincoln's estimate, as we shall see, were conceded to McClellan, but which were actually cast for Lincoln.

In October, Maryland had voted upon her new constitution, the chief feature of which was the final extinction of slavery; and out of a total of 60,000 votes the majority in favor of the new law was a bare 375, and that result had been carried to the Court of Appeals on the theory that the vote of the soldiers in the field could not legally be counted.

The Pennsylvania, Ohio and other State elections took place on October 11, only two days before the incident described below. On that evening Lincoln stayed in the telegraph office until after midnight for the purpose of receiving promptly the results of the elections—his last message being as follows:

> *Washington,* Oct. 11, 1864.
> GENERAL SIMON CAMERON, Philadelphia:
> Am leaving office to go home. How does it stand now?
> A. LINCOLN.

Cameron's reply was hopeful but not conclusive. The following day Grant telegraphed to the War Department for news of the Pennsylvania election. Lincoln being in the telegraph office when the despatch was received, answered it thus:

> October 12, 1864.
> LIEUT. GENL. GRANT, City Point, Va.:
> Pennsylvania very close and still in doubt on home vote.
> A. LINCOLN.

Such in general were the conditions throughout the country as they appeared to Lincoln when, on the evening of October 13, 1864, he made his regular visit to the War Department telegraph office, which for over three anxious years had been his safe retreat and lounging-place, and where he had so often calculated the wavering chances of war and peace. Major Eckert and the cipher-operators were all there, and we could not fail to notice that the President looked unusually weary and depressed as he sat down to scan the political field and consider the probabilities of his reëlection, three weeks later.

After the results of the State elections two days before had been fully discussed, the conversation begun by him turned to the Presidential election, and he expressed himself as not being at all sure of reëlection. He referred to special conditions in some of the States as affording ground for the fear that McClellan might slip through. In fact his cautious spirit led him to underrate his own strength, and to exaggerate McClellan's chances, and after pondering the matter a short while, he reached for a cipher telegraph-blank and wrote his own careful estimate of the electoral vote as shown by the facsimile published for the first time in "The Century Magazine" for August, 1907.

He entered in one column the names of the eight States which he conceded to McClellan, giving him 114 electoral votes. In a second column he entered the names of the States which he felt sure would cast 117 votes for the Administration. This total showed only three more votes than he allowed McClellan. He did this from memory, making no mistake in the number

Office U. S. Military Telegraph.

WAR DEPARTMENT.

Facsimile of Lincoln's autographic estimate of the electoral vote of 1864

The original autograph, now owned by the author of this volume, was written by Lincoln in the War Department telegraph office, October 13, 1864, three weeks before the election, and was printed for the first time in "The Century Magazine" for August, 1907. The headings: "Supposed Copperhead Vote" and "Union Vote for President," as well as the addition of "Nevada," with "3" votes, and the corrected total "120" are in the handwriting of Major Eckert.

of electoral votes to which each State was entitled, excepting that he omitted Nevada, which
was about to come into the Union, and her three
votes were added in Eckert's handwriting. (The
President's proclamation admitting Nevada is
dated October 31, 1864.)

It is hard to believe to-day that Lincoln allowed himself in his calculations so narrow a margin as three votes out of 231, but the proof is
absolute.

The actual result of the election was of course
very different from Lincoln's figures. McClellan received only twenty-one votes, two of the
three States, Delaware and Kentucky, being
original slave States, the other being New Jersey. Lincoln received 212 votes instead of his
estimate of 117. One Nevada vote was not
counted owing to a technicality. In 1860 he had
received 180 votes.

Those who are familiar with Lincoln's written
papers will not be surprised at the neatness of this
memorandum in his own handwriting, which
shows no erasure or blot, every word being legible, although in the lapse of time some of his
pencil-marks have become somewhat blurred and
indistinct. It was his custom when writing a

note or making a memorandum, as the cipher-operators had observed, to take his pen or pencil in hand, smooth out the sheet of paper carefully and write slowly and deliberately, stopping at times in thoughtful mood to look out of the window for a moment or two, and then resuming his writing. In this respect he was wholly different from Stanton, whose drafts or letters and memoranda were jotted down at a terrific pace, with many erasures and interlineations.

I still have in my possession the original draft (partly in my handwriting) of Stanton's General Orders to the army, dated April 16, 1865, announcing the death of the President, which is so full of corrections in his own bold hand as to be almost unreadable; but all of Mr. Lincoln's papers, written by himself, were models of neatness and accuracy.

It is of more than passing interest to note that on the very day on which Lincoln was setting down his conservative estimate of the political situation and of the trend of Northern opinion adverse to his administration, Jacob Thompson, the Confederate agent in Canada, wrote to Jefferson Davis that in his opinion "the reëlection of Lincoln is almost certain." Thompson's letter in cipher, dated Clifton, Canada, October 13, 1864, reached the War Department at the hands of Thompson's messenger (who was also in our secret service), on Sunday, October 16, and was translated by the cipher-operators.[1]

Lincoln's fears proved to have been unfounded, and were no doubt the result of peculiar circumstances and conditions operating upon an anxious mind normally disposed to introspection. Let us, if we can, imagine his thoughts at this time of sore depression. We may suppose that his mind reverted to Valley Forge at that critical period of the Revolution, in February, 1778, when news came of the alliance between France and the United States which had been secured through the influence of Franklin, the patriot and philosopher.[2]

[1] See chapter V and also General Eckert's testimony in "The Trial of the Conspirators," compiled by Pitman, page 42.

[2] John Hay, in his essay on "Franklin in France," says of the reception of that treaty:

"It was the sunburst to the colonies after a troubled dawn. The tattered and frost-bitten soldiers of Valley Forge were paraded to receive the joyful news, . . . and shouted, 'Long live the King of France!' Washington issued a general order saying 'It had pleased the Almighty Ruler of the universe propitiously to defend the cause of the United American States, and by finally raising up a powerful friend among the nations of the earth to establish our liberty and independence upon a lasting foundation.' This act of France gave us a standing abroad which we had hitherto lacked." —"The Century" for January, 1906.

Now, in 1864, at what probably seemed to Lincoln the crucial hour of our Republic, he no doubt reflected upon the ambitious efforts of Napoleon III to set up a monarchy upon our southwestern borders by means of French bayonets, in contrast with the generous act of Louis XVI, nearly eighty years before, in signing a "treaty of universal peace and true friendship," which should bind his heirs and successors.

Without doubt Lincoln also dwelt seriously upon the awful sacrifice of human life in the conduct of the war, and particularly upon Grant's sanguinary struggle in the Wilderness and on the James, with Richmond still defiant; and he may well have wondered whether the people of the North were not weary of the deluge of blood, with no stoppage of the flow in sight. David R. Locke (Petroleum V. Nasby) in his "Reminiscences" says of Lincoln in 1864:

He was as tender hearted as a girl. He asked me if the masses of the people of Ohio held him in any way responsible for the loss of their friends in the Army.

Lincoln doubtless thought of the desertion of his standard by some of his own former supporters, and of the lukewarmness of others; of the

many unjust criticisms of his policy in the newspapers, and of their slurs and falsehoods which he
was powerless to answer or combat. Truly, like
the Saviour, he had "endured the contradiction of
sinners." And we must remember also that Lincoln was possessed of a natural melancholy, a
morbid tendency to take undue blame upon himself when subjected to criticism. All things then
being considered, it is perhaps not so very strange
that on that evening of October 13, 1864, in his
accustomed seat at Major Eckert's desk, he
should have been ready to give up the ship if God
so willed it. But God did not so will it, for on
the night of November 8, he received the welcome
news of his reëlection while in the War Department telegraph office, where only three weeks before he had been almost ready to concede McClellan's election. He was not unduly elated at the
glad result, but serene and dignified, and was still
mindful of the feelings of others, as is shown by
the closing part of his speech to the assembled
multitude on that most eventful occasion, so often
quoted, but well worth repeating in this connection:

So long as I have been here I have not willingly planted
a thorn in any man's bosom. While I am deeply sensible

to the high compliment of a reëlection, and duly grateful, as I trust, to almighty God for having directed my countrymen to a right conclusion, as I think, for their own good, it adds nothing to my satisfaction that any other man may be disappointed or pained by the result. May I ask those who have not differed with me to join with me in this same spirit towards those who have.

XXI

CONSPIRATORS IN CANADA

IN the spring of 1863 Clement L. Vallandigham of Ohio was arrested by General Burnside for his words and acts, which seemed to the commanding general of the Department of the Ohio to be treasonable. Vallandigham was a prominent "Peace Democrat," and at the time of his arrest was an avowed candidate for the governorship of his State; and, in fact, he was nominated at the State Convention a little later. Vallandigham was tried by a military court, convicted and sentenced, but assumed the rôle of martyr to the cause of free speech, which was then a popular rallying-cry for a certain wing of the Democratic party. The criticisms of some of the newspaper opponents of the Administration were so bitter that a very embarrassing situation was created. The Washington authorities did not approve of Burnside's action; but as an accomplished fact it was indorsed by Lincoln, who, as a way out of the dilemma, proposed the exile of Vallandigham through the lines of the Confederacy.[1]

Lincoln could not foresee all the consequences of his edict of May 19, 1863, banishing the talkative Ohio politician; but looking backward now, the writer of these lines is of the opinion that the death of our first martyred President may be traced to its inception, at least, indirectly, to Vallandigham's conferences with the Richmond authorities during his enforced exile. We may well believe that with his persuasive tongue he was able to convince Davis of a very strong peace sentiment in the North, which could be fostered and encouraged to the great benefit of the South by the plans which, after Vallandigham's return North, were inaugurated by him and his sympathizers, and which in course of time led to arson and other crimes against society at large. In their reflex influence upon the minds of certain zealots and fanatics these plans and their resultant

[1] See on page 345, Vol. II, of "The Complete Works," Lincoln's letter of June 12, 1863, to Erastus Corning and others who, at a public meeting at Albany, May 16, had secured the passage of resolutions censuring the Administration for the alleged unconstitutional arrest of Vallandigham.

deeds furnished the inspiration which, in the writer's belief, finally resulted in the tragedy of April 14, 1865.

Let us go over the trail from Vallandigham's sojourn in the Confederacy in 1863 to the early summer of 1864, when it became known to our Government through the medium of its secret service that President Davis had appointed special commissioners to reside in Canada, ostensibly for the purpose of actively coöperating with the leaders of the peace party in the North, and their open and secret allies, in the creation and development of peace sentiments, so that a path might be opened for effective peace negotiations between the Richmond and Washington governments. While this was made to appear as the principal duty of the commissioners, and to that extent it was a laudable service, their zeal and varied inclinations led them to initiate and actively support other measures which were not even hinted at in their official instructions, and which there is no good reason to believe were approved by President Davis or his cabinet, although the official correspondence between Richmond and Canada published since the close of the war tends to show that some, at least, of the Richmond authorities had definite knowledge of the desperate acts of their Canadian representatives.

Taking the official record in order, as shown by the copies and extracts given herein with such explanation as may be necessary for an intelligent understanding of each transaction, one is amazed at the wide scope and devilish purpose of the deep-laid plans for the destruction of life and property, some of which, however, were fortunately discovered in time to prevent their being fully carried out. The first communication is this:

Richmond, Va., April 7, 1864.

HON. JACOB THOMPSON, Macon, Miss.

(Care of Gov. Charles Clark).

If your engagements will permit you to accept service abroad for the next six months, please come here immediately. JEFFERSON DAVIS.

Thompson evidently fell in with the scheme in the mind of Davis, who had meantime conferred with several other persons whom he wished to include in the commission, for we next find the following:

Richmond, Va., April 27, 1864.

Hon. Jacob Thompson,

SIR: Confiding special trust in your zeal, discretion, and patriotism, I hereby direct you to proceed at once to Canada, there to carry out such instructions as you have received from me verbally, in such manner as shall seem most to conduce to the furtherance of the interests of the Confederate States of America, which have been entrusted to you.   Very respectfully & truly yours,

JEFFN. DAVIS.

Similar letter to Hon. C. C. Clay, Jr.

In addition to Jacob Thompson and C. C. Clay, Jr., Davis selected Professor James P. Holcombe and George N. Saunders, and these four commissioners proceeded to Canada, which they made their headquarters during the remainder of the war, keeping up communication with Richmond by means of letters carried to and fro by secret agents, and also by "personals" in one of the New York dailies, which were inserted by one of their agents in New York City, the Richmond authorities having facilities for regularly obtaining copies of these newspapers through the lines. The Confederate commissioners also corresponded from time to time with certain peace agitators in the North, and by July they had so far imposed on the credulity of Horace Greeley as to induce that patriotic and honest but misguided man to implore President Lincoln to allow the four Confederate commissioners to come to Washington for an interview. John Hay, Lincoln's secretary, was sent to New

York for conference with Greeley, and afterward to the Canadian side at Niagara Falls, where Thompson, Clay, Holcombe, and Saunders were then staying, armed with a safe conduct to Washington and return for those gentlemen, subject to certain prescribed conditions, as follows:

July 18, 1864.

To Whom it May Concern:

Any proposition which embraces the restoration of peace, the integrity of the whole Union, and the abandonment of slavery, and which comes by and with an authority that can control the armies now at war against the United States, will be received and considered by the executive government of the United States and will be met by liberal terms on other substantial and collateral points, and the bearer or bearers thereof shall have safe conduct both ways.

Abraham Lincoln.

As is well known Greeley's chimerical project resulted in failure, as the commissioners were not able to meet the simple and reasonable conditions prescribed by the President.

Our Government next became aware of the pernicious schemes of the conspirators—for such they must be called—in the field of active coöperation with C. L. Vallandigham and other Northern malcontents in their plan of forming in Indiana, New York, Ohio, Illinois, and other

States a secret order, whose members were to be enrolled under military rules, bound with formidable oaths, and ultimately provided with arms and ammunition for active service in support of the plans of the organization. These plans contemplated, among other things, opposition to army drafts, release of Confederate prisoners wherever possible, burning of Northern cities, and general devilment for the purpose of harassing the Federal authorities, the expectation being that an appreciable number of Union troops would be drawn from the armies at the front to protect the threatened cities and frustrate the plans of the "Copperheads," as they were called. There was also held before the eyes of certain ambitious leaders of the movement the glittering prospect of a new Confederacy to be composed of certain States in the then Northwest, which at an opportune time were to secede from the Union; and a wild hope was cherished by some of the eastern leaders of the movement that even the Empire State might secede and set up a separate government on the Atlantic seaboard.[1]

[1] For full details concerning these various secret orders, known as the Sons of Liberty, Knights of the Golden Circle, McClellan Minute Guard, etc., see Judge Advocate General Holt's report to the Secretary of War dated October 8, 1864, printed in the Rebellion Records, Series I, Vol. VIII, p. 930.

It was rumored that the membership of the secret band in New York City alone amounted to 20,000, all suitably officered and armed. In Thompson's report to the Confederate authorities, of December 3, 1864, he estimated the whole membership of the order at 60,000. It was reported by the secret agents of the War Department that some of the New York State officials were in sympathy with the movement, but it was not believed that Governor Seymour or his subordinates had any previous knowledge of the villainous plans for setting fire to New York City, or for the assassination of Lincoln. However, all was not clear sailing for the commissioners, and one of them, at least, became discouraged, as the following letter shows:

St. Catharines, Canada, West,
September 12, 1864.

HON. J. P. BENJAMIN, *Secretary of State,*
Richmond, Va.

· · · As to revolution in the North-west or any where in the United States, I am growing skeptical. The men who gave us strongest assurances of the purpose of the "Sons of Liberty" to rush to arms . . . are now in prison or fugitives in Canada. . . . C. C. CLAY, JR.

Meanwhile the War Department was not idle, and through the services of a secret agent, who was also in the employ of Thompson, kept itself posted on all the important movements of the conspirators.

In chapter V an account has been given of Thompson's cipher-despatch dated Clifton, Canada, October 13, 1864, addressed to Jefferson Davis at Richmond, and the reply, also in cipher, dated Richmond, October 19. These despatches were intrusted to our agent, above referred to, and by him as he passed through Washington were shown to Major Eckert, who brought them, each in its turn, to the War Department, where the cipher-operators quickly translated them into English. Thompson's despatch included these words:

We again urge the immense importance of our gaining immediate advantages. We now look upon the re-election of Lincoln in November as almost certain.

Davis in reply used the following language:

Your letter of 13th at hand. There is yet time enough to colonize many voters before November.

Genl. Longstreet is to attack Sheridan without delay and then move north toward unprotected points. . . . He will endeavor to assist the Republicans in collecting their ballots. Be watchful and assist him.

JEFFN. DAVIS.

Unlike Lincoln, Davis was not disposed to be facetious in his correspondence, but his remark about Longstreet assisting in the collection of Republican ballots, which probably referred to the soldiers' vote, had in it a touch of humor. It turned out, however, that in that very week at Cedar Creek, Sheridan was able to dash their hopes.

While in certain directions the plans of the conspirators were being thwarted, other schemes were inaugurated which were dastardly and villainous in the extreme. One source of information as to such plans was our consul at Halifax, who reported as follows:

Halifax, Nova Scotia, November 1, 1864.

Hon. Wm. H. Seward, Secretary of State:

It is secretly asserted by secessionists here that plans have been formed and will be carried into execution by the rebels and their allies, for setting fire to the principal cities in the Northern States on the day of the Presidential election.   M. M. Jackson, United States Consul.

Another and more significant bit of news was contained in a letter dated Syracuse, N. Y., November 2, 1864, and addressed to Hon. William H. Seward, Secretary of State, Washington, which inclosed a copy of an order just issued by John A. Green, Adjutant-General of the State of New York. This order, after referring to the general election to be held on November 8, and the rights of the people to an "untrammeled franchise," advised the public and the local authorities in each county and election district that "No military interference can be permitted with the election" and that "The Federal Government is charged with no duty or responsibility whatever relating to an election to be held in the State of New York." A postscript to Holmes's letter was as follows: "There is great reason to fear that Lincoln will be assassinated soon."

Vague rumors of a plot to kidnap or assassinate the President had previously reached the War Department, but had been given little credence until just about this time a photograph of Lincoln had been received by Mrs. Lincoln through the mail which showed red ink-spots on the shirt-front, with a rope around the neck, the ends being drawn tautly upward. On one of his visits to the cipher-room Lincoln drew this photograph out of his high hat and told us that it had caused Mrs. Lincoln some anxiety which he did not share, as he had long ago become accustomed to seeing caricatures of himself. He added some words of surprise and sorrow that any human being could be so devoid of feeling as thus to wound the heart of an innocent woman.

A duplicate of this mutilated picture of Lincoln came by chance into the possession of Eckert under the following circumstances. While on his way to Cortlandt Street Ferry on November 26, 1864, Eckert found in a street car an unsealed envelop containing, among other papers, a letter giving directions, evidently referring to a kidnapping plot and also a picture of Lincoln with a rope around his neck and red ink-marks on the bosom of the shirt. These papers were afterward discovered to belong to Payne, the assassin, —see chapter XXVII.

XXII

THE ATTEMPT TO BURN NEW YORK

AS explained in the previous chapter, one of
Thompson's messengers who traveled between Canada and Richmond, was also in our
secret service, and the War Department was
therefore frequently advised of the plans of the
conspirators.[1] This man had reported that the
rumor mentioned in Consul Jackson's letter of
November 1, 1864 (on page 296), of a purpose
to set fire to certain Northern cities was correct,
but that the work would not be attempted on
Election Day, November 8, but several weeks later; and that due notice would be given by him
when the actual date was fixed. Later advices indicated the week after Thanksgiving as the probable time. Nothing further, however, being received from our spy, Major Eckert went to New

[1] See "The Trial of the Conspirators," compiled by Pitman, p. 24,
also the quotation from my war diary in chapter V.

York on Thanksgiving Day, November 24, and on the following morning called on Major-General Dix, commanding the Department of the East, for a conference. The latter had already been advised by Secretary Stanton of the machinations of the Confederate commissioners and their emissaries, but was wholly incredulous of the news about the burning of the city.

With the aid of the police department of the city Dix had already used every available means to track the conspirators, but without success, and the scheme appeared so diabolical that he concluded it was wholly imaginary. Eckert tried to convince him, but could not, that there was solid ground for the rumors, and that the danger was not only real but imminent. Superintendent Kennedy and Inspector Murray of the police department were called in conference, and they too proved to be unbelievers.

Eckert therefore left them for the purpose of returning to his hotel to prepare a cipher-message to Secretary Stanton, asking for further instructions. Upon entering a Broadway omnibus, his eyes encountered those of our secret service man from Canada. Neither showed any recognition of the other, but when Eckert left the stage at the St. Nicholas Hotel the man also got out and followed him into the hotel and up-stairs to his room. All this time no word had been spoken by either. After the key was turned in the door, the man said that as there was not sufficient time to get the information to Washington by means of a New York "News" personal, the usual channel of communication, he had hurried from Toronto to New York to communicate to the War Department the fact that the conspirators intended to set fire to twelve or more New York hotels, whose names he gave, that very Friday evening. A lunch was ordered for the man, who was ravenously hungry and tired, having traveled for over twenty-four hours, and after his meal he was told to lie down, which he did, falling asleep almost instantly. Eckert locked him in and went back to Dix with his fresh confirmatory evidence, and both the military and civil authorities then accepted the situation and took immediate steps to thwart the plans of the conspirators. Plainclothes men, policemen and soldiers by the hundred were quickly distributed about the city, with particular reference to the hotels that had been specially named by our spy as starting-points for the general conflagration.

Thirteen hotels were selected to be fired, they being the Astor, United States, Fifth Avenue, Everett, St. Nicholas, Lafarge, Howard, Hanford, Belmont, New England, St. James, Tammany and Metropolitan. Rooms in these hotels were taken by the members of the band, several of whom registered at two or more places. The plan they adopted, and which was carried out that evening, November 25, 1864, was as follows: At the hour agreed upon, or as soon after as possible, the party in each case placed his door-key in the keyhole on the outside, and then, after a suitable disposition of the bedding and furniture, started a fire by breaking a bottle of liquid having the qualities of Greek fire, and which had been prepared beforehand by one of the band familiar with that class of chemicals. In a few cases a clockwork device was the medium, set to go off within about an hour after being wound up. In either case the conspirator having completed his work left his room, locked his door, and disappeared. In addition to the fires at the hotels named there was an alarm in Barnum's Museum, and two hay barges in the North River at the foot of Beach Street were also set on fire; but, fortunately, because of the activity of the military and civil authorities, who were so accurately informed in advance regarding the scheme, none of these dastardly attempts to cause a destructive conflagration proved successful. Had they all or even a majority of them succeeded, one's imagination weakens in the effort to picture the awful loss of life and property that almost certainly would have resulted. Two reasons for the failure, both referring to traitors in their camp, are indicated in Thompson's report to his principals (which will be quoted later), the first being a defect in the qualities of the Greek fire, and the other a premature disclosure of the plot to the Federal authorities by some one in the confidence of the Confederate commissioners. The second of these reasons had a real foundation, whatever may have been true of the other.

For obvious reasons, General Dix requested the newspapers not to publish the names of suspected or arrested persons, but the following were, however, mentioned, the names, no doubt, being fictitious. At the Astor House, a man named Haynes; at the Howard, one named Horner; and at the Belmont a man who had registered as Lieut. Lewis, U.S.A. The New York

Hotel Keepers' Society offered a reward of $20,000 for the arrest and conviction of the miscreants; but while there were numerous arrests (including certain residents of the city), evidence sufficient to convict them could not be secured. Only one of the active conspirators was ever apprehended, namely, Captain Robert C. Kennedy of the Confederate army, who had, with all the others, escaped to Canada, the day or day after the fires were started. Kennedy returned to the United States in December, 1864, and was arrested in Cleveland, Ohio. His trial took place at Fort Lafayette, in New York harbor, under General Orders No. 14, dated January 17, 1865. The commission lasted twenty-three days and was presided over by Brigadier-General Fitz Henry Warren, and Kennedy was hanged on March 25, 1865. In the sentence of the military court the crime was characterized as follows:

. . . The attempt to set fire to the city of New York is one of the greatest atrocities of the age. There is nothing in the annals of barbarism which evinces greater vindictiveness. . . . In all the buildings fired, not only non-combatant men, but women and children, were congregated in large numbers, and nothing but the most diabolical spirit of revenge could have impelled the incendiaries to act so revoltingly.

THE ATTEMPT TO BURN NEW YORK

The real agents in the plot, on their arrival in Canada, reported to Thompson and Clay, with accounts of their unsuccessful efforts. In Thompson's letter of December 3, 1864, to Judah P. Benjamin, the Confederate Secretary of State, he mentions the attempts to start conflagrations not only in New York but also in certain other Northern cities. This remarkable report from a high commissioner to a government claiming to have been actuated by motives of the highest order, contains these cold-blooded statements:

. . . I have relaxed no effort to carry out the objects the Government had in sending me here. . . . Money has been advanced to Mr. Churchill of Cincinnati to organize a corps for the purpose of incendiarism in that city. I consider him a true man and although as yet he has effected but little, I am in constant expectation of hearing of effective work in that quarter. . . . Having nothing else on hand, Colonel Martin expressed a wish to organize a corps to burn New York city. He was allowed to do so and a most daring attempt has been made to fire that city, but their reliance on Greek fire has proved a misfortune. It cannot be relied on as an agent in such work. I have no faith whatever in it and no attempt shall hereafter be made under my general directions with any such material. . . . During my stay in Canada a great amount of property has been destroyed by burning. The information brought me as to the perpetrators is so conflicting and contradictory that I am satisfied nothing can certainly be known. Should claims

305

be presented at the War Office for payment for this kind of work, not one dollar should be advanced on any proof adduced until all the parties concerned may have an opportunity for making out and presenting proof. Several parties claim to have done the work at St. Louis, New Orleans, Louisville, Brooklyn, Philadelphia and Cairo. . . . I infer from your Personal in the New York News that it is your wish I should remain here for the present and I shall obey your orders. Indeed I have so many papers in my possession, which in the hands of the enemy would utterly ruin and destroy very many of the prominent men in the North, that a due sense of my obligations to them will force on me the extremest caution in my movements. . . . The attempt on New York has produced a great panic which will not subside at their bidding. . . .[1]

John Wilkes Booth, the assassin, has not been certainly connected with the conspiracy to burn New York, but he was in that city on the day the fires occurred. In the New York papers of November 25, 1864, an advertisement appeared of a performance that night at the Winter Garden Theater in aid of the fund for the erection of a bronze statue of Shakspere (now standing on the Mall in Central Park). Shakspere's "Julius Cæsar" was the play announced, and the

[1] For further details of the attempt to burn New York City see "Confederate Operations in Canada and New York," by John W. Headley, who claims to have held a commission as captain in the Confederate army, and to have been assigned by President Davis to special secret service under Thompson and Clay, Confederate commissioners in Canada.

three brothers, Edwin, Junius and John Wilkes Booth, were to act together, the last named taking the part of *Mark Antony*. While the play was in progress, word reached the audience that Barnum's Museum and several hotels were on fire. There was great excitement, and people rushed to the exits to escape from the building. Edwin Booth came on the stage and urged the audience to remain seated as the Winter Garden Theater was not on fire and there was absolutely no danger. His speech had the effect of calming the frightened people, and the play then went on to the end, although the audience was somewhat depleted.

While John Wilkes Booth may not have had previous knowledge of the plot to burn New York it is certain that his associate, Lewis Powell—or Payne, as he was called—was acquainted with the diabolical scheme, for after his arrest in April, 1865, he confessed that he had been selected to set fire to one of the hotels on that November night, but had refused on principle to act, his reason being that while he was willing to take the life of a high official of the Government for the good of the cause, he would not join in anything that would tend to the needless destruction of property and the sacrifice of innocent lives.

At the trial of the conspirators in the assassination, Sanford Conover testified that in April, 1864, Surratt brought to Montreal and delivered to Thompson cipher-despatches from Jefferson Davis and Judah P. Benjamin, approving of the plot to kidnap Lincoln and his cabinet. Thompson said (as Conover testified), "This makes the thing all right." Doubt is thrown on this testimony by the fact that Thompson's appointment as commissioner in Canada was dated April 27, 1864, and there could not have been time for him to reach Canada, communicate with Richmond and receive back in "April" the despatches mentioned by Conover. The Official Records, however, show that in the weeks of excitement and tension immediately following the death of the President, the Judge-Advocate-General of the War Department believed his Bureau had substantial proof of the complicity of the Confederate government and its Canadian commissioners in the assassination plot. Judge Holt's report to the Secretary of War (see Rebellion Records, Ser. II, Vol. 8, p. 977) bears this indorsement:

THE ATTEMPT TO BURN NEW YORK

Bureau of Military Justice, War Department,
Washington, D. C., May 2, 1865.

Respectfully returned with report that the testimony which has been under consideration by this Bureau indicates that Jefferson Davis, Geo. N. Saunders, Jacob Thompson, Clement C. Clay and others . . . were in complicity with the assassins of President Lincoln and their accomplices who committed the crimes referred to.

J. HOLT, Judge Advo. Genl.

The above is quoted not to revive or kindle anew war-time animosities, but merely to complete this account, and the writer may add that, having read with care Judge Holt's report, he does not discover in it evidence to satisfy him that either President Davis or any member of his cabinet had guilty knowledge of John Wilkes Booth's plot to murder the President.

XXIII

GENERAL GRANT wrote three separate orders, one after the other, removing General Thomas from command of the Army of the Cumberland. President Lincoln suspended the first, General Logan did not deliver the second because Thomas had meantime advanced against Hood and fought and won the battle of Nashville, and Major Eckert suppressed the third.

Before Grant came east to take general command of the army, March, 1864, he was doubtless under the impression, which was generally prevalent[1] (at least the cipher-operators so believed), that Administration influences in Washington

[1] Captain David Lowry, now of Pittsburg, who was Adjutant of the 5th Brigade, Army of the Ohio, is authority for the statement that "Grant's acceptance of the command of the United States army in March, 1864, was well-known among the staff to be on condition of absolute freedom of control from Washington influences." See also Lincoln's letter to Grant April 30, 1864, at the opening of Grant's first campaign in the east, in which he said, "The particulars of your plans I neither know nor seek to know."

were frequently allowed to interfere with what was the better judgment of military men, and it was also understood that he was not favorably disposed toward Thomas.[1]

Mr. Carnegie told me in May, 1906, that as Grant passed through Pittsburgh on his way to Washington in March, 1864, he said to Grant that he presumed Thomas would be placed in command of the army in the west, and that Grant replied, "No; Sherman is the man."

During the ensuing months of the year, Halleck, Chief of Staff at Washington, had, as the cipher-operators believed, caused Grant's unfriendly feeling toward Thomas to be strengthened, and both, we knew, were of the opinion that Thomas in the west, as McClellan had been in the east, was too cautious to take the initiative, and too much disposed to inactivity. Fearing that Hood would cross the Cumberland and reach the Ohio before Thomas made up his mind

[1] It will be recalled that after the battle of Shiloh, in the spring of 1862, Halleck virtually shelved Grant, his second in rank, placing Thomas in command of four of Grant's divisions. In his Memoirs, Vol. I, p. 377, Grant says: "For myself I was little more than an observer. Orders were sent to the right wing or reserve, ignoring me, and advances were made from one line of intrenchments to another, without notifying me. My position was so embarrassing, in fact, that I made several applications during the siege [of Corinth] to be relieved. . . ."

to attack him, Grant sent a telegram from City Point on December 9, 1864, directing Halleck to prepare an order and telegraph it to Nashville, relieving Thomas, and placing Schofield in command. The order was made out in the name of the President, but was not sent because the President, who once before had defended Thomas against public criticism (as expressed in the Maxwell "crazygram," printed in chapter XII), now supported him against his (Lincoln's) own military advisers, and Grant's order was suspended by Lincoln, after being prepared by Assistant Adjutant-General Townsend as follows:

(GENERAL ORDERS No.—)

War Department, Adjutant General's Office, Washington, D. C., December 9, 1864.

In accordance with the following dispatch from Lieutenant-General Grant, viz: "Please telegraph order relieving him [Gen'l Thomas] at once and placing [Gen'l] Schofield in command. Thomas should be directed to turn over all dispatches received since the Battle of Franklin to Schofield. The President orders:

I. That Maj.-Gen'l J. M. Schofield assume command of all troops in the Departments of the Cumberland, the Ohio, and the Tennessee.

II. That Maj.-Gen'l George H. Thomas report to Gen'l Schofield for duty and turn over to him all orders and dispatches received by him, as specified above.

By order of the Secretary of War.

312

Nicolay and Hay say that "the authorities took the responsibility of delaying the order." Major Johnson, Stanton's private secretary, says "the order was prepared by Halleck but held by him until a reply could be received from Thomas to Halleck's telegram of December 10, referring to Grant's dissatisfaction at the delay." The truth probably is that Lincoln, Stanton, and Halleck conferred together, and that the concensus of their opinion was to allow Thomas one more opportunity to move against Hood before Grant's order was executed; but the writer believes that Lincoln's judgment was the controlling factor.

From December 9 until December 13 Grant and Halleck were in daily correspondence about the suspended order, and on the latter date Grant wrote his second order relieving Thomas, and sent it by the hand of Logan to be delivered in person, provided, when Logan arrived at Nashville, Thomas had not yet advanced. (See Special Orders 149, City Point, Virginia, December 13, 1864.) Before Logan was a day's journey away, however, Grant became still more anxious and started in person for Nashville via Washington, as shown by the following telegrams:

City Point, Va., December 14, 1864, 3 P.M.

MAJOR-GENERAL MEADE: I am unexpectedly called away. . . .   U. S. GRANT, Lieutenant-General.

(Same to Major-General Ord.)

City Point, Va.,
December 15, 1864, received at 3:15 P.M.

MAJOR-GENERAL H. W. HALLECK, Chief of Staff: Lieutenant-General Grant left last evening for Washington and will probably reach there this afternoon.

JNO. A. RAWLINS,
Brigadier-General and Chief of Staff.

Grant arrived in Washington December 15, in the afternoon, and found that the wires to Nashville were interrupted, as shown by the following local despatches to Thomas, and that there was nothing to indicate that Thomas had yet moved toward the enemy:

Nashville, Dec. 14, 1864, 10:20 P.M.

GENERAL THOMAS: The telegraph line stopped working north of Gallatin at about 5 this P.M.   J. C. VANDUZER.

Nashville, December 14, 1864, 11 P.M.

GENERAL THOMAS: The line between Clarksville and Bowling Green is also cut, which severs connection with Louisville entirely for to-day. I will endeavor to have the Clarksville route reëstablished in morning. . . .

J. C. VANDUZER.

A conference was held in the War Department on the evening of December 15, between Lincoln, Stanton, Grant, and Halleck. Major Eckert being called in for consultation regarding the telegraphic situation, reported that nothing had been received from Thomas for twenty-four hours. Grant expressed his continued anxiety and finally told the President that he intended to continue on his journey to Nashville and take command in person, meantime relieving Thomas and placing Schofield in immediate command until his arrival.

Grant then wrote his third order removing Thomas, and although Lincoln and Stanton were strongly opposed to such action, they were forced to consent because of Grant's urgent importunity. The final order for the removal of Thomas was then handed to Eckert for transmission, Grant going to Willard's Hotel to prepare for his departure.

Eckert says he then returned to the telegraph office, where in fact he had been on duty constantly day and night for nearly a week. After conversing for a while with Pittsburgh, the repeating office for Louisville, he learned that the line to Nashville by one route had been repaired and that messages were being exchanged. With General Grant's final despatch in his hands Eckert was in a quandary. Should he put it on the wires or not? Recalling the protests of the President and the Secretary of War only an hour before, against the removal of Thomas, he concluded to hold the telegram until he could hear from VanDuzer. So he waited for over an hour until finally at 11 P.M. (Dec. 15) the following telegrams came in cipher, the translation being in my handwriting:

Nashville, Tenn., Dec. 14, 1864, 8 P.M.

MAJOR-GENERAL H. W. HALLECK, Washington, D. C.: Your telegram of 12:30 P.M., to-day is received. The ice having melted away to-day, the enemy will be attacked to-morrow morning. . . . GEORGE H. THOMAS,

Major-General U. S. Vols., Commanding.

Nashville, Dec. 15, 1864, 10:30 P.M.

MAJ. T. T. ECKERT: Our line advanced and engaged the rebel line at 9 this A.M. (Then follows a long eye-witness account of the first day's battle resulting in an initial victory for our army.) . . . J. C. VANDUZER.

Eckert says he ran down-stairs with the two telegrams in his hand and started for Stanton's residence on K Street, in the ambulance, which was always in readiness at the door of the War

Department. Stanton appeared at the second story window and called out, "Is that you, Major? What news?" "Good news," was the answer. Stanton shouted "Hurrah," and Eckert says he could hear Mrs. Stanton and the children also shouting "Hurrah."

The Secretary appeared at the front door in a few moments and rode with Eckert to the White House. Eckert says he will never forget the tall, ghostly form of Lincoln in his night-dress, with a lighted candle in his hand, as he appeared at the head of the second story landing when the two callers were ushered up-stairs by the doorkeeper. The President was, of course, highly delighted to receive the news of Thomas's victory.

While in the ambulance with Secretary Stanton on his way to the White House, Eckert took out of his pocket Grant's last order relieving Thomas and handed it to Stanton without saying a word. The Secretary asked whether it had been sent. Eckert replied, no, that he had held it on his own responsibility, partly because the wires were not working well at the time he received it from Grant, and partly because he wanted to hear further from VanDuzer, and he hoped to receive later information that the weather had

317

moderated, thus allowing Thomas to begin his advance. The Major added: "Mr. Secretary, I fear that I have violated a military rule and have placed myself liable to be court-martialed." Secretary Stanton put his arm around Eckert's shoulder and said, "Major, if they court-martial you, they will have to court-martial me. You are my confidential assistant, and in my absence were empowered to act in all telegraph matters as if you were the Secretary of War. The result shows you did right." While at the White House Stanton showed Grant's last order removing Thomas to the President and told him Eckert had suppressed it. Lincoln replied that Eckert's action met with his hearty approval.

Meantime a copy of VanDuzer's telegram had been sent to Willard's Hotel and upon its receipt, Grant handed it to Beckwith with the remark, "I guess we will not go to Nashville." He then wrote the following telegram:

Washington, D. C., December 15, 1864, 11:30 P.M.

MAJOR-GENERAL THOMAS, Nashville, Tenn.: I was just on my way to Nashville, but receiving dispatch from Van-Duzer, detailing your splendid success of to-day, I shall go no farther. . . . U. S. GRANT, Lieutenant-General.

Shortly afterward Grant received a long despatch from Thomas, from which the following extracts are taken:

> *Nashville, Tenn.,* December 15, 1864, 9 P.M.
> Received 11:25 P.M.

MAJ.-GEN. H. W. HALLECK, Washington, D. C.: I attacked the enemy's left this morning and drove it from the river below the city . . . about 8 miles. Have captured . . . 1000 prisoners and 16 pieces of artillery . . . I shall attack the enemy again to-morrow . . . GEO. H. THOMAS.

> Major-General U. S. Vols. Commanding.

Grant then sent the following telegrams:

> *Washington, D. C.,* December 15, 1864, 11:45 P.M.

MAJOR-GENERAL THOMAS, Nashville, Tenn.: Your dispatch of this evening just received. I congratulate you and the army under your command for to-day's operations and feel a conviction that to-morrow will add more fruits to your victory.   U. S. GRANT, Lieutenant-General.

> *Washington, D. C.,* December 15, 1864, 11:50 P.M.

BRIG.-GEN. J. A. RAWLINS, City Point, Va.: I send you dispatch just received from Nashville [Thomas to Halleck]. I shall not now go there. Will remain absent, however, until about Monday.   U. S. GRANT, Lieutenant-General.

When Lincoln came to the telegraph office the next morning, he sent the following fine despatch to Thomas:

LINCOLN IN THE TELEGRAPH OFFICE

Washington, D. C., December 16, 1864, 11:25 A.M.

MAJOR-GENERAL THOMAS, Nashville, Tenn.: Please accept for yourself, officers, and men, the nation's thanks for your good work of yesterday. You made a magnificent beginning. A grand consummation is within your easy reach. Do not let it slip.   A. LINCOLN.

Logan heard of Thomas's great victory at Louisville and sent this message:

Louisville, Ky., December 17, 1864, 10 A.M.

LT.-GENERAL U. S. GRANT, Burlington, N. J.: Have just arrived. . . People here jubilant over Thomas's success . . . It would seem best that I return to join my command with Sherman.   JNO. A. LOGAN, Major-General.

In consequence of the great victory over Hood, Secretary Stanton, on December 19, urged Thomas's appointment as major-general in the regular army, but Grant, apparently still inimical to Thomas, wired Stanton, December 20:

I think Thomas has won the major-generalcy, but I would wait a few days before giving it, to see the extent of damages done. . . .

The later reports from Thomas, however, were so very gratifying that Grant could no longer withhold his approval, and on December 24, 1864,

Thomas received his commission as major-general in the regular army to date from December 15.

In this connection, it is of interest to note that in February, 1868, President Johnson offered to appoint Thomas, lieutenant-general of the army. Thomas telegraphed the President from Pittsburg declining the high honor, and stating that he "had done nothing since the Civil War to merit the compliment, and it was too long after the war to consider the appointment as a reward for anything he had done during the war."

When Thomas made a visit to Washington in the summer of 1865, Secretary Stanton sent Eckert to the depot to meet him and bring him to the War Department in Stanton's own carriage, sending his baggage to his house, where Thomas was invited to stay while in the capital. When Thomas entered Stanton's office the latter greeted him most cordially and after discussing the battle of Nashville and the incidents referred to above, Stanton produced Grant's third and last order of December 15, 1864, removing Thomas from his command, and then turning to Eckert said, "This is the man who withheld that order and saved you from the mortification of a summary removal."

XXIV

THE ABORTIVE PEACE CONFERENCE AT
HAMPTON ROADS

VERY little has ever been published concerning the only Peace Conference to which this country was a party, at which our Government was represented by the President in person and also by the Secretary of State—and that little is comprised in a few brief letters and telegrams submitted to Congress by Lincoln in response to a resolution calling for information on the subject. Of what actually took place at the conference itself (February 3, 1865), Lincoln gave an account in these few lines:

On the morning of the 3d, the three gentlemen, Messrs. Stephens, Hunter, and Campbell, came aboard of our steamer, and had an interview with the Secretary of State and myself, of several hours' duration. No question of preliminaries to the meeting was then and there made or mentioned. No other person was present; no papers were exchanged or produced; and it was, in advance, agreed that the conversation was to be informal and verbal merely.

On our part the whole substance of the instructions to the Secretary of State, hereinbefore recited, was stated and insisted upon, and nothing was said inconsistent therewith;

while, by the other party, it was not said that in any event or on any condition, they ever would consent to reunion; and yet they equally omitted to declare that they never would so consent. They seemed to desire a postponement of that question, and the adoption of some other course first which, as some of them seemed to argue, might or might not lead to reunion; but which course, we thought, would amount to an indefinite postponement. The conference ended without result.

The foregoing, containing as is believed all the information sought, is respectfully submitted.

There was also a preliminary conference with the Confederate commissioners at which the President was represented by Major Eckert, and of what occurred at that conference beyond the formal exchange of letters no account whatever has been given to the public. In fact, Eckert's reticence in regard to all confidential Civil War matters with which he had to do has been so marked as justly to entitle him to the sobriquet of the "Silent Eckert" bestowed upon him by Major Johnson, Stanton's private secretary. However, after the lapse of more than forty years, Eckert has unlocked his memory-box and brought to light some incidents of the Civil War drama in which he played an important, though subordinate part in relation to Lincoln, the principal actor.

One of these incidents has for its subject the Peace Conference at City Point and Hampton Roads of February, 1865. Following the re-election of Lincoln in November, 1864, the peace agitators in the North ceased their active efforts and, in his Annual Message to Congress on December 6, Lincoln alluded to the question in the briefest manner as follows: "In stating a single condition of peace, I mean simply to say, that the war will cease on the part of the Government whenever it shall have ceased on the part of those who began it."

This postulate referring to a vital subject could not have been stated more clearly, or in shorter terms, in fact, it is axiomatic. Mr. Francis P. Blair, Sr., was one of the most earnest and unselfish supporters of the peace movement. His fine old residence at Silver Spring, Maryland, not far from where the battle of Fort Stevens had taken place the previous July, was set on fire by Early's artillery and was later converted into a hospital for our wounded soldiers, a large number of whom were thus hospitably cared for. Blair fancied he discerned something between the President's lines in reference to peace, and made the latter believe, or at least hope, that if given the opportunity to see Davis in person he could work out a plan that would meet the simple conditions named, and at the same time enable the Confederate leaders to "save their faces."

The patient Lincoln trusted his old political friend and believed in his wisdom and skill; and, unwilling to cast aside the poorest chance to bring the war to an end, he gave Blair, on December 28, 1864, a safe conduct through our lines and return, against the protest, however, of Stanton. Blair was soon back in Washington with a letter from Davis, dated January 12, which was shown to the President, who gave Blair authority to say to Davis that he had been, and should continue to be "ready to receive any agent whom he or any other influential person now resisting the national authority may informally send to me with the view of securing peace to our common country."

This allusion to "our common country" was made because Davis had referred in his letter to "the two countries," an idea perhaps suggested or at least fostered and strengthened in Davis's mind by the memory of Gladstone's remarkable speech at Newcastle-upon-Tyne, in which the dominant British Cabinet Minister spoke of Jefferson Davis as having "created not only an army and a navy, but a nation."

Lincoln's letter to Davis (of January 18, 1865) was taken to Richmond by Blair and delivered on January 21. On the 28th Blair was again in Washington, and Davis had started his three commissioners, Messrs. Stephens, Hunter, and Campbell, on their way toward Washington via City Point. They reached our lines on January 29, but were not permitted to enter; General Ord, in the temporary absence of General Grant, telegraphing to Washington for instructions. On Grant's return to his headquarters, January 31, he received a communication from the commissioners dated Petersburg, January 30, which he forwarded to Washington; but before his despatch was received, the President, upon Stanton's suggestion, had already selected as his representative to meet the Confederate agents, Major Eckert, who had a personal acquaintance with one of them.[1] The instructions to Lincoln's ambassador on this mission were as follows:

[1] Stephens had saved Eckert from the hands of a Southern mob in July, 1861, as related in chapter IX. When Eckert told Lincoln of this incident the latter said that he remembered Stephens in Congress and believed him to be a fair man.

PEACE CONFERENCE AT HAMPTON ROADS

Executive Mansion, Washington, January 30, 1865.
Major Thomas T. Eckert:

SIR: You will proceed with the documents placed in
your hands, and, on reaching General Ord, will deliver him
the letter addressed to him by the Secretary of War; then,
by General Ord's assistance, procure an interview with
Messrs. Stephens, Hunter, and Campbell, or any of them.
Deliver to him or them the paper on which your own letter
is written. Note on the copy which you retain the time of
delivery and to whom delivered. Receive their answer in
writing, waiting a reasonable time for it, and which, if it
contain their decision to come through without further condition, will be your warrant to ask General Ord to pass
them through, as directed in the letter of the Secretary of
War to him. If, by their answer, they decline to come, or
propose other terms, do not have them passed through.
And this being your whole duty, return and report to me.

Yours truly,   A. LINCOLN.

Observe the careful wording of these instructions. To the average man it would seem that in
view of the experience, ability, and proved honesty of Blair, Lincoln would have ordered Grant
to pass the commissioners through the lines and
thence to Washington, or at least that he would
have trusted the Lieutenant-General of the army
to meet them and learn whether their credentials
came within the scope of Lincoln's clearly expressed conditions. But the subject was so complicated and so fraught with contingent dangers,
and Stanton was so strenuous in his objections to

the whole scheme, that only Lincoln himself or some one fresh from his councils who possessed his absolute confidence could be trusted to meet the shrewd and wily emissaries. He did not designate a member of his cabinet for the responsible service, but selected the Chief of the War Department telegraph staff.

Mr. Robert T. Lincoln in a letter dated June 22, 1907, writes as follows:

"After the visit of Mr. F. P. Blair, Sr., to Richmond, an effort was made by some gentlemen, sent by Mr. Davis from Richmond, to come through our lines and proceed to Washington for an interview with my father. It is a well known matter, of course, which occurred in January, 1865. I remember my father telling me one evening all that had occurred up to that time in the matter, and his indicating to me that he was not feeling quite comfortable as to the way in which the matter was being handled at army headquarters at City Point; and that, therefore, he had that day sent 'Tom Eckert,' as he affectionately called him, with written instructions, to handle the whole matter of the application of these visitors from Mr. Davis to get into our lines. He said that he had selected 'Tom Eckert' for this business because—to use his language as nearly as I can remember it—'he never failed to do completely what was given him to do, and to do it in the most complete and tactful manner, and to refrain from doing anything outside which would hurt his mission.' He was so emphatic in expressing this reason for sending Eckert that it made a deep impression upon me, and I never see General Eckert without thinking of it."

Meantime, in expectation that the Confederate commissioners would not hesitate to accept the conditions outlined in his January 18 letter, Lincoln had sent Secretary Seward to Fort Monroe with the following instructions:

Executive Mansion, Washington, January 31, 1865.
HON. WILLIAM H. SEWARD, Secretary of State:

You will proceed to Fort Monroe, Virginia, there to meet and informally confer with Messrs. Stephens, Hunter, and Campbell, on the basis of my letter to F. P. Blair, Esq., of January 18, 1865, a copy of which you have. You will make known to them that three things are indispensable, to wit:

1. The restoration of the national authority throughout all the States.

2. No receding by the executive of the United States on the slavery question from the position assumed thereon in the late annual message to Congress, and in preceding documents.

3. No cessation of hostilities short of an end of the war, and the disbanding of all forces hostile to the government.

You will inform them that all propositions of theirs, not inconsistent with the above, will be considered and passed upon in a spirit of sincere liberality. You will hear all they may choose to say, and report it to me. You will not assume to definitely consummate anything. Yours, etc.,

ABRAHAM LINCOLN.

Eckert left Washington January 31, reaching City Point the following afternoon, and at 10 P.M. forwarded this despatch:

City Point, Virginia, February 1, 1865, 10 P.M.

HIS EXCELLENCY A. LINCOLN, President of the United States:

I have the honor to report the delivery of your communication and my letter at 4.15 this afternoon, to which I received a reply at 6 P.M. but not satisfactory.

At 8 P.M. the following note, addressed to General Grant, was received:

"City Point, Virginia, February 1, 1865.

"Lieutenant-General Grant:

"SIR: We desire to go to Washington city to confer informally with the President, personally, in reference to the matters mentioned in his letter to Mr. Blair, of the 18th of January, ultimo, without any personal compromise on any question in the letter. We have the permission to do so from the authorities in Richmond.

"Very respectfully yours,

"ALEX. H. STEPHENS,
"R. M. T. HUNTER,
"J. A. CAMPBELL."

330

At 9.30 P.M., I notified them that they could not proceed further unless they complied with the terms expressed in my letter. The point of meeting designated in above note would not, in my opinion, be insisted upon. Think Fort Monroe would be acceptable. Having complied with my instructions, I will return to Washington to-morrow unless otherwise ordered.   THOS. T. ECKERT, Major, etc.

When Lincoln received Eckert's telegram stating that the reply of the Confederate commissioners was "not satisfactory" he felt that as they were unwilling, or unable, to meet the prescribed conditions it was useless to do anything further in the matter, and he therefore decided to recall both Seward and Eckert; but before doing so the following cipher-despatch, timed a half hour later than Eckert's, was received:

City Point, Virginia, February 1, 1865, 10.30 P.M.
HON. EDWIN M. STANTON, Secretary of War:
Now that the interview between Major Eckert, under his written instructions, and Mr. Stephens and party has ended, I will state confidentially, but not officially—to become a matter of record—that I am convinced, upon conversation with Messrs. Stephens and Hunter, that their intentions are good and their desire sincere to restore peace and union. I have not felt myself at liberty to express even views of my own, or to account for my reticency. This has placed me in an awkward position, which I could have avoided by not seeing them in the first instance. I fear now their going back

without any expression from any one in authority will have a bad influence. At the same time, I recognize the difficulties in the way of receiving these informal commissioners at this time, and do not know what to recommend. I am sorry, however, that Mr. Lincoln cannot have an interview with the two named in this despatch, if not all three now within our lines. Their letter to me was all that the President's instructions contemplated to secure their safe-conduct, if they had used the same language to Major Eckert.

U. S. GRANT, Lieutenant-General.

Lincoln therefore wisely determined to go in person to meet the commissioners,[1] and accordingly left for Hampton Roads about noon, February 2. On his arrival late that night he found things *in statu quo.* Lincoln adds, in his explanation to Congress, "Here I ascertained that Major Eckert had literally complied with his instructions, and I saw, for the first time, the answer of the Richmond gentlemen to him, which, in his despatch to me of the 1st, he characterizes as 'not satisfactory.'"

The following are the communications exchanged between Eckert and the Richmond gentlemen at the preliminary conference at City Point:

[1] They had meantime informed Grant of their willingness to accept Lincoln's conditions and had proceeded to Hampton Roads to await the President's arrival.

PEACE CONFERENCE AT HAMPTON ROADS

Messrs. Alex. H. Stephens, J. A. Campbell and *R. M. T. Hunter,*

GENTLEMEN:—I am instructed by the President of the United States to place this paper in your hands, with the information that if you pass through the United States military lines, it will be understood that you do so for the purpose of an informal conference on the basis of the letter, a copy of which is on the reverse side of this sheet, and that, if you choose to pass on such understanding, and so notify me in writing, I will procure the commanding general to pass you through the lines and to Fortress Monroe, under such military precautions as he may deem prudent, and at which place you will be met in due time by some person or persons, for the purpose of such informal conference. And, further, that you shall have protection, safe-conduct, and safe return in all events.

THOMAS T. ECKERT, Major and Aide-de-camp.
City Point, Virginia, February 1, 1865.

F. P. Blair, Esq.   *Washington,* January 18, 1865.

SIR: You having shown me Mr. Davis's letter to you of the 12th instant, you may say to him that I have constantly been, am now, and shall continue ready to receive any agent whom he, or any other influential person now resisting the national authority, may informally send to me, with the view of securing peace to the people of our one common country.

Yours, etc.   A. LINCOLN.

City Point, Virginia, February 1, 1865.
Thomas T. Eckert, Major and Aide-de-camp,

MAJOR: Your note, delivered by yourself this day, has been considered. In reply, we have to say that we were furnished with a copy of the letter of President Lincoln to Francis P. Blair, Esq., of the 18th of January, ultimo, another copy of which is appended to your note. Our instructions are contained in a letter, of which the following is a copy:

"*Richmond,* January 28, 1865.

"In conformity with the letter of Mr. Lincoln, of which the foregoing is a copy, you are to proceed to Washington city for informal conference with him upon the issues involved in the existing war, and for the purpose of securing peace to the two countries.

"With great respect, your obedient servant,

"JEFFERSON DAVIS."

The substantial object to be obtained by the informal conference is to ascertain upon what terms the existing war can be terminated honorably.

Our instructions contemplate a personal interview between President Lincoln and ourselves at Washington city, but with this explanation we are ready to meet any person or persons that President Lincoln may appoint, at such place as he may designate. Our earnest desire is that a just and honorable peace may be agreed upon, and we are prepared to receive or to submit propositions which may, possibly, lead to the attainment of that end.

Very respectfully yours,   ALEXANDER H. STEPHENS,
R. M. T. HUNTER,
JOHN A. CAMPBELL.

And now we come to Eckert's account, given to me in conversation in the spring of 1907, of what took place at his interviews with the three Confederate Peace Commissioners at City Point on February 1, 1865, on board the steamer

River Queen, the only persons present being Stephens, Hunter, Campbell and Eckert.

"Quite a little time," he says, "was occupied by Stephens asking me how I was, what I had been doing, etc., because he had met me before in 1861 and knew my cousin George in Congress. I sat between Stephens and Hunter. Stephens was very civil in his reception, more so than the others. He asked if they might not begin to discuss the subject. I said 'Yes, what is the subject you want to discuss?' He said, 'We of the South lay great store by our State rights.' I turned to him and said, 'Excuse me, but we in the North never think of that, we cannot discuss that subject at all.'

"I told them that all the proceedings of the conference must be in writing. I then submitted a copy of my instructions from the President which they took saying they would like to consider it and reply later. Hunter was the chief spokesman, but my communications were always to Stephens, his name being the first on the list of three. Campbell had the least to say. He was, however, a close listener. Before the conference we came very near getting into a difficulty that would have forced me to have done something that might have raised a row, because General Grant wanted to be a party to the conference. I told him no. I said, 'You are the commanding general of the army. If you make a failure or say anything that would be subject to criticism it would be very bad. If I make a mistake I am nothing but a common business man and it will go for naught. I am going to take the responsibility, and I advise you not to go to the conference.' He finally said, 'Decency would compel me to go and see them.' I said that for the purpose of introduction I should be pleased to have him go with me but not until after I had first met the gentlemen. Grant was vexed with me because I did not tell him exactly what my mission was.

"Grant went with me on my second visit a few hours later and after he was introduced, one of the commissioners, I am sure it was Hunter, said to Grant, 'We do not seem to get on very rapidly with Major Eckert. We are very anxious to go to Washington, and Mr. Lincoln has promised to see us there.' General Grant started to make reply when I interrupted him and said, 'Excuse me, General Grant, you are not permitted to say anything officially at this time,' and I stopped

him right there. I added, 'If you will read the instructions under which I am acting you will see
that I am right.'

"After listening a while to what the commissioners were saying Grant got up and went out.
He was angry with me for years afterward, and
this has been a source of sincere regret to me, because in his responsible position as commanding
general of the army he had some reason for
chagrin at the action of a mere major in questioning his ranking authority in the presence of
representatives of the government whose army
he was fighting. But at the time I gave no
thought to this feature of the case, remembering
only my explicit orders written and oral from the
President. When Grant was stopped from making a reply to Hunter he and the other commissioners doubtless thought that if they could have
presented the matter direct to Grant they would
likely get his approval. This view is sustained by
Grant's telegram of 10.30 P.M., February 1, 1865.

"At 9.30 P.M. I informed the commissioners
that they could not proceed further unless they
complied with the terms recited in my letter of
instructions, their formal reply to which had
been delivered to me at our earlier interview and

to inform General Grant in case they concluded to accept the terms. I then withdrew and sent my cipher-despatch to President Lincoln dated 10 P.M. Feb. 1, advising him that the reply of the Peace Commissioners was 'not satisfactory.' The originals of all writings at this conference with the three commissioners were taken to Fort Monroe and handed to Secretary Seward."

One of the dangers that Stanton foresaw in the President's meeting with the Confederate agents was the fear that Lincoln's great kindness of heart and his desire to end the war might lead him to make some admission which the astute Southerners would wilfully misconstrue and twist to serve their purpose; and then if the conference were fruitless they would throw the burden of failure upon the President. As events turned out it was shown that Lincoln was fully competent to deal with the ablest and most adroit politicians of the South. Their report to Davis of the results of the conference could not have been ambiguous if we may judge from what he said in his message to the Confederate Congress of March 13, 1865, as follows:

Our commissioners were informed that the Government of the United States would not enter into any agreement or

338

treaty whatever with the Confederate States, nor with any single state, and that the only possible mode of obtaining peace was by laying down our arms, disbanding our forces, and yielding unconditional obedience to the laws of the United States, including those passed for the confiscation of our property and the constitutional amendment for the abolition of slavery. It will further be remembered that Mr. Lincoln declared that the only terms on which hostilities could cease were those stated in his message of December last, in which we were informed that in the event of our penitent submission, he would temper justice with mercy and that the question whether we would be governed as dependent territories, or permitted to have a representation in *their* Congress was one on which he could promise nothing but which would be decided by *their* Congress after our submission had been accepted.

We may conclude, therefore, that the main effect of the Hampton Roads Peace Conference was the demonstrating to Jefferson Davis and the Southern leaders that their only hope of success lay in Lee's army, which even then was fast diminishing in numbers and effectiveness, and which in a little over two months after the conference surrendered to Grant.

The news of the visit of President Lincoln and Secretary Seward to Hampton Roads to meet the Confederate Peace Commissioners had been spread abroad by telegraph, and the newspapers were full of references to the matter, many persons believing, and all hoping, that a practical basis of settlement would be reached and the war soon ended. The financial market, in its nervous expectancy, reflected the wavering opinions and hopes of the public, and if the meeting had resulted favorably, there would have been instant response on the gold and stock exchanges of New York and elsewhere, and those possessing the earliest news would be able to buy securities and gold and make large profits.

To save time, the President's party came up the Chesapeake Bay, instead of by the longer route up the Potomac. Secretary Stanton had provided a special engine and car to meet the party at Annapolis, and when they reached the old railroad station, the platform was crowded with people, all eager to catch a glimpse of the President. In the crowd there were many newspaper reporters interested in obtaining definite news, or even a hint, from Lincoln, Seward, or Eckert, as to the outcome of the momentous meeting. On the platform Eckert recognized an acquaintance, who managed to draw him aside and, in a hurried conversation, which he said must be strictly confidential, asked him for the result of the conference, at the same time placing in his hands an envelop, saying that the contents would recompense him for his trouble.

After some parleying, Eckert returned to the car, and in Lincoln's presence opened the envelop and showed him a certified check for $100,000, telling him how it came into his hands. Lincoln asked who gave it to him.

Eckert replied: "I am not at liberty to say, but when the train is ready to leave, I will be on the platform, and hand the envelop to the man from whom I received it, so that you can see who he is." This was done, Eckert telling the man that he was obliged to decline the offer, and could give him no news of the conference. Lincoln saw the transaction, and recognized the man as one prominent in political affairs, and who had held a responsible official position in one of the western States.

Upon returning to the car, Lincoln remained silent for a long time, but afterward, when he and Eckert could converse together without attracting Seward's special attention, or that of Robert S. Chew, his private secretary, the only other occupants of the car, it was agreed that neither should disclose the incident to any one excepting only Secretary Stanton, Eckert contending that the effect on public opinion generally, and especially as it related to the Administration, of an announcement of such an offer having been made, would be very injurious at a time of such extreme tension, and that if the public were to learn of the failure of the Peace Conference without at the same time receiving Lincoln's own clear explanation, they would be inclined to criticize him for having once more defeated possibly well-meant efforts to bring the war to an end.

Upon reaching Washington, Secretary Seward's carriage took him direct to his home, while Eckert rode in the President's carriage. At the White House they met Stanton, and gave him a full account of the recent Peace Conference, and also of the incident of the certified check, and all three agreed that, for obvious reasons, they would keep the affair strictly confidential between themselves. It is believed that no mention of the incident has ever been made prior to the account which appeared in "The Century Magazine" for May, 1907, nor has the name of the person who made the offer ever been disclosed.

XXV

LINCOLN'S LAST DAYS

DURING the last three weeks of Lincoln's
life, that brief period in which at last he
felt slipping from his shoulders the burden that
for four years had pressed so heavily upon him, he
could anticipate in the near future a happy, re-
united country. What gladness must have filled
his heart as with Mrs. Lincoln and his beloved
Tad he journeyed down the quiet Potomac and
up the placid James! He had received word
from Grant of his purpose to close in upon Lee
and bring the war to an end, and then followed
this despatch, dated March 20:

HIS EXCELLENCY A. LINCOLN: Can you not visit City
Point for a day or two? I would like very much to see you,
and I think the rest would do you good.
　　　　　Respectfully yours, etc.,
　　　　　　　U. S. GRANT, Lieutenant-General.

He eagerly responded to the call and started
on the *River Queen,* convoyed by the little

steamer *Bat,* Thursday, March 23, arriving at City Point the following evening.

Grant directed Beckwith, his cipher-operator, to report to the President and keep him in touch by telegraph with the army in its advance movement, and with the War Department at Washington. It may, therefore, be truthfully said that for the next two weeks out of the three remaining to him, Lincoln lived "in the telegraph office," for he and Beckwith were almost inseparable and the wires were kept busy with despatches to and from the President. Beckwith's tent adjoined the larger tent of Colonel Bowers, which Lincoln made his headquarters.

It was by telegraph on Monday, after reaching City Point, that Lincoln indorsed Stanton's order of exercises to be observed at Fort Sumter on the anniversary of its surrender, in which many notable persons, including Colonel Robert Anderson, Admiral Dahlgren, Assistant Adjutant-General Townsend, Captain Gustavus V. Fox, the Rev. Henry Ward Beecher, the Rev. R. S. Storrs, and others were to participate.

The following telegram shows Lincoln's close attention to details and the tenacity of his memory:

LINCOLN'S LAST DAYS

City Point, Va., March 27, 1865, 3:35 P.M.

HON. SECRETARY OF WAR, Washington, D. C.:

Yours enclosing Fort Sumter order received. I think of
but one suggestion. I feel quite confident that Sumter fell
on the 13th, and not on the 14th of April, as you have it.
It fell on Saturday, the 13th; the first call for troops on
our part was got up on Sunday, the 14th, and given date
and issued on Monday, the 15th. Look up the old almanac
and other data and see if I am not right.   A. LINCOLN.

The President's recollection was correct, as the
records proved. Another illustration of Lincoln's
aptitude for fixing dates is shown in his remark
one day that it was his habit to fasten in his mind
the name of the week-day on which the month
came in, as he was thus reminded that the 15th
and 29th occurred on the same day of the week.
He then looked forward to the first day of the
following month as falling on a certain day of the
week, and so on through the whole year.

On the night of Grant's general advance
against Lee there was a severe thunder-storm,
rain falling in torrents, with blinding lightning
flashes. Grant had not intended the grand movement to begin until later, but when the storm
broke he quickly decided that one effect would be
to drive the enemy to cover wherever possible, and
so he told his cipher-operator at the front, A. H.

Caldwell, to transmit the order that had already been prepared for the purpose, addressed to Meade, Sheridan, and the corps commanders, directing them to begin the advance at once, simultaneously at all points, without regard to the violent storm then raging. Grant sent an additional telegram to each commander containing these four words only: "Let the fur fly." Caldwell retained in his possession this laconic despatch in Grant's handwriting, and, so far as known, it has not been heretofore published. In May, 1865, when Caldwell was in charge of the Richmond telegraph office, he exhibited the original to Mr. William H. Eckert, now of New York, who recently told me of the incident.

Mrs. Lincoln remained at City Point one week, returning to Washington on April 1, leaving little Tad with his father. Grant's forward movement progressed so well that on Sunday morning the President telegraphed to Mrs. Lincoln some details of our great success. The original is shown in facsimile on page 347.[1]

Upon Lincoln's arrival at City Point, March 24, Grant had offered him the choice of his two

---

[1] Mrs. Lincoln came back to City Point on April 6, with Senators Sumner and Harlan and Mrs. Harlan and made a trip to Richmond.

favorite horses, "Cincinnati" and "Little Jeff."
Lincoln selected the former, being the larger of

Facsimile (reduced) of Lincoln's despatch to Mrs. Lincoln
of 7:45 P. M., April 2, 1865

the two, as better suited to his tall form, and during his stay he frequently rode Cincinnati around
the camp.   He was a good rider and greatly en-

joyed this recreation, and when Grant went to the front to personally direct the general assault upon Lee's army along a line of over thirty miles, he left a trusted groom in charge of Cincinnati, so that if the movement should prove successful, the President might ride out to the front. Cincinnati was richly caparisoned with all the Lieutenant-General's embellishments and insignia of rank, and although the President did not fully appreciate the magnificence of his mount, he admired the splendid action of the matchless war-horse.

The following account of Cincinnati and Little Jeff, two of Grant's favorite horses, is from Beckwith's pen. The third one was called Egypt.

"Grant's famous Kentucky thoroughbred chestnut gelding 'Cincinnati,' was presented to him in the hotel at St. Louis where the two Grants met for the first time—by chance.

"The Cincinnati Grant sent his card, without explanation, requesting General Grant to call at his room. Quite puzzled, General Grant was conducted to his namesake's room, where the mystery was solved by the sorry grunting of a wealthy invalid, who said: 'General, I have a horse that I shall never again be permitted to ride. I would not sell this kind and beautiful animal to any one, but your appreciation of a really good horse induces me to offer him to you as a present.'

"The majestic animal reached Chattanooga, richly blanketed, in charge of a groom, in December, 1863. It was not, however, until the Wilderness Campaign, that 'Cincinnati' became filled with the martial spirit and frantic to participate in the turmoil of battle. In quietude this famous animal seemed gentle and spiritless, but the battle sounds stirred him with enthusiasm. No artist could paint the beauty of this horse in the midst of action, when the curb was required to hold him back; and this was the horse that bore Mr. Lincoln as quietly as a sheep to and from Petersburg, April 3, 1865.

" 'Little Jeff' was a black, shapely-limbed pony, 14 hands high, formerly owned by Mrs. Jefferson Davis, and was captured at Grand Gulf, Miss., in the early part of 1863. A proposition at Chattanooga to purchase this pony resulted in Grant's response: 'We shall not remain long enough for you to require a purchase. Exercise any one of my horses that you desire; they 'll be all the better for it.' I preferred 'Little Jeff' to 'Egypt' or 'Cincinnati,' and while the pony was speeding, his carriage was so perfect in his pace that I could have threaded a needle. On April 2, 1865, the Petersburg line was broken, and while our army was moving on in pursuit of Lee, Grant lingered at Petersburg with 'Little Jeff,' impatiently awaiting Lincoln's arrival. He came the following morning, and after an hour's conference with the Lieutenant-General, returned to City Point on 'Cincinnati.' This was Lincoln's last horseback ride. Meantime, 'Little Jeff,' carrying Grant, was speeding on to overtake the pursuing columns of the Army of the Potomac. Grant rode 'Little Jeff' through the Appomattox campaign, as he had also done at Vicksburg, and Chattanooga.

"When Grant became President in 1869, these two faithful animals were duly installed with honors in the White House stables. Subsequently 'Little Jeff' gave Grant an occasional morning ride, but I never witnessed equally meritorious distinction for 'Cincinnati,' whose lofty spirit was demeaned by the dragging of the White House carriage, a duty which he so spurned that his fretful annoyance gained respectful recognition, and another horse was chosen to wear the unwelcome harness."

In September, 1906, I sent a picture of Little

Jeff to Mrs. Jefferson Davis, thinking it would be a pleasure, after a lapse of so many years, to look once more upon the form of her old horse. The following acknowledgment in her own beautiful handwriting reached me later:

Hotel Gramatan, Bronxville, N. Y., Sept. 19th, 1906.
David H. Bates, Esq.

MY DEAR SIR: Many thanks for the interesting picture of one of our well known breed of horses in which Mr. Davis and I took much interest. They were a cross of a noted Canadian racing pacer called Oliver, with several blooded American and English mares. I think they were all taken except one inferior gelding. They were without exception horses of wonderful speed and endurance and gaited by nature with the long pace which was so speedy and at the same time easy to the rider.

Excuse, please, my tardy acknowledgement of your kind attention in sending the engravings, and believe me

Respectfully and truly yours,
V. JEFFERSON DAVIS.

Mrs. Davis came to New York a few days after writing this letter, was taken ill, died on October 16, and was buried at Richmond beside her husband on October 19.

UPON Lincoln's return from Petersburg, he found awaiting him a telegram from the Secretary of War, pointing out the dangers which the

President was likely to meet if he went to the front, as his early morning message had stated he would do.

In part Stanton said: "Ought you to expose the Nation to the consequences of any disaster to yourself in the pursuit of a treacherous and

Facsimile (reduced) of Lincoln's cipher-despatch, in which he announced the fall of Petersburg and Richmond

dangerous enemy like the rebel army?" In Lincoln's reply to this thoughtful warning, which is given in facsimile on page 353 he says: "I will take care of myself."

Alas, with all his precautions and in spite of all the safeguards placed around his person by the Secretary of War and by General Grant, he was destined to meet death at the hands of an assassin, eleven days later.

The despatch above referred to was the last one sent by the President before he went to Richmond the following day, and before his death, so far as is recorded, he sent only seven others.

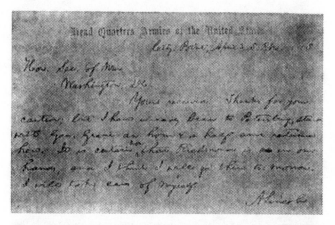

Facsimile (reduced) of Lincoln's despatch of 5 P.M., April 3, 1865

On April 4, Lincoln left City Point for Richmond, accompanied by Beckwith, the faithful cipher-operator, who recently sent me the following account of the journey.

"At 8 A.M., Tuesday, April 4, 1865, I received orders from Mr. Lincoln to accompany him to the late capital of the Confederacy, which had fallen into our hands the day before. I at once repaired to the dock, where an escort of cavalry and a four-horse ambulance were being embarked on the transport *Columbus,* and sat down at the captain's desk for the purpose of completing some cipher-translations, supposing the President was already on board. The captain of the transport soon discovered my whereabouts and nervously informed me that the *River Queen,* with the President and Rear-Admiral Porter on board had dropped down the river in search of me and was then passing up. Without a moment's loss of time I ran ashore and hailed the nearest tug which then steamed up the James and by means of signals overtook the *River Queen,* near Bermuda Hundred, where I was taken aboard and reported to the President. Admiral Porter, little Tad and Captain Penrose of the army were with him. The last named had been assigned by Secretary Stanton to protect the President during his stay in Virginia.

"When we arrived at the lower side of the 'obstructions'[1] in the James, the *River Queen* tied

---

[1] It should be explained that the Confederates, during the long siege of their capital, had placed obstructions in the winding channel of the James, between Richmond and City Point, leaving a narrow passage only, through which small vessels might pass, and which could be quickly closed when so desired.

up, while the President betook himself to the Admiral's eight-oared barge in waiting for him above the obstructions in tow of a tug. Mr. Lincoln directed me to follow with the cavalry escort and ambulance, if we could make the passage of the obstructions, and if not, then to bring them up to Richmond overland. When the President had left, I called the captains of the *River Queen* and *Columbus* into council, and they thought my suggestion feasible to drop down the stream about 500 feet, force on full steam and jam through the rushing current in the narrow opening, but alas, while almost at the upper end of the channel, we were swept around and firmly held, as if spiked to the piling.

"We were now stuck in the narrow opening. There are cheerful outlooks in nearly every condition, but I must confess to a momentary loss of hope and anticipated pleasure, while thinking that I was to be deprived of seeing the entry into Richmond of our beloved President. While in the pilot-house, I detected the gold bands on the sleeves of a man of small stature aboard a tug coming down the James. As he came into closer vision, I observed that the sturdy sailor was none other than Admiral Farragut on the deck of his tug, giving personal orders for the relief of our beleaguered vessel. As Farragut dropped slowly down, I heard his word of command, 'Get your hawsers ready.' The sergeant in command of the escort on our boat reëchoed the order, 'Men, get your harses ready,' adding in a lower tone, 'Phwat does he want of harses in the wather?'

"The Admiral's tug soon pulled us through, and we proceeded rapidly to our destination at the Rocketts, two miles below Richmond. Here we found General Weitzel's aide-de-camp awaiting us. The President's party had arrived a short time before, and with an escort consisting of about a dozen sailors, had gone to Jeff. Davis's abandoned house, known as the 'Confederate Mansion,' and which was then occupied by General Weitzel commanding, and by General Shepley, Military Governor of Richmond.

"Upon landing at the Rocketts, I lent my horse and an extra one to the two captains, who were eager to enter the city in style, only to learn a little later that both horses, frightened by the noise and excitement in the streets, had run away with them. As for myself, in charge of the President's cavalry escort, which I felt sure would be needed in the Southern capital, all my energy was called forth to maintain unbroken lines on our journey from the wharf up the hill to Davis's former home. The enthusiasm of the colored people was something indescribable. They cheered us continually as we moved along, my ambulance preceding the cavalry escort. As our cavalcade approached the Confederate Mansion, Mr. Lincoln was seen on the piazza, and his first words to me, as the loud cheering continued, were to the effect that I had been stealing somebody else's thunder.

"The President then took a drive around the streets of Richmond, and was everywhere greeted by the negroes with noisy ejaculations of joy. There seemed to be a sort of freemasonry among them, so that the news of the President's coming had spread like wildfire. In the afternoon our entire party left the mansion, the President in a carriage, and I maintaining my position at the head of the cavalry escort, immediately following, until we reached the landing on the James, where Admiral Porter's barge conveyed the President to the flagship *Malvern* for the night, after which I reported to General Shepley for quarters and rations for my horses and men.

"At 9 o'clock the next morning, April 5, I was

on hand with my escort at the landing waiting for the President, who soon came ashore in the Admiral's barge. A second drive around the city was then taken, and after a visit to headquarters and a conference with Generals Weitzel, Shepley, and others, including Charles A. Dana, Assistant Secretary of War, and several members of the Virginia Legislature, we headed for the wharf again, and the President and party, including myself, boarded the Admiral's barge which was in readiness with the eight well-armed sailors to convey us to City Point, towed by a tug, as Mr. Lincoln had specially requested. At the mouth of the Dutch Gap Canal, the tug cut loose and passed around the nine-mile bend, while the sailors shipped their oars and took us quickly through the canal. Arriving at City Point, Mr. Lincoln immediately repaired to his accustomed desk in Colonel Bowers's tent, and I to my post of duty in the telegraph tent adjoining, where a number of ciphers for the President were awaiting translation."

As indicated in Beckwith's account, Lincoln, upon his return to City Point, found a batch of telegrams, including some from Grant at the front telling of the continued progress of his army in the pursuit of Lee's disheartened and fast disintegrating forces.

At noon, the following day, Lincoln telegraphed to Grant that Secretary Seward had been seriously injured by being thrown from his carriage in Washington, and that this, with other matters, would take him to Washington soon. Otherwise it is to be presumed, that notwithstanding Stanton's warning, he would have gone to Appomattox to be present at the surrender of Lee's army. The same day he telegraphed General Weitzel at Richmond on the subject of a meeting of the "gentlemen who have acted as the Legislature of Virginia," for the purpose of taking measures "to withdraw the Virginia troops from resistance to the General Government." Lincoln remained at City Point until April 8, when he returned on the *River Queen* to Washington, where he arrived April 9, at which time he received Grant's welcome despatch announcing the capitulation of Lee.

And now, let us go back to the morning of April 3, when Lincoln's despatch from City Point gave us in the War Department the first news of the capture of Petersburg and Richmond. Shortly after that message was received we were startled to hear our comrade, William J. Dealy, at Fort Monroe, say over the wire, "Turn down for Richmond." To one not a telegrapher these words would be Greek, but we all knew what was meant, and operator Thomas A. Laird at once turned down the armature spring so that it might respond to the weaker current from the more distant office and the signals thus be made plainer to the ear. Then came the inquiry, "Do you get me well?" "Yes, go ahead." "All right. Here is the first message for you in four years from

Richmond, Va., April 3, 1865.

Hon. Edwin M. Stanton, Secretary of War, Washington, D. C.: We took Richmond at 8:15 this morning. . . The city is on fire in two places. . .

G. Weitzel, Brig.-Gen'l Comd'g.

Weitzel sent a similar message to Grant at the front, the original of which is still in the possession of the operator who transmitted it over the field wire—Mr. William B. Wood, now of New York City.

When Laird received the words, "From Richmond," he jumped up and ran into the cipher-room, leaving Willie Kettles, a lad of fifteen, the youngest operator in the office, to copy the despatch while Laird spread the glad tidings by word of mouth. Looking out of the windows at the people who were passing, the cipher-operators leaned as far out as possible and shouted, "Richmond has fallen."

During the following week the wires were kept busy with messages relating to the task of restoring order in the former capital of the Confederacy and with other messages from Grant possessing a deeper interest, until on April 9, we were rejoiced to hear of the surrender at Appomattox. We knew then that the war had ended, and a new era had begun. Lincoln had already started from City Point, reaching Washington on the evening of the 9th. The political situation was uppermost in his mind, and in order that he might begin at once "to bind up the Nation's wounds," he sent immediately for Governor Pierpoint, of Virginia, his first telegram after arrival being the following:

Executive Mansion, Washington, April 10, 1865.

GOVERNOR PIERPOINT, Alexandria, Va.: Please come up and see me at once.　　　　　A. LINCOLN.

On the following evening, at the White House, he delivered his carefully prepared, written speech, touching particularly on the Louisiana situation. This was his last public address, and the writer had the pleasure of listening to it on his way home from the War Department.

On the morning of Wednesday, April 12, he came over to the telegraph office and wrote two telegrams, both relating to Virginia legislative matters, and to complete this record they are given in full below:

Washington, D. C., April 12, 1865.

MAJOR-GENERAL WEITZEL, Richmond, Va.: I have seen your dispatch to Colonel Hardie about the matter of prayers. I do not remember hearing prayers spoken of while I was in Richmond; but I have no doubt you have acted in what appeared to you to be the spirit and temper manifested by me while there. Is there any sign of the rebel legislature coming together on the understanding of my letter to you? If there is any such sign, inform me what it is; if there is no such sign, you may withdraw the offer. A. LINCOLN.

Weitzel's reply not being conclusive, Lincoln then wrote his last telegraphic despatch, using for the purpose a Gillott's small barrel pen—No. 404—borrowed from Albert Chandler:

Washington, D. C., April 12, 1865.

MAJOR-GENERAL WEITZEL, Richmond, Va.: I have just seen Judge Campbell's letter to you of the 7th. He assumes, as appears to me, that I have called the insurgent legislature of Virginia together, as the rightful legislature of the State, to settle all differences with the United States. I have done no such thing. I spoke of them, not as a legislature, but as "the gentlemen who have acted as the Legislature of Virginia in support of the rebellion." I did this on purpose to exclude the assumption that I was recognizing them as a rightful body. I dealt with them as men having power de facto to do a specific thing, to wit: "To withdraw the Virginia troops and other support from resistance to the General Government," for which, in the paper handed Judge Campbell, I promised a specific equivalent, to wit: a remission to the people of the State, except in certain cases, of the confiscation of their property. I meant this, and no more. Inasmuch, however, as Judge Campbell misconstrues this, and is still pressing for an armistice, contrary to the explicit statement of the paper I gave him, and particularly as General Grant has since captured the Virginia troops, so that giving a consideration for their withdrawal is no longer applicable, let my letter to you and the paper to Judge Campbell both be withdrawn, or countermanded, and he be notified of it. Do not allow them to assemble, but if any have come, allow them safe return to their homes.

A. LINCOLN.

When this despatch was passed over to us, we quickly transcribed its contents in the cipher-book, line after line and column after column, little thinking that it was the last message we should ever receive from his hands. Soon it was in form for transmission to the cipher-operator at Richmond, and then the end of our association with the great President had come.

XXVI

THE ASSASSINATION

IMMEDIATELY after Lee's surrender, and without waiting to witness the details attending the transfer of the enemy's arms and property, General Grant started for Washington, where he arrived on April 13. That evening had been set apart for an illumination of the city in honor of our victories, and the expected end of the war. The chief interest centered about the White House, and Secretary Stanton's residence on K Street, at both of which places large crowds of people assembled. Extra precautions were taken by the authorities to protect the President and Lieutenant-General against expected attempts to kidnap or kill them, because of secret service reports that plans had been made to accomplish such evil designs during the excitement of that occasion. Grant was present at Stanton's reception and, but for the safeguards provided, it is more than likely that the efforts of O'Laughlin, one of the conspirators, to enter Stanton's house and execute his murderous task, might have been successful. John C. Hatter, now of Brooklyn, one of the War Department telegraph staff, testified at the trial of the conspirators in May, 1865, that one of them—Michael O'Laughlin— was in the crowd at Stanton's house the night of the illumination, and had tried to enter. In fact, he reached the front hall, but Hatter, who was uneasy over his presence, induced him to leave.

It was mainly on the strength of Hatter's testimony that O'Laughlin was found guilty. He died in prison at Dry Tortugas, Florida, September 23, 1867.

On the day of the illumination, Mrs. Lincoln made plans for a small theater-party on the following evening, Friday, April 14, to see Laura Keene play the part of *Florence Trenchard* in "Our American Cousin." Lincoln reluctantly acceded to Mrs. Lincoln's request that he should be present, and suggested that General and Mrs. Grant be invited to join the party.

The invitation was given and accepted, but when Stanton heard of it he made a vigorous protest, having in mind the numerous threats of assassination which had come to his notice through secret service agents and otherwise.

Lincoln made light of all these signs, but Stanton realized the seriousness of the situation, and told Grant of his fears, urging him not to go to the theater and, if possible, to dissuade Lincoln from going. It was Stanton's idea that if it were announced that the Lieutenant-General and the President were to attend Ford's Theater together there would be a large crowd present, and evil-disposed persons would be better able to carry out their plans.

Grant agreed with Stanton, and said he only wanted an excuse not to go. He concluded, therefore, to send word to Lincoln that as he had not seen his daughter Nellie for a long time he would withdraw his acceptance of the invitation and start on Friday afternoon for Burlington, New Jersey, where his daughter was attending school.

On the morning of the 14th, Lincoln made his usual visit to the War Department and told Stanton that Grant had cancelled his engagement for that evening. The stern and cautious Secretary again urged the President to give up the theater-party, and, when he found that he was set on going, told him he ought to have a competent guard. Lincoln said: "Stanton, do you know that Eckert can break a poker over his arm?"

Stanton, not knowing what was coming, looked around in surprise and answered: "No; why do you ask such a question?" Lincoln said: "Well, Stanton, I have seen Eckert break five pokers, one after the other, over his arm, and I am thinking he would be the kind of man to go with me this evening. May I take him?"[1]

Stanton, still unwilling to encourage the theater project, said that he had some important work for Eckert that evening, and could not spare him. Lincoln replied: "Well, I will ask the Major myself, and he can do your work to-morrow." He then went into the cipher-room, told Eckert of his plans for the evening, and said he wanted him to be one of the party, but that Stanton said he could not spare him. "Now, Major," he added, "come along. You can do Stanton's work to-morrow, and Mrs. Lincoln and I want you with us."

Eckert thanked the President but, knowing

[1] The incident of breaking the stove pokers is described in chapter IX.

Stanton's views, and that Grant had been induced to decline, told the President he could not accept because the work which the Secretary referred to must be done that evening, and could not be put off.

"Very well," Lincoln then said, "I shall take Major Rathbone along, because Stanton insists upon having some one to protect me; but I should much rather have you, Major, since I know you can break a poker over your arm."

It is idle to conjecture what might have been the result if the alert and vigorous Eckert had accompanied Lincoln to Ford's Theater that night. Had he done so the probabilities are that in view of Eckert's previous knowledge of the plot to kidnap or kill the President, Booth might have been prevented from firing the fatal shot, and Lincoln spared to finish his great work.

As is well known Lincoln went to the theater in the evening with Mrs. Lincoln, Miss Harris, daughter of Senator Ira Harris of New York, and Major Rathbone, a stepson of the senator.

During the course of the play, a few minutes after ten o'clock, John Wilkes Booth entered the theater lobby and passed round the dress-circle to the door of the box where Lincoln's party were seated, picked up a bar of wood that he had previously provided and placed it in position for use as a brace. When he entered the box and closed the door after him the brace fell into a slot in the wall, thus preventing the door from being opened from the outside.

At 10:20 P.M. Booth, using a Derringer pistol and exclaiming: *"Sic semper tyrannis"* as he fired, shot the President in the back of his head, and then, shaking himself loose from Major Rathbone who had grappled with him, jumped over the box to the stage, about seven feet below. As he fell the spur which he wore caught in the folds of the American flag which draped the front of the box and caused him to break his ankle.

The whole affair was so sudden and startling that the crowded audience appeared to be dazed, and although some of the clearer-headed persons tried to seize the assassin the confusion was so great that he managed to escape through the left-hand exit from the stage, and, mounting a horse that was being held ready by Spangler, one of the conspirators, rode off unmolested toward the bridge over the eastern branch of the Potomac, where he was met by Herold, another conspirator. Together they rode through lower Maryland, while the whole North, aroused to fury, was trying to track them and the other assassins: Payne, who murderously assaulted Secretary Seward; Atzerodt, to whom was assigned the task of killing Vice-President Johnson; O'Laughlin, who was to kill Grant, and the other conspirators who took minor parts in the great tragedy.

I remember the long night of Friday, April 14, that black day in our country's history, when the hate and cruelty embodied in four years of bloody war culminated in a stroke of madness, aimed at the life of one who had only "charity for all with malice toward none." Although I was on duty in the cipher-room that evening, I have no distinct remembrance of anything that occurred prior to the moment when some one rushed into the office with blanched face saying, "There is a rumor below that President Lincoln has been shot in Ford's Theater." Before we could fully take in the awful import, other rumors reached us, horror following fast upon horror: the savage attack upon Secretary Seward, and the frustrated efforts to reach and kill Vice-President Johnson, Secretary Stanton and other members of the Government. As the successive accounts crystallized, a fearful dread filled our hearts, lest it should be found that the entire cabinet had been murdered. After an hour of this awful suspense, we received word from Major Eckert, who had gone quickly to Secretary Stanton's house on K Street, and from there with the Secretary to the house on Tenth Street, opposite the theater, to which the President had been carried after having been shot by John Wilkes Booth. This message merely assured us of the present safety of Stanton, while confirming our worst fears concerning the President. Two of my comrades were in the audience at the theater, Thomas A. Laird, now of Buffalo, and George C. Maynard, now assistant curator of the Smithsonian Institute. Laird ran to Eckert's house on Thirteenth Street to give him the news, while Maynard came to the War Department. Both men remained on duty all night with Chandler and myself.

A relay of mounted messengers in charge of John C. Hatter was immediately established by Eckert, and all night long they carried bulletins in Stanton's handwriting addressed to General Dix, New York City, which were at once given to the Associated Press and flashed over the wires throughout the country. As these bulletins were spelled out in the Morse telegraph characters, our hearts were stunned and yet seemed to be on fire. The awfulness of the tragedy hushed us into silence. As the hours slowly passed, hope revived fitfully as some sentence offered faint encouragement that the precious life might perhaps be spared to complete its chosen work; but at last, about 7:30 A.M., April 15, the tension gave way, and we knew that our beloved President was gone from us forever.

The news of the tragedy reached Grant at Philadelphia, as he was about to take the ferryboat for Camden. He continued his journey to Burlington with Mrs. Grant, returning to Washington immediately with Beckwith, his cipher-operator. The latter remained in Washington until April 22, when he was ordered to the lower Potomac to establish communication with the several parties in that vicinity who were searching for Booth, for the capture of whom the large reward of $100,000 had been offered. It was reported that Booth's route of escape was through Maryland, toward Point Lookout, and a force, including 600 colored troops, commanded by Major James R. O'Beirne, was sent from Washington to capture the assassins. Beckwith went with this detachment and opened an office at Port Tobacco, from which place he sent a number of telegrams, one of which gave the Washington authorities the earliest authentic clue to Booth's immediate whereabouts, and in part read as follows:

Port Tobacco, Md., April 24th, 1865.

10 A.M., received 11A.M.

MAJOR ECKERT: Have just met Major O'Beirne, whose force has arrested Doctor Mudd and Thompson. Mudd set Booth's left leg (fractured), furnished crutches, and helped him and Herold off. They have been tracked as far as the swamp near Bryantown. . . .   S. H. BECKWITH.

Stanton ordered a small body of picked men under Lieutenant E. P. Doherty of the 16th New York Cavalry to start for Port Tobacco, leaving Washington on the steamer *John S. Ide,* at four o'clock, arriving at Belle Plain, seventy miles below Washington, at ten o'clock. The men and their horses disembarked, and the whole party struck out on the trail, and by midnight they had tracked Booth and Herold across the river into

23   **373**

War Department
Washington City

April 16 1865.

General;

The distressing duty has devalued upon the Secretary of War ~~and see~~ to announce ~~through~~ ^you^ to the armies of the United States, that at twenty two minutes after seven o'clock on the morning of ~~yesterday~~ ^day of April 1865^ the fifteenth ^instant^, Abraham Lincoln, President of the United States died of a mortal wound inflicted upon him by an assassin.

The armies of the United States ~~will~~ share with their fellow citizens the feelings of grief and horror inspired by this most atrocious murder of their great and beloved President and Commander-in-Chief ~~and will~~ ^a great national calamity^ with profound sorrow will mourn his death as.

~~Your will direct that the~~ ^other^
Head Quarters of every Department ^be^ ^both and Stations be^ draped in mourning for thirty days, and ^appropriate^ ~~that~~ the ~~personal~~ honors ~~prescribed~~

Facsimile, on this and the following page, of the manuscript of Secretary Stanton's order to the armies for honoring the memory of the murdered President

The original is in the possession of David Homer Bates who first wrote the message from Stanton's dictation, after which the latter revised it extensively with his own hand

Virginia, where they were discovered concealed in a barn, which was set on fire for the purpose of forcing the fugitives from its shelter, and, as is well known, Booth was shot by Sergeant "Boston" Corbett, of Company L, 16th New

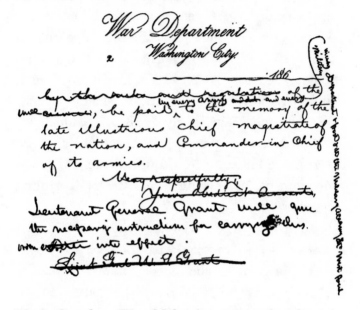

York Cavalry, Herold having surrendered previously.

Corbett was born in London. He was a member of the old Attorney Street Methodist Church, New York, before he enlisted. The writer met him one night in the summer of 1865 at Foundry

Church, Fourteenth and G streets, Washington, where he testified regarding his religious experience. He appeared to be very quiet and rather morose. Years afterward his mind gave way, and he was committed to an asylum, where he died.

It is believed that all of the conspirators were apprehended. As before stated, John Wilkes Booth was shot near Port Royal, Virginia, on April 26. Lewis Thornton Powell (alias Payne), George A. Atzerodt, David E. Herold, and Mrs. Mary E. Surratt, were hung at the Washington arsenal July 7, 1865. Samuel Arnold, Edward Spangler, Michael O'Laughlin, and Dr. Samuel A. Mudd were sentenced to imprisonment for varying terms at Dry Tortugas, Florida.

John H. Surratt, who had evaded arrest, went abroad, served in the Papal Zouaves at Rome, was apprehended, and escaped, and later went to Egypt, where he was arrested, brought to the United States and, in 1867, placed on trial for his part in the conspiracy. The jury disagreed, and when he was arraigned the second time he was discharged by the court.

XXVII

IN a previous chapter reference was made to the finding by Eckert on November 26, 1864, the day after the attempt of the conspirators to burn New York City, of a letter addressed to a man called Payne with directions regarding the assassination of certain persons, and also a picture of Lincoln with a red ink-mark around the neck and down the shirt-front. The connection of Payne the assassin with these documents was made certain six months afterward, on his own confession.

Payne's real name was Lewis Thornton Powell. He enlisted in the Confederate army from Florida, where his father, a Baptist minister, then resided. At Gettysburg, in July, 1863, he was wounded and taken prisoner. He escaped from the hospital in Baltimore, after falling in love with his nurse, and returned to the Confederate army, but about a year later came North, either to meet his sweetheart, or as a deserter or spy, probably the latter, in view of his connection with the Lincoln picture above referred to, and also in view of his association with Booth in the plot to kill Lincoln and his cabinet.

Payne was a remarkable man, mentally and physically. His limbs and muscles were finely formed and developed, and when in the prisoners' dock on trial, clad as to upper garments only in a tight-fitting knit shirt, his stalwart figure was almost gladiatorial in its clean-cut robustness. His face was sphinx-like in its immobility, and the steady gaze of his dark, expressive eyes gave one the impression of a man of coldly-calculating, daredevil disposition, whom fate had decreed to reckless deeds and now to death, and who was without remorse. This naturally stolid man, fired with the spirit of revenge by the fate of his native South and the death of his two brothers killed in battle, was but a tool in the hands of the impulsive and romantic Booth.

Until then no high official of our Government had ever suffered attack by would-be assassins. The shock to the country was terrific. Might not others of our rulers also be struck down as Lincoln and Seward had been, and our Ship of State be driven from its moorings without pilot or anchor? Great fear and anxiety were felt by every one, and chiefly by Stanton, who deemed it a matter of vital importance to unravel quickly the threads of the murderous plot, and thus prevent further trouble. But how to proceed was a puzzle. Booth was dead, Atzerodt was foreign-born, stupid, and hard to understand. Herold, Arnold, Spangler, Mrs. Surratt, and O'Laughlin all acted subordinate parts and, it was reasoned, might not know of Booth's real plans. Payne was the only one of the seven supposed to have enjoyed the full confidence of the arch conspirator, and he was silent and imperturbable, answering no questions, refusing all but a bare modicum of food, and even resisting one of the demands of nature. In this latter respect, the inactive period was prolonged to an extraordinary extent, every possible means being employed by the attending physician to induce normal action.

Secretary Stanton sent Assistant Secretaries Dana and Eckert to the monitor *Saugus,* where Payne was confined in irons, in the hope that he might be led to talk. Dana soon tired of the task, but Eckert persevered in his efforts to break down the barriers between them, and for several days kept vigil, remaining with the prisoner almost constantly during the day, and for hours uttering no word, but keeping his eyes upon Payne and waiting for the moment of victory over the assassin's iron will. One day the provost marshal in command tried to have a picture taken of Payne, who moved his head from side to side to hide his face. The officer, angered by his failure, struck at Payne's arm with his sword or cane. Eckert told the officer he had no authority for striking a prisoner, or even for taking his picture. In this he was upheld by Secretary Stanton, who directed that Payne should be placed in Eckert's custody, and he so remained until the day of his execution. At the next meeting of the two, Payne said that the remark to the officer who struck him was the first sympathetic expression he had heard for many months.

When Eckert told Payne of his finding the letter hereinbefore referred to, Payne said that it had been lost at the time of the conspirators' attempt to burn the city in November, 1864. He added that he knew of the scheme, and had been designated to set fire to one of the hotels, but had refused to be a party to a crime involving injury and probably death to innocent parties who had no connection with the Government, and had, instead, gone to the Winter Garden Theater to see the three Booths in Shakspere's "Julius Cæsar."

Under instructions from the Secretary of War each of the conspirators on the *Saugus* was fitted with a hood over the head, with an opening for the nose and mouth, so that they might not communicate with each other. Their place of confinement was in the anchor-well at the bow of the boat. They were manacled, but were not confined separately in rooms or cells, there being no such facilities on the vessel.

Payne had asked for some tobacco, which Eckert did not have, but he obtained some before his next visit, and then in Payne's presence cut off a piece and put it into his own mouth, meantime watching Payne, whose eyes were fixed on the coveted morsel. Eckert then cut off a liberal piece and slipped it through the opening in the hood into Payne's mouth. The prisoner said that he never had anything to taste so good as that piece of tobacco.

When the time came to remove the prisoners to the arsenal prison, Eckert accompanied Payne with the guard. Payne's feet had swollen so that he could not wear his shoes, and a pair of carpet slippers were provided which gave him much relief. As they neared the gang-plank of the vessel it was necessary for each one to lower his head to prevent being struck by a cross-piece, the tide being very low. It was pitch-dark, the transfer being made at night. Payne could not see the obstruction and Eckert placed his hand on Payne's head and pressed it down so as to prevent his striking the cross-piece.

It was after one of these incidents that Payne broke down, and confided many details of Booth's plot, which were of such a character as to lead to the belief that, with the exception of John H. Surratt, who was apprehended in Egypt two years later, all the conspirators were then under lock and key, and that no further trouble might be expected from that source.

Even after Eckert had obtained Payne's confidence, the latter still withheld information bearing on his own part in the conspiracy, waiting for a promise not to testify against him. He was told that such a promise could not be made, but later Payne gave a few details.

One Baltimore rendezvous was in a gambling-place on Monument Square near Guy's Hotel. The secretary of the meeting was a physician on

Fayette Street, near-by. Eckert went to Baltimore by the first train, and consulted the doctor for indigestion, and while he went into an adjoining room to write a prescription, Eckert quietly pocketed a picture of the good physician, which was standing on the mantelpiece, and on his return to Washington showed the picture to Payne, who identified it. Eckert also went to the Washington rendezvous, on D Street, near the railroad station, and inquired for a room for meetings. A colored woman in charge offered him the very room which Payne had described, and said it had been used for meetings. From her story, it was learned just when Booth and his band had been there, although she evidently had no inkling of the diabolical plot which was being laid by her tenants. The room was large and had a grate at one end. It had not been cleaned up thoroughly, papers and dust having been swept toward the hearth and under the grate. Eckert poked with his cane until he had separated the scraps of paper from the debris and afterward, by pasting the pieces together, made out portions of a resolution evidently having reference to an abduction, and which, it was believed, had been written by Booth.

Among the debris was also found a scrap of paper bearing the name of Mudd. Dr. Mudd living in lower Maryland had set Booth's broken ankle during his flight toward Virginia and had been arrested on April 21 as one of the conspirators. On the trial, Mudd was found guilty and sentenced for life to Dry Tortugas but was pardoned by President Johnson in 1869, after nearly four years' imprisonment.

Payne told Eckert of three occasions when he was close to Lincoln and could have shot him if so inclined. Once, during the winter of 1865, Booth and Payne had walked through the White House grounds in the daytime. Booth urged Payne to send a card in to Lincoln, using any name that he might see fit, and when he went into the room to shoot the President. Payne said he refused, and Booth berated him soundly for cowardice.

At another time, when Lincoln was making a speech from the White House, Booth and Payne were in the crowd of listeners and Booth asked Payne to take out his revolver and fire. Payne said, "No, I will not do it." Again Booth damned Payne and urged him to commit the deed then and there, saying that the crowd was so great that it could be done without detection, but Payne was obdurate, not yet having screwed his courage up to the point of murder. It is more than likely this was on April 11, on the occasion of Lincoln's Louisiana speech, which I heard him deliver.

The third occasion was under the following circumstances: Payne suddenly turned to Eckert and said, "Major, were you not the man walking with the President through the White House grounds late one frosty night last winter?" Payne said that he was secreted behind the bushes in front of the old conservatory where the executive offices now stand, waiting for Lincoln to return from the War Department. There had been a light rain and it then got colder and there was a crust of ice so that it crackled under one's foot. Payne said he heard footsteps from the direction of the War Department, and when the persons got nearly opposite where he was hiding he saw Lincoln and another man coming along the walk, and heard the President say, "Major, spread out, spread out, or we shall break through the ice."

The two then stopped, and Lincoln told of an incident when he was a young man. The nearest grist-mill to his father's house was seven or eight miles distant and the custom was to take the grain to the mill and wait for it to be ground and then carry the meal back home, leaving a percentage for the miller. He said on one occasion during a very cold spell he and a party of neighbors were returning from the mill with their bags and they came to the Sangamon Creek, which was frozen over so that they could cross on it, but when they were part way over the ice cracked, and some one said, "Spread out, spread out, or we shall break through the ice." Eckert told Payne that he recalled the incident, that he was with President Lincoln that night, and had walked home with him many other nights from the War Department to the White House.

John C. Hatter, heretofore mentioned, told me in July, 1907, that near the end of 1864 he accompanied the President from the War Department to the White House at two o'clock in the morning. The weather had changed from rain to sleet and there was a coat of ice on the ground. When the gate outside the War Department (opposite the present executive offices) was opened to let the President pass through they heard a sound as of some one running along the fence, and over the frozen ground.

Upon examining the fence they found three

palings removed which Hatter said were not out of place in the evening when he came on duty. Mr. Lincoln said: "What was that noise?" Hatter answered that it sounded like some one running through the bushes toward the conservatory.

The President asked Hatter not to say anything to any one about the incident, and they resumed their walk to the White House. Hatter says that he never mentioned the subject, except to Secretary Stanton, who had heard of it through some other source and asked for the facts.

In reply to my inquiry on the subject, Rear-Admiral Asa Walker, superintendent of the Naval Observatory at Washington, wrote me on July 30, 1907, that the Observatory records show the following:

December 14, 1864. Commenced hailing at 12:25 A.M., and changed to rain in 20 minutes after, and sleet.

January 21, 1865. Began raining moderately at 8:50 A.M. Changed soon into sleet, continuing until 9 P.M. or later. Stopped before midnight. . . . The formation of a crust on the snow would probably not be mentioned in our records.

It seems probable that in the last two cases mentioned by Payne, his purpose was frustrated by the fact that Lincoln had a companion on his journey through the White House grounds. It is also likely that Lincoln's departure for City Point, on March 23, 1865, prevented the conspirators from carrying out their murderous plans at that time.[1] They were on the watch, however, and within five days after his return to Washington they finally succeeded.

[1] See the account of William H. Crook in "Harper's Magazine" for June, 1907, page 48.

XXVIII

SECRETARY STANTON'S private secretary, Major A. E. H. Johnson, in conversation with the writer in April, 1907, said that in dealing with the public, Lincoln's heart was greater than his head, while Stanton's head was greater than his heart. This characterization, though general, contains a great deal of truth. But we must not forget that the crystallized opinion of the present generation is that on all the important questions of public policy and administrative action, where Stanton's views were opposed to those of Lincoln, the latter dominated his energetic War Secretary. Indeed, one of Lincoln's latest biographers has entitled his volume "Lincoln, Master of Men," and has marshaled facts and documents which seem to demonstrate that on essential points Lincoln's will was stronger than Stanton's.

It is a fact, however, that during the three and

a quarter years of their close official relations the two men worked in almost entire harmony. There never appeared, to the writer's observation, any real conflict between them. It suited both to treat the public each in his own characteristic way, and when in any case the pinch came, each knew how far to yield to the other without sacrifice of prerogative.

One incident may be cited to show the opposing characteristics of the two men. The scarcity and very high price of cotton, especially toward the end of the war, had the effect of leading certain Northerners to engage in the somewhat questionable work of buying up cotton through certain agencies in the border States with the resultant effect of supplying needed funds to the South and establishing lines of communication which were used in many cases for conveying military information to the enemy. Accordingly, the War Department issued stringent orders on this subject which were, of course, criticized by the cotton speculators, one of whom, about May, 1864, appealed to Lincoln for the purpose of inducing him to overrule Stanton's order in his particular case and allow a large amount of cotton, already bought and paid for, to come through our lines. Lincoln heard the man's story and declined to intervene, but upon being further importuned gave his autograph card with an introduction to Stanton. The man went over to the War Department, presented the card and told his story, whereupon Stanton tore up the President's card, threw it into the waste-basket, and said: "The orders of this Department will not be changed."

The speculator, who was a man of considerable prominence, went immediately back to the White House and told of his reception, using strong language and censuring Stanton severely.

"Mr. President," said he, "what do you think Stanton did with your card?"

"I don't know," said Lincoln, "tell me."

"He tore it up and threw it into the waste-basket. He is not a fit man to be your Secretary of War."

"Did he do that?" replied Lincoln; "well, that 's just like Stanton."

In the afternoon, in the presence of Major Eckert, the President gave the Secretary of War an account of the incident, evidently with great enjoyment, and without taking the slightest exception to Stanton's course.

There was a marked contrast between Lincoln's manner, which was always pleasant and even genial, and that of Stanton. The latter's stern, spectacled visage commanded instant respect and in many cases inspired fear. In receiving visitors, and they were legion, Stanton seldom or never sat down, but stood before a high desk as the crowd passed before him and one by one presented their requests or complaints, which were rapidly disposed of. He was haughty, severe, domineering, and often rude. When I think of him in the daily routine of his public audiences, the characterization of Napoleon by Charles Phillips, the Irish orator, comes to mind: "Grand, gloomy, and peculiar."

The almost overwhelming burden of the great struggle for the life of the nation was ever pressing upon Stanton's heart and brain, and he even begrudged the time which he believed was wasted in ordinary civilities and was impatient with every one who failed to show like zeal and alertness with himself. He was not blessed with Lincoln's happy faculty of story-telling or exchanging badinage, which to the latter was a God-given means of relief from the awful strain to which he was subjected. And yet there were

From a photograph by Davis and Eickemeyer, taken in May, 1907

Charles Almerin Tinker
Cipher-operator, War Department
telegraph office, 1861–1869

David Homer Bates
Manager and cipher-operator, War Department telegraph office, 1861–1866

Thomas Thompson Eckert
Chief of the War Department Telegraph
Staff, 1861–1866

Albert Brown Chandler
Cashier and cipher-operator, War Department telegraph office, 1863–1866

times when even Stanton would soften and when he would disclose a kindly nature, the knowledge of the possession of which would come as a sharp surprise to any one fortunate enough to be present on such an occasion.

One instance in my recollection occurred after what seemed to me an unusual outburst of temper visited upon my innocent head. This was in connection with the receipt of the sensational Sherman-Johnston Peace Agreement which reached Washington on April 21, 1865 (only six days after Lincoln's death), the contents of which were of such an extraordinary character as to cause Stanton to become intensely excited. In fact, every high official of the Government, not excluding General Grant, was amazed at Sherman's action in signing such an agreement. Major A. E. H. Johnson has told me that Secretary Stanton on one occasion, when he was discussing the subject, said that President Johnson at the historical conference on the evening of April 21, in Representative Hooper's house,[1] after hearing Stanton read over his "Nine Reasons why the Sherman-Johnston Agreement

[1] President Johnson had not yet moved into the White House. The Hooper house was later altered into a hotel—the Shoreham.

should be rejected by the Government," remarked that Sherman was a traitor.

In preparation for this hastily called cabinet meeting, Stanton called me in from the cipher-room and asked me to write from his dictation, the regular clerical staff of the secretary's office having gone home for the day. Although as a telegrapher I was a rapid penman, my task was not an easy one, for the great War Secretary's sentences came tumbling from his lips in an impetuous torrent and it was impossible for me to keep up the pace he set. In fact, even a short-hand writer would probably have stumbled, so that breaks were frequent and equally annoying to both of us. I did my best, but lost some words and transposed others, so that the fiery dictator was forced to go back several times in his train of thought and reconstruct sentences, and in doing so here and there he used phrases different from those in his original composition. The final result was therefore unsatisfactory, and Stanton in his eagerness snatched the manuscript from my hands, with some remarks that would not look well in print.

Taking a pen in his hand and dipping it vigorously into the inkstand he proceeded to rewrite a considerable part of the document himself. Having done this, he read it over to me carefully and then had me write a new copy entire, while he paced back and forth across the room impatient of the fast-speeding minutes, and occasionally looking over my shoulder to see how far I had progressed. At last the final copy was ready, and I handed it to him and started to go into the cipher-room adjoining, when he called me back and, placing his hand affectionately on my shoulder, said, "I was too hasty with you, Mr. Bates. The fault was mine in expecting you to keep up with my rapid dictation; but I was so indignant at General Sherman for having presumed to enter into such an arrangement with the enemy, that I forgot everything else. I beg your pardon, my son."

Another incident occurs to my mind, showing how very thin was the outer crust of his harsh manner and how readily at times it could be broken so as to reveal the inherent kindness of his heart.

One evening, in the summer of 1864, I rode out to the Soldiers Home with important despatches for the President and Secretary of War, who were temporarily domiciled with their families in cottages on the grounds of the Home. I found Stanton reclining on the grass, playing with Lewis, one of his children (now living in New Orleans). He invited me to a seat on the greensward while he read the telegrams; and then, business being finished, we began talking of early times in Steubenville, Ohio, his native town and mine. One of us mentioned the game of "mumble-the-peg," and he asked me if I could play it. Of course I said yes, and he proposed that we should have a game then and there. Stanton entered into the spirit of the boyish sport with great zest, and for the moment all the perplexing questions of the terrible war were forgotten. I do not remember who won.

My comrade, Wilson, tells of a somewhat similar experience with Lincoln, in his "From the Hudson to the Ohio" (page 46). In the fall of 1861, Wilson had gone to the White House with an urgent despatch from Governor Morton of Indiana, which the President concluded to answer by means of a direct wire-talk from the War Department. Wilson adds:

Calling one of his two younger boys (Willie or Tad) to join him, we three started. . . . It was a warm day, and Mr. Lincoln wore as part of his costume a faded linen duster

which hung loosely around his long gaunt frame; his kindly
eye was beaming with good nature. . . . We had barely
reached the gravel walk before he stooped over, picked up a
round, smooth pebble and shooting it off his thumb, chal-
lenged us to a game of "followings," which we accepted.
Each in turn tried to hit the outlying stone which was constantly being projected onward by the President.   The
game was short but exciting . . . and when the President
was declared victor it was only by a hand-span. . . . He
softened our defeat by attributing his success to his greater
height and longer reach of arm.

Although to his family and chosen friends,
and, on rare occasions, to others, Stanton disclosed a warm, tender heart, yet in the daily
routine of the War Department he was intensely
in earnest, and required of every one else a like
zeal and devotion and an utter sacrifice of self
and of personal comfort whenever the interests
of the Government were concerned. He hated
disloyalty and had no patience with critics of his
administration. Accordingly he was brusk and
many times rude to newspaper men, members of
Congress and others who applied to him for news
or favors or who called upon him in support of
claims that had already been rejected.

In contrast, Lincoln freely told to callers the
contents of despatches from the armies, and
there were some occasions on which he disclosed

to the public in advance information relating to army manœuvers of special importance, which leaked through to the enemy, with the result of defeating our plans. So it came to pass that we were ordered by Stanton not to place in the cipher-drawer copies of despatches which told of expected army movements, or which related to actual or impending battles, until after he had first seen them; and in some instances the Secretary retained both copies to make sure their contents should not be prematurely published.

Lincoln's keen eyes soon discovered that there was undue reticence in our attitude toward him, and without criticizing our course, he would ask us occasionally, with twinkling eyes, whether the Secretary of War did not have some later news, or if there were not "something under the blotter." Of course we could not deceive him and he would then go to the adjoining room and ask Stanton if he had anything from the front. Sometimes he addressed Stanton as "Mars," but while the stern Secretary gave no indication of displeasure at this playful allusion to his official character, he did not, on the other hand, allow a smile to brighten his face.

Early in February, 1862, the morning after

the interview referred to in chapter IX, when Stanton, in the presence of President Lincoln and Governor Brough of Ohio, tore up Eckert's resignation, Lincoln called on the latter at McClellan's headquarters and, referring to the interview, said that he was glad to have been able to testify concerning Eckert's attention to duty, adding that Stanton's manner was very peculiar, but that he was all right when people came to know him. He said that he was a most remarkable man; that he first became aware of his great abilities when they met years before in Cincinnati in the McCormick Reaper case, in which Lincoln and Stanton had been retained for the defense; and that after he had heard Stanton's masterly presentation of that case he said to one of his associates that he was going home to study law, as he had found out, after hearing Stanton, that he knew very little about it.

In his "Recollections of President Lincoln" (page 186), L. E. Chittenden says that at the moment of Lincoln's death, Stanton uttered this eulogy: "There lies the most perfect ruler of men the world has ever seen."

In August, 1865, Stanton left Washington for a few weeks' vacation, the first he had been permitted to take for five years. I accompanied him as cipher-operator. He visited Simeon Draper, Collector of the Port, and a Mr. Duer at New York, Isaac Bell at Tarrytown, a Mr. Minturn at The Highlands, New Jersey; Samuel Hooper at Boston, and a Mr. Hone at Newport. This respite was greatly enjoyed by Stanton. During Stanton's absence on this trip our chief, General Eckert, the Assistant Secretary, became the Acting Secretary of War. Stanton's death occurred December 24, 1869, the year following his protracted and bitter struggle with President Johnson, and at the very time that President Grant had offered him the much-coveted prize of a seat on the Supreme Court bench. He lived and died a relatively poor man. In the writer's opinion it is a nation's shame that his extraordinary services to his country in her time of stress and need have not been suitably recognized by the erection of a monument to his memory at the nation's capital. General McClellan has been so honored recently, and at Richmond Jefferson Davis and Generals Lee and Stuart are also remembered, but our own great War Secretary to whom the country owes so much has apparently been forgotten.

Eckert always commanded the full confidence

of President Lincoln and Secretary Stanton, and was intrusted with military and state secrets and charged with special commissions not at first disclosed to the cipher-operators, who were justly proud of their Chief.

Although holding a commission Eckert never wore an officer's uniform. His appointment as Assistant Secretary of War, really took effect in March, 1865, although the official date is given as July 27, 1866. In this connection, and as showing the high appreciation in which he was held by both Lincoln and Stanton, it is proper to state that in August, 1865, when the Western Union and American Telegraph companies were about to be consolidated, he was offered a prominent position with the joint companies and tendered his resignation to Secretary Stanton, who was about to leave Washington on the vacation referred to on page 401. Stanton started to write an acceptance, but Eckert observed that he was evidently laboring under strong feeling, and said that if the Secretary preferred to have him remain for another year, he would do so. Stanton gladly accepted this offer and laid aside the document on which he was engaged. He then resumed his vacation plans, placing Eckert in charge as Acting Secretary of War from August 15, to September 23, 1865. I was selected as cipher-operator to accompany Stanton on this trip, which occupied five weeks.

A year later when Eckert entered the service of the Western Union Company, Stanton handed him an envelop containing the partly finished acceptance of his resignation, dated August 7, 186 , and another autographic communication over his signature bearing only the year date, 1866. The latter had been written by Stanton in anticipation of Eckert's departure and laid aside until July 31, 1866, the day Eckert left Washington for his new duties, and Stanton did not then stop to insert the full date.

Stanton's remark at the time these letters were delivered to Eckert was, "Don't open the envelop until you reach New York." The second of these communications is here shown in facsimile.

War Department
Washington City,
Aug. 7, 186 .

My Dear Friend:

The acceptance of your resignation as Assistant Secretary of War is one of the most painful events of my life, not only because it severs official relations that have given me great aid and comfort in the performance of my duties,

Facsimile (reduced) of Secretary Stanton's letter accepting
Major Eckert's resignation

but also sunders to some extent the close personal relations and daily intercourse between us that has so long existed. It would be a vain effort to express the full confidence and depth of affection my heart entertains towards you. The highest and most responsible trust of the Government during the war you, as Superintendent of Military . . .

War Department
Washington City,
186 .

My Dear Sir:

It is with very great regret that I am constrained out of regard for your own personal interest and welfare to accept your resignation as Acting Secretary of War and Superintendent of Military Telegraphs. My personal and official intercourse with you will always be among the most pleasing recollections of my life. Your zeal, fidelity and laborious diligence for years to the prejudice of your health and comfort, contributed much to the successful operations of this Department during the War of the Rebellion. You have had and well deserved my unlimited confidence. To your discretion and patriotic fidelity the most important and confidential interests of the Government were often entrusted, and the trust reposed in you was never betrayed or perverted. You had the good fortune to have enjoyed the personal regard and confidence of our late beloved President Abraham Lincoln to a degree seldom bestowed.

It is with feelings of profound sorrow, and with my thanks for your inestimable aid, that I bid you an official farewell. Yours truly,

Edwin M. Stanton,
Secretary of War.

Brevet Brig General Thomas T. Eckert.

On August 1, 1866, General Eckert entered the service of the Western Union Telegraph Company as general superintendent of the eastern division, afterward becoming general manager, and later president. He is now chairman of the board, and although eighty-six years of age, is still active and vigorous. While he is stern and at times implacable toward those who have deviated from the path of rectitude, below the surface there beats a heart full of warm affection for his chosen friends and of unswerving loyalty to whatever cause he may espouse. The surviving members of his staff of cipher-operators in the War Department—Tinker, Chandler, and myself—have been associated with him in business positions of trust and responsibility for many years. The quartet has not yet been disturbed by the grim reaper Death, although we sometimes fancy we can hear him sharpening his scythe, as we journey down the narrowing lane of life.

THE writer could wish that this desultory account of "Lincoln in the Telegraph Office" were more worthy of the subject. The task, though somewhat arduous, has been a pleasant one. It has called back to memory conversations and incidents through which there was revealed to the cipher-operators in the War Department telegraph office, more fully perhaps than to others, Lincoln's simple yet varied and lofty character, which has since become the object of wonder and admiration of the civilized world: his marvelous tact in the handling of men and the settlement of complex questions; his skilful leading of public opinion into broader channels; his control of great events; his gathering up of the fruits of political conflict, and, above all, his boundless charity for and deep sympathy with the common people.

Ever since the first announcement in "The Telegraph Age" of a purpose to prepare an account of Lincoln in the telegraph office, the writer's comrades in the military telegraph service in all parts of the country have freely tendered full and interesting data in their own experience, and this occasion is availed of to thank them most sincerely for their valuable help; the only regret being that the limits of this volume have made it necessary to leave out so much that would have been of general interest.

APPENDIX

APPENDIX

To Chapter II

In Senate Document Number 251, Fifty-eighth Congress, 2d Session, may be found a general, but quite clear, idea of the organization, scope, and service of the United States Military Telegraph Corps during the Civil War. The documents therein quoted by General Ainsworth begin with the order of Simon Cameron, Secretary of War, dated April 27, 1861, placing Colonel Thomas A. Scott in charge of railways and telegraphs and end with an extract from the annual report of Edwin M. Stanton, Secretary of War, dated November 22, 1865.

To Chapter VII

See Page 110

The full story of the mutilation of McClellan's telegram to the Secretary of War of June 28, 1862, is told for the first time by Major A. E. H. Johnson, Stanton's confidential clerk and custodian of military telegrams during the war, in a letter to the writer. He says:

When the telegram was received in cipher and translated, Major Eckert, chief of the War Department telegraph staff, sent for Colonel Edwards S. Sanford, military supervisor of telegrams, and asked him to decide what should be done. The charge against Secretary Stanton contained in the two paragraphs at the close of the despatch was false and while it was doubtful whether the censor had authority to suppress a telegram from the commanding general of the army addressed to the Secretary of War, yet this one contained such an outrageous untruth that the censor thought he ought not to allow himself to be used to hand it to the Secretary in that form. Colonel Sanford thereupon caused the despatch, minus the offensive words, to be recopied and delivered to Secretary Stanton, who took it in person to President Lincoln. Neither Lincoln nor Stanton knew of the mutilation and both acted upon it in ignorance of the terrible charge against them which it had previously contained. The first copy of the telegram as received was destroyed. The mutilated copy published in the Rebellion Records was taken from the collection made to be delivered to Stanton at the close of the war. It may also be found on page 302, Vol. I. of the Report of the Committee on the Conduct of the War, in connection with General Hitchcock's testimony in the McDowell court of inquiry.

To Chapter VIII

See Page 118

The "Story of the *Monitor*" by William S. Wells (late engineer United States Navy), pages 14 and 77, mentions a conference at Washington in 1861 between President Lincoln, Captain G. V. Fox, Assistant Secretary of the Navy, and other members of the Naval Board, and John A. Griswold, John F. Winslow, and Cornelius S. Bushnell (the last three later becoming the contractors for building Ericsson's turret vessel, the *Monitor*). At this conference a pasteboard model of Ericsson's invention was shown, and its merits and peculiar advantages discussed.

Colonel William Conant Church, in his "Life of John Ericsson," page 249, also refers to this conference, and quotes from a letter of Bushnell dated March 9, 1877, to Gideon Welles, Secretary of the Navy, containing the following extract:

All were surprised at the novelty of the plan; some advised trying it, others ridiculed it. The conference was finally closed by Mr. Lincoln remarking: "All I have to say is what the girl said when she put her foot into the stocking, 'It strikes me there's something in it.'"

In a foot-note Colonel Church says:

Mr. Bushnell was given a pasteboard model of the *Monitor,* admirably illustrating the easy method of training the guns by rotating the turret. It was this that struck Mr. Lincoln and which he held in his hand when he remarked about the girl and her stocking.

It is of interest to recall that Lincoln's early experience with light-draft flat-boats on shallow western rivers qualified him to speak with authority on the subject when the model of the *Monitor* was shown to him.

Major A. E. H. Johnson, who was employed in Edwin M. Stanton's patent law office before the war, and who still practises his profession in Washington, D. C., writes, June 7, 1907, that the model of Lincoln's invention described in Letters Patent, Number 6469, granted

APPENDIX

May 22, 1849, for a "Method of Lifting Vessels over Shoals," is still preserved in the Patent Office at Washington. Major Johnson adds that "instead of being a freak invention as claimed by some, it was a pioneer conception in the art of navigation, and the air-tight compartments of our great sea-going ships are valid proofs of the utility of Lincoln's air-chamber device. If this be true, Lincoln should be classed among the great inventors of the nineteenth century."

The basic value of Lincoln's invention is emphasized by the salvage of the twelve-thousand-ton vessel, the *Bavarian*, shipwrecked in the St. Lawrence near Quebec on the night of November 3, 1905, after repeated efforts had been made to float her by various methods. When more than one hundred and fifty thousand dollars had been expended by the owners, the *Bavarian* was turned over to the underwriters, who also spent a large amount of money without satisfactory result. Then Robert King and William Witherspoon, two young engineers who had done more or less tunnel and caisson work by means of compressed air, tackled the problem, and on November 16, 1906, the great *Bavarian* was raised and a half million dollars saved to the underwriters. In their last analysis the methods employed in this case resemble, in principle, the somewhat crude devices in the patent of Abraham Lincoln.

See Page 123

CAPTAIN SAMUEL H. BECKWITH, General Grant's cipher-operator, has recently sent the writer a copy of one of President Lincoln's characteristic laconic despatches, which he does not recall having seen in print, as follows:

APPENDIX

GENERAL PHILIP H. SHERIDAN,
       Winchester, Virginia.

General Grant telegraphs me that if you push the enemy you can force Early out of the Shenandoah Valley—Push him.   A. LINCOLN.

The copy bears no date, but Beckwith says, "I witnessed the writing and transmission of the despatch, which to my knowledge has not been heretofore published. I think it was before Fisher's Hill where Sheridan did 'push him,' capturing nearly all of Early's guns. When Sheridan's despatch announcing this victory was handed to Grant, I inquired if there was anything more that Sheridan could take. Grant's silent, pleasant smile assured me of his victory over the wise men at Washington who had claimed that Sheridan was 'too young' for the great responsibilities which Grant had placed upon him."

To Chapter XII

See Page 159

THE following incident indicates Lincoln's great interest in Rosecrans's victory at Stone's River:

In January, 1863, not long after the battle, Rosecrans wrote a letter to the President stating his position in detail and the need of reinforcements, which was carried to Washington by Captain George C. Kniffin of General Crittenden's staff, and handed to Lincoln in person. In his War Paper, Number 47, read at the meeting of the Loyal Legion, Commandery of the District of Columbia, on March 6, 1903, Colonel Kniffin gives an account of that interview from which the following extract is taken:

An intense earnestness exhibited itself in his anxious inquiry, "Are you from Murfreesboro?" "Yes, Mr. President; and I am the bearer of an important despatch from General Rosecrans," which I handed to him at once, and noting the legend "Personal" on the envelop, he placed it in his pocket. We were alone in the room. He motioned me to a seat and pushed a sheet of paper toward me with the remark: "Now tell me all about it." "About what?" Suddenly the thought occurred to me to describe the battle of Stone's River. . . . Improvising a ruler with my staff sword, I drew two lines crossing each other at an acute angle, which represented the railroad and turnpike leading from Nashville to Murfreesboro. I then drew, from memory, a map which I still think was a tolerably correct representation of the topography of the country. I aligned the troops under Rosecrans across the turnpike and railroad as they went into bivouac on the night of December 30, 1862. I stationed the batteries of artillery and gave the position of the cavalry. Then I gave as nearly as possible the position and strength of the enemy. The President took an absorbing interest in my work as it progressed, asking questions, which I answered as intelligently as possible. I then described the battle, how we repulsed the final charge of Breckenridge and drove them back pell-mell into Murfreesboro and compelled Bragg to evacuate the place. I spoke rapidly, and during my recital the President sat motionless. When I had finished, for the first time I raised my head and looked about me. Standing, peering over each other's shoulders at the map of the battle-field which I had drawn, listening so intently that I was not aware of their presence, was an august assembly, members of the cabinet and of the

Senate and House, all of sufficient prominence to be admitted to the President's room without the formality of an introductory card. I was greatly embarrassed, but was speedily reassured by the kindhearted President, who introduced me to each gentleman present.

To Chapter XIII

The following despatches relate to the transfer of Hooker's two army corps to Chattanooga for the reinforcement of Rosecrans:

Camden Station, Md., Sept. 27, 1863.
Edwin M. Stanton,
      Secretary of War,
          Washington, D. C.
Our agent at Grafton has orders to hold all the 3rd Division, 11th Corps, until General Schurz arrives.
                 W. P. Smith.

War Department, Washington, D. C.
          Sept. 27, 1863, 9:40 p.m.
Major-General Carl Schurz,
      Fairmont, W. Va.
Major-General Hooker has the orders of this department to relieve you and put under arrest any officer who undertakes to delay or interfere with the orders and requisitions of the railroad officers in charge of the transportation of troops.
          Edwin M. Stanton, Secy. of War.

APPENDIX

Sept. 27, 1863, 9:40 P.M.

W. P. SMITH, General Manager,
>   *Baltimore & Ohio Railroad Co.,*
>>   *Camden Station.*

I have telegraphed Schurz that he will be relieved and put under arrest if he undertakes to interfere with the trains. You need not have furnished him an extra but let him and any of the other officers who lag behind get along the best they can.

EDWIN M. STANTON, Secy. of War.

Baltimore, Md., Sept. 27, 1863, 11 P.M.

EDWIN M. STANTON,
>   Secretary of War,
>>   *Washington, D. C.*

. . . It is only by a wilful delay by our operator at Grafton of Schurz's message to Fairmont that the detention of the troops there was avoided.

W. P. SMITH.

The above official correspondence from the Rebellion Records, Vol. **XXIX,** will surely indicate that the successful movement of so large a body of troops for so great a distance in an incredibly short period of time was only possible by keeping the transportation wholly under the control of the railroad officers themselves. It also shows how narrow an escape General Carl Schurz had from being placed under arrest for his attempted interference with the trains. Immediately upon Schurz's arrival at Bridgeport, Alabama, October 1, 1863, he wrote a long letter to Secretary Stanton explaining his action, which communication was forwarded to Washington by General Howard, corps commander,

420

with an indorsement favorable to Schurz. There is no record that Stanton ever replied to Schurz's letter.

To Chapter XIV

In a letter to the editor of "The Century Magazine," Captain D. V. Purington, of Chicago, says:

Mr. Bates's reference in the July "Century" [1907] to the fact that not all the stories attributed to Mr. Lincoln were really his, calls to my mind a little incident that corroborates Mr. Bates's position.

Early in the winter of 1864–5, President Lincoln visited the Army of the Potomac and the Army of the James. General Godfrey Weitzel was at that time commanding the 25th Army Corps, and Dutch Gap was within the limits of his command. Mr. Lincoln desired to see this particular work of the army engineers. Arrangements were made, and he was escorted from corps headquarters by General Weitzel and his entire staff, of which the writer was a junior member. On the return of the party, Mr. Lincoln was invited to lunch with the General and his staff. It was my privilege to be seated at the table immediately opposite the President, and to listen to the conversation between him and General Weitzel. After we had all enjoyed some story of Mr. Lincoln's (which I am sorry to have forgotten), General Weitzel said: "Mr. President, about what proportion of the stories attributed to you really belong to you?"

Mr. Lincoln replied: "I do not know; but of those I have seen, I should say just about one half."

The percentage of genuine to the whole number of so-called Lincoln stories has probably decreased considerably since the President's estimate of "about one half."

To Chapter XVIII
See Page 252

Brigadier-General J. P. S. Gobin, in a paper read at the memorial meeting of the Pennsylvania Commandery of the Military Order of the Loyal Legion, Philadelphia, February 13, 1907, makes the following reference to Lincoln's presence at Fort Stevens on July 12, 1864:

L. E. Chittenden, in his "Reminiscences" says that when he reached the Fort, he found the President, Secretary Stanton and other civilians. A young colonel of artillery, who appeared to be the officer of the day, was in great distress because the President would expose himself and paid little attention to his warnings. He was satisfied the Confederates had recognized him, for they were firing at him very hotly, and a soldier near him had just fallen from a broken thigh. He asked my advice, says Chittenden, for he said the President was in great danger. After some consultation the young officer walked to where the President was looking over the edge of the parapet and said: "Mr. President, you are standing within range of five hundred rebel rifles. Please come down to a safer place. If you do not, it will be my duty to call a file of men and make you."

"And you would do quite right, my boy," said the President, coming down at once. "You are in command of this fort. I should be the last man to set an example of disobedience." He was shown to a place where the view was less extended, but where there was almost no exposure. As Mr. Chittenden was present and speaks from personal knowledge, this is assumed to be a correct statement.

APPENDIX

To Chapter XX

See Page 281

PRESIDENT LINCOLN's proclamation announcing the admission of Nevada into the Union was signed and dated October 31, 1864, immediately after the full text of Nevada's constitution had been telegraphed from Nevada City to Washington. The transmission of this long document required the use of the wires all day October 30 (Sunday), and all that night. This course was taken in order that Nevada's electoral vote might be counted in the Republican column.

To Chapter XXVI

JEFFERSON DAVIS, in his "Rise and Fall of the Confederate Government," page 683, says concerning Lincoln's assassination, the news of which was received by him from General Sherman on April 18, 1865, at Charlotte:

For an enemy so relentless in the war for our subjugation, we could not be expected to mourn, yet, in view of the political consequences, it could not be regarded otherwise than as a great misfortune to the South. . . .

To Chapter XXVIII

See Page 395

THE following communication from Major A. E. H. Johnson is of historic interest in connection with the fierce controversy between President Johnson and Secretary Stanton, in which Generals Grant and Sherman were also involved:

Washington, D. C., August 23, 1907.
Mr. David Homer Bates, New York City.

DEAR SIR: Referring to your request to give you what information I have of the cabinet meeting April 21, 1865, at which the Sherman-Johnston terms of surrender were rejected, and particularly, whether President Johnson spoke of Sherman as a "traitor" at that meeting, I know that Secretary Stanton, in speaking of the matter some years after, said that Johnson referred to the terms as being "close to treason." I never heard Secretary Stanton speak of that cabinet meeting but once, and that was at the time President Johnson brought General Sherman to Washington to help him get rid of Stanton as Secretary of War. The President knew that Sherman would be glad to pay Stanton back for what he did in publishing his "nine reasons" for the rejection of the agreement, and as the reasons were published at the time in the name of the President, he caused the White House reporters to deny that he knew of Stanton's reasons until he saw them in the press the morning of their publication and that he had authorized their publication, so that Sherman might see it as the President wanted, that he might use him in the Johnson-Grant-Sherman fight to oust Stanton. The occasion when the Secretary spoke of this cabinet meeting and what was said of Sherman, was to Senator Wilson of Massachusetts and Congressman Kelley of Pennsylvania, who were discussing with the Secretary the presence of Sherman in Washington in connection with the President's efforts to oust Stanton. Stanton told them that the President wanted Sherman to think that he had nothing to do with the publication of the reasons for the rejection of the terms and that the President was using the reporters for that purpose; but that he was taking good care not to tell them that at that meeting he had said of the terms that they were "close to treason" and that Sherman was a "traitor"; and that the terms would put the rebel leaders, fresh from treason, in control of Congress and in the making of the laws.

This was just what the President then wanted to do by ousting Stanton; and while all the cabinet denounced the terms, the President's denunciation was the strongest; and it was the President who directed that General Grant be ordered to go at once to take command of the army and give battle again to Joe Johnston.

Yours very truly,

A. E. H. JOHNSON.

INDEX

A

Act of January 26, 1897: Military Telegraphers' Certificates, 36
Anderson, Robert, 344
Arnold, Samuel, 379
Atlantic Cable, 257 *et seq.*
Atwater, Henry H., 253, 265
Atzerodt, George A., 83, 370 *et seq.*

B

Baker, Edward D., 93 *et seq.*
Baldwin, George W., 46
Barr, Samuel F., 21
Battle of Antietam, 142; Bull Run, 88, 118; Chickamauga, 158; Fort Stevens, 250; Fredericksburg (campaign), 58; Gettysburg, 154; Nashville, 310; Stone's River, 159; Vicksburg (siege), 155; Wilderness, 244
Beauregard, P. T., 91
Beckwith, Samuel H., 8, 56, 344 *et seq.*, 372 *et seq.*
Beecher, Henry Ward, 241, 344
Bell, Isaac, 402
Benjamin, Judah P., 72 *et seq.*, 81, 85, 294, 305
Black Hawk War, 122
Blair, Francis P., Sr., 324 *et seq.*
Boker, George H., 225
Booth, Edwin, 307
Booth, John Wilkes, 83, 306, 369, 378
Booth, Junius Brutus, 307
Bovay, A. E., 150
Bowers, T. S., 187, 344, 358
Boyd, Joseph W., 47
Bragg, General, 163 *et seq.*
Bragg, Thomas, 153
Bright, John, 196

Brough, John, 136, 401
Brown, Samuel M., 14
Buell, M. V. B., 47, 212
Burnside, Ambrose E., 58 *et seq.*, 287
Burt, Silas W., 190
Bushnell, C. S., 247
Butler, Benjamin F., 19, 21, 28, 86

C

Cable, Atlantic, 257 *et seq.;* to Gulf of Mexico, 257 *et seq.*
Cadwallader, General, 237, 238
Caldwell, A. H., 56, 107, 346
Cameron, Simon, 16, 20, 54, 88, 277
Cammack, J. H., 72 *et seq.*
Campbell, J. A., 322 *et seq.*, 362, 363
Carnegie, Andrew, 14, 20, 92, 173, 179, 311
Carpenter, F. B., 141, 189, 210
Chandler, Albert Brown, Lincoln at Fort Stevens, 252; Lincoln's anxiety after Gettysburg, 157; Lincoln's last despatch, 362; on duty night of April 14, 1865, 371; operates new signals, 265
Chase, Salmon P., 143
Cheney, J. W., 39
Chittenden, L. E., 401
Church, W. C., 117
Cipher-codes, Confederate, 68; Federal, 49
Clay, Clement C., 80 *et seq.*, 291 *et seq.*
Clowry, Robert C., 35
Cochrane, 269
Colburn, A. V., 107
Confederate, attempt to burn New York, 299; cipher-codes, 68; operator on Union wire,

INDEX

INDEX

Great Britain, recognition of South, 159, 160
Greeley, Horace, 291, 292
Green, John A., 297

H

Hackett, James H., 223
Hall, Edward A., 270
Halleck, Henry Wager, 143, 155, 174 et seq., 311 et seq.
Hamilton, George A., 237
Hamlin, Hannibal, 268
Hardie, James A., 249, 362
Hardin, M. D., 253-254
Harlan, Secretary, 187
Harrison, Burton N., 203
Hatter, John C., 365, 371, 386, 387
Haupt, Herman, 119 et seq.
Hay, John, 30, 275, 283, 291
Helms, General, 163
Henry, Joseph, 265
Herold, David, 369, 379
Hewitt, Abram S., 270
Hill, Adams, 242
Hill, Benjamin H., 72 et seq.
Hill, Frederick Trevor, 6
Hitchcock, General, 112
Holcombe, J. P., 85, 291 et seq
Holmes, ——, 297
Holt, Joseph, 293, 309
Hone, ——, 402
Hood, General, 310
Hooker, Joseph, 175 et seq.
Hooper, Samuel, 395, 402
Howard, General, 9
Howard, Joseph, 239 et seq.
Howe, Julia Ward, 225
Howell, A., 181
Hunter, R. M. T., 322

I

Ingalls, Rufus, 64

J

Jackson, Andrew, 6
Jackson, M. M., 296, 299
Janvier, Francis de Haes, 225
Jaques, Charles W., 92, 93

Jefferson, Thomas, 6
Johnson, A. E. H., 48, 81, 109, 112, 146, 195, 313, 323, 389, 395
Johnson, Andrew, 130, 267, 321, 370, 384, 395
Johnston, Joseph E., 69

K

Keene, Laura, 365
Keith, Alexander, Jr., 72 et seq.
Kelley, William D., 224
Kellog, Sanford Cobb, 170
Kellogg, Mrs. F. B., 170
Kelton, J. C., 68
Kennedy, Robert C., 304
Kennedy, superintendent of police, 300
"Kerr, Orpheus C.," 186 et seq.
Kettles, William E., 360

L

Laird, Thomas A., 360, 371
Leaming, Wallace, 238
Lee, Robert E., 182, 205, 402
Lieber, Francis, 203
Lincoln, Abraham, Atlantic cable, recommends, 257; brief national career, 6; calls Stanton "Mars," 400; commends Grant, 123; commends Rosecrans, 159, 162; commends Thomas, 169, 320; dates, method of determining, 345; dissatisfaction with McClellan, 101 et seq.; dissatisfaction with Meade, 156; dreams, influenced by, 215; estimate of 1864 electoral vote, 279; forebodings of defeat in 1864, 267; Fort Stevens, at Battle of, 252; last horseback ride, 350; last story told in telegraph office, 206; last telegraphic despatch, 362; lecture on "Discoveries and Inventions," 222; love for his children, 208; love of Shakspere, 223, 226; manner con-

INDEX

INDEX

Stephens, Alexander H., 126, 322 *et seq.*
Stewart, Frank, 46
Stone, Amasa, 30; Charles P., 94
Storrs, Richard S., 344
Strouse, David, 16, 27
Sumner, Charles, 346
Surratt, John H., 83, 376, 382; Mary E., 376, 379
Swaim, James M., 261
Swett, Leonard, 270

T

Thomas, George H., 162 *et seq.*, 310 *et seq.*
Thompson, Jacob, 76, 79, 168, 282, 290, 299
Tinker, Charles Almerin, delivers Lincoln's despatch of September 23, 1863, to George H. Thomas, 171;
diary of May, 1863, 155; May, 1864, 245; September, 1864, 175;
explains Morse telegraph to Lincoln, 4; helps Lincoln to remember a name, 145; learns Swaim's new signal code, 262; Lincoln's last story told in telegraph office, 206; operates new signals, 264, 265; takes charge of seized telegraph office, 236
Townsend, E. D., 47, 88, 344
Trimble, Isaac R., 16

U

United States Military Telegraph Corps, commended, by General Grant, 11; Quartermaster-General Meigs, 12; Secretary Stanton, 11; Senator N. B. Scott, 13; Congress grants members, certificates of honorable service, 36; organization and staff, 14

V

Vallandigham, C. L., 287 *et seq.*
VanDuzer, J. C., 314, 316
Verdin, Doctor, 130
Villard, Henry, 242

W

Wade, Jeptha H., 125
Walker, Asa, 387
Wallace, Lew, 237, 250
Ward, Artemus, 186 *et seq.*
War Department, building, 146; library, 39
telegraph office locations, 26, 38, 87; plan, 144; staff, 393
Warren, Fitz Henry, 304
Watson, Peter H., 139, 176
Weitzel, Godfrey, 356 *et seq.*
White, Horace, 242, 267
Whiting, William, 155
Whiton, William H., 177
Wilkes, Charles, 97 *et seq.*
Wilkeson, Samuel, 247
William II, German Emperor, 12
Wilson, William Bender, 45, 88, 199, 398
Winans, Ross, 87
Wing, Henry E., 244
Wintrup, John, 207
Wiswell, General, 236
Wood, William B., 360
Wool, John E., 116
Worden, John L., 117
Worl, J. N., 235 *et seq.*
Wright, David M., 150 *et seq.*; H. G., 255

432

Printed in the United States
78923LV00001B/2

9 780803 261259